the
CLOUD GROWS THIN

the CLOUD GROWS THIN

A memoir

MICHAEL LAFLEUR

Copyright © 2025 Michael LaFleur

All rights reserved. No part of this publication may be reproduced, distributed, or transmitted in any form or by any means, including photocopying, recording, or other electronic or mechanical methods, without the prior written permission of the author.

First Edition

ISBN: 979-8-9999281-6-0 (Paperback)

Printed in the United States of America

For Christina, Ezra, and Ethan who showed me grace when I could not see its face.

CHAPTER ONE

Even in death, my mother had found a way to abandon me.
My sister called me at work on a Tuesday afternoon.
"Mom's dead," she said. No hello, no small talk. Just those two words.

I sat down in my office chair. "When?"

"Yesterday. Marilyn found her."

"Are we able to go see her?"

There was a pause. "No. She prearranged everything with some company called the Neptune Society. They already came and got her."

"What do you mean, they got her?"

"She's already gone. She's been cremated." My sister's voice was flat, like she was reading from a grocery list. "Marilyn said she was very specific about it. The documents said no family until after it was done."

I held the phone against my ear and stared at my screen. The same stuff I had been working on when the phone rang was still open, the everything looking exactly the same as it had five minutes ago when I thought my mother was still alive.

"Neither of us gets to see her?"

"No."

She was gone—again.

But this time was different. This time it was permanent.

+ + +

I had flown into Colorado to help my sister with the unavoidable cleanup that happens after a family member dies. As I checked into the hotel in Fort Collins, the desk staff asked me if my stay was for business or pleasure. I answered, "Neither. My mother just died, and I am here for that." There was a pause in the conversation that I had never felt before. The silence turned the conversation from cordial to awkward, but a different sort of awkward than I had ever experienced before.

That was the first time in my life that I was forced to say that someone I was related to had died, and I had no idea the impact those words had on an unsuspecting listener.

The desk clerk fumbled with her pen, shuffled some papers, and then told me she was sorry to hear that, and she got quiet again.

It was an uncomfortable few minutes as she finished getting me my key. She told me how sorry she was again, and I headed up to my room.

When I traveled for work, I tried to stay at the same hotel chain as often as I could. I chose one hotel brand and stuck with it because of familiarity. No matter what city in the United States I was staying, I knew that when I opened the door, the layout of the room, the positions of the beds, the location of the desk, the type of TV, would be the same as it had been in the last hotel I stayed at. There was a strange comfort in that—the kind of reliable predictability I had learned to create for myself when no one else would. In the Air Force, they'd taught us that controlling your environment was the first step in surviving chaos. Same room layout, same procedures, same result. It was a survival mechanism I'd carried into civilian life, this need to impose order on uncertainty.

After I got into the room, I set my suitcase down on the rack, dropped my backpack on the desk, and then looked at my phone to find my sister had texted saying that she had landed in Denver and was on her way to get a rental car. That gave me over an hour to wait, so I went out into the neighborhood, as the sun hovered just above the peaks of the Rocky Mountains to the west.

The mountains were silhouetted against a fiery sunset, their jagged outlines etched in sharp relief. The rays seemed to grow long and gold as the sun neared the mountain tops, bathing the landscape in a warm glow. As soon as the sun would dip behind the peaks the air would take to crispness, hinting at the approaching night. As I walked, the cottonwoods, elms, and pines swayed gently in the late afternoon breeze, their leaves and needles creating what sounded like a whispered message.

It had been less than three weeks since I had last been to Fort Collins, but before that, it had been over twenty years since I had been to the place.

Time had transformed Fort Collins beyond recognition, but as I walked, the hotel's location began to feel familiar. Then I realized why. Just a block away was the edge of the downscale apartment complex my mother had lived in over twenty-five years earlier. The managers of that complex had given me a short-term maintenance job while I waited for my time to ship out to the Air Force in 1985.

As I walked under the shade of the trees along the boulevard, I felt the struggle of the affluence of the upscale hotel I was staying in and the bleak meagerness of the downscale apartments I had come from. Around the complex, I could smell the early mornings when I added chlorine to the pool before residents would be up and sunning themselves or splashing in the water. I could feel the cold aluminum pole of the vacuum as I cleaned the pool. And I could sense the searingly bright noonday sun spent on the roof of the buildings sealing cracks. I remembered the tense evenings with my mother, who had agreed to let me stay with her for the two and a half months it would take for my spot in Air Force basic training to open up.

+ + +

I had just gotten back to my room, when I got a call from my sister, Bonnie. I answered, "Hey. How was the trip?"

"Fine. We just checked in to the hotel," she said. "Dean and I are on a special diet, and we need to eat within the next half-hour or so."

"Oh, there's a nice restaurant here in my hotel, would that work?"

"No, while Dean was driving, I found a place where we can eat."

"Should I meet you there? Where is it?" I asked. She gave me the address, and I made my way down to get my rental car.

The restaurant they chose was in a strip mall, but the exterior had a façade of dark stained wood. The interior was dimly lit for the dinner service and the tones were deep green and deep, red brown. Fort Collins is not a huge city by any means, but by the time I got to the restaurant, Dean and Bonnie had already been seated at a booth with overstuffed, leather upholstery. And they had already ordered their food without me being there. It was nearly 8pm, and I had eaten much earlier in the evening, so I simply slid into the booth they were in, and I ordered a drink.

We made small talk about travel and work, and they politely asked about my wife and my sons. I was in a slightly maudlin mood, and I risked telling my sister that I was proud of her. I was proud of how far she had come from the runaway I knew when I was eleven. How far she had come from the ward of the state she was when she was in her late teens. How she had gotten her GED, then her bachelor's degree, her masters, and then had earned her Ph.D.

"Maybe it's because I have been thinking about everything we went through with Mom," I told her. "But before we talk about anything else, I have to tell you how proud I am of you. Everything you've done is amazing."

Her response was to avoid looking at me and to keep eating in silence. It was the same silence she'd mastered as a child, the kind that could make you disappear even when you were sitting right there. I recognized it because I'd learned it too—we'd both developed ways of vanishing without leaving the room. But I'd thought that somehow, all these years later, after everything she'd accomplished, we might have moved past the need to protect ourselves from each other.

Even in the dim light of the restaurant, I could see the look on Dean's face go from slightly shocked at my saying what I said, to disappointed when Bonnie didn't respond. They finished their meal. I finished my drink, and we agreed to meet at my mother's apartment the next morning.

When I walked across the parking lot to my rental car to drive to the back to the hotel, I was reminded of how impossibly mild a late summer evening in the foothills of the mountains can be. It was one of those Rocky Mountain nights where, even in the city, it seemed like I could see every star in the heavens, and there was just a slight blue over the mountains to the west where the sun had not too long ago set. I rolled down all windows in the car, just to feel cool air, because cool air was better than feeling nothing at all.

Back to the hotel, as I walked past the front desk, I was greeted with, "Hello, Mr. LaFleur. Welcome back."

I waved and said, "Thanks."

I got to my room and found a large gift basked full of fruit, pastries, chocolate, a bottle of wine, and a card that expressed the sympathy of the staff of the hotel at the loss of my mother. This would be the only sympathy card I was to receive, even after I returned home to Minnesota.

+ + +

My mother had a small set of co-workers in Fort Collins, and my cousin, who was my mother's niece, and her family lived in town, so we had a small memorial service for her at a meeting space in the apartment complex she had recently moved in to.

She was not religious, so my sister found some acquaintance of my mother who had posted something vaguely Christian on his Facebook page and asked him to say some words. He spoke about eternal rest and peace, about forgiveness and love—words that felt hollow in that sterile conference room.

I found myself wondering if forgiveness was something you could choose, or something that simply happened to you. Whether my mother deserved it. Whether I was capable of it.

The room looked like a typical multipurpose space, perhaps a business conference room, except that the wall to the back of the room was full of windows that overlooked a courtyard that was well groomed and full of late summer flowers.

I think the pathetic little memorial service was what made me cry.

At the end of the ceremony, my mother's primary care doctor introduced herself to me, and said she thought my mother was brave. I am sure I was polite in my response, but I stood there trying to make sense of the woman who was younger than me, with tattoos visible on her arms, making judgements about my mother's fortitude. This young doctor didn't know the woman I knew as my mother.

Walking back to the hotel from the parking lot that evening, I thought about the doctor's assessment of my mother's bravery. Maybe faith was like that too—other people could see virtues in you that you couldn't see in yourself. Maybe grace worked the same way.

+ + +

The day after the memorial, we set about putting my mother's things and affairs in order. she had no retirement savings or pension before she died, living the best she could on on Social Security and wages from a part-time job. But she had managed to save over twenty thousand dollars.

When she was diagnosed, and my sister and I learned of the prognosis, we convinced her to move to a luxury assisted living facility. There was no way she could possibly outlive her savings, and it was okay if every dollar would go toward the rent.

There was no will to sort through, and there was no need for probate. She had not left anything behind that hinted at what she wanted to happen to the few belongings and the little money she had, but there was no fight or argument.

As we walked into the apartment, Bonnie said to me, "There is some of Mom's stuff that I want," the tone hinting that she felt there might be an argument.

I simply said, "I don't want anything. You can take anything you want." After a moment's pause, I added, "Take everything."

The apartment was a one-bedroom unit with a small living room adjoining a kitchen. It looked to me that my mother had lived in it for years, she had settled into it so well, so quickly. In reality, she had been in the space for less than two weeks. I didn't recognize anything in the apartment as being anything from my early childhood. There were no family heirlooms, no hanging family photos, nothing from my past. My sister, however, seemed to find sentimental value in things I simply didn't recognize—an end table, a tablecloth, a pillow. Any of these might have given her the impression that she should keep it.

While my mother's recent move was mostly unnoticeable in how she ordered and arranged what meager furniture she had, there were still boxes that had been moved in that had been unpacked.

Bonnie and Dean went through boxes looking for sentimental things, I was searching for documents, because I was concerned that someone might steal her identity once her obituary was printed and cause a legal issue down the road. My plan was to find anything that could be used by someone to create a fake identity and make sure to get it shredded before I returned home. I gathered the three boxes that were full of documents to the center of the small living room floor.

It didn't make sense that a woman who had nothing legally complex in her life would have thought to keep as many documents as she had kept. People in our circumstances usually learned to travel light, to keep what mattered and discard the rest. But she had burdened herself with this accumulation of paper, and before long I was making three piles on the living room floor.

One was for documents that had sensitive information that could be used in id theft and would need to be destroyed by shredding. Another pile was obviously harmless documents that could simply be thrown away. And the third was for letters, or cards, or things that might be significant in some emotional way.

I wasn't sure what I would do with the third pile. Besides, I was completely disengaged from this task. It was as if I approached it the way I'd been trained to handle any mission—methodically, emotionally detached, focused on the objective. Sort, categorize, complete. Don't think about what it means; just execute the task. It was easier that way.

There was little need to invest any emotion in going through the first box. As I went through it, the box was mostly banking records and tax returns. There was nothing of significance. They were merely papers that had rows of numbers and figures on them. These all went into a pile destined for the shredder. I shoved the empty box aside for later use and pulled the second box closer to me.

The first papers I pulled out turned out to be from lawyers and courts.

While still not emotionally invested, I soon found myself reading these papers with a bit of curiosity. The story they told jogged my memory. Over twenty years prior, my mother had filed for bankruptcy, and the papers I was looking at chronicled the journey through the process from the start to the terms of her settlement.

I felt slightly like a voyeur reading these, and even though they contained little sensitive information a criminal could use, I put them in the shred pile.

The next section in this box was full of yellowed legal documents much like the others. The first ones I looked at were all dated in the year 1977—the year my parents got divorced.

In the first few documents was the divorce decree itself with the seal of the court on top. My parents' divorce was not the simple matter it had seemed at first glance. It went through the court system, with a judge specifying the terms of the divorce.

I had known that a judge was involved in the divorce, but I had never seen the decree. My parents had no property of value to divide, and I knew that even at the time the divorce was going on. The decree ordered my father to give my mother a large portion of his Navy retirement for the rest of her life. And there were other details of the divorce that I didn't really pay attention to.

The section on custody, visitation, and child support was well known to me as well. My sister and I were put into the custody of my father, and since he was the primary income earner, there was no child support defined. As for visitation, this was undefined as well. My father had sole custody of Bonnie and me, with no indication that my mother would even see us.

The sun that had been streaming onto that apartment floor went dim, as if a thunderhead was brewing. I began to feel a cold, heavy knot in my stomach while reading the judge's decision. I shifted my sitting position, and I could feel my heart rate increase. I wanted to get out of that living room. I paused for a few moments, and then placed the decree into the shred pile.

The next set of papers that followed the decree seemed to be a set of random correspondence between my mother and her lawyer, and her lawyer and the judge. I was about to put the entire set in the throw away pile, but for some reason, I started riffling through the stack, not knowing what I was looking for, but feeling a prickling sensation across the back of my neck that compelled me to look. That's when I came across a letter that had my name in the first paragraph. I began to feel nauseated as I read the contents of the letter.

I had spent my entire life from the time I was eleven to the time I was forty-five—the age I was when going through those boxes—believing that I had cruelly turned away from my mother and chosen to live with my father after the divorce. Whenever my mother wanted to manipulate me, or, in those early days of the divorce, make me cry in remorse for what she told me I had done, she would tell me how hurt she was that I had chosen to leave her all alone and go live with my father. This letter to the judge revealed that this had all been a lie. I had not chosen to live with my father. I had not had a choice in the matter at all.

In the first paragraph of the letter, my mother's lawyer explained to the judge that my mother would not be contesting custody of me: "Mrs. LaFleur has expressed that, due to her vulnerable and fragile state at this juncture, she does not feel capable of effectively raising her son. Furthermore, she perceives no foreseeable relief from this condition. She has encountered significant difficulties managing and understanding her son's emotional and behavioral issues, which have become increasingly challenging. Consequently, Mrs. LaFleur does not wish to pursue custody at this time."

The words on the page seemed to pulse with their own terrible light. My vision narrowed until nothing existed except those typed sentences that dismantled my entire childhood story.

The room fell away—Dean and my sister were still there, sorting through doilies and napkins and old photos of cats, their voices a distant murmur—but I was utterly alone in a way I hadn't felt since I was eleven years old.

My hands began to shake. The same hands that had sorted through documents with precision moments before now trembled as they held the evidence of my mother's betrayal. I set the letter down carefully, afraid I might tear it, afraid I might lose this proof of what I'd always suspected but never dared to name. Since the letter was from a lawyer to a judge in support of a case traversing its way through court, in my hands I had legal proof that my mother had not wanted me. I had always suspected this, but here was solid proof.

I was forty-five years old, sorting through my dead mother's belongings, when I discovered the legal proof that she had never wanted me.

For thirty-four years, I had believed I was the one who cruelly chose to leave her. The truth was much heavier: the choice was not mine to make.

I did not say anything to my sister about what I had found because I didn't want to start a fight, which, based on our history, was a certainty. I sat with the letter in my lap for a few minutes, sometimes looking at the words on the page, sometimes gazing off into space.

CHAPTER TWO

As I have aged, one of the most difficult lessons I have learned in life is that we don't often get what we think we deserve. Finding out that my mother actively plotted with her lawyer to convince the judge that she was not capable of caring for me, her ten-year-old son, was a thunderclap that shattered the narrative I had built around my life. Recognizing that I was unwanted by my mother caused a visceral tightening of my chest, sent cold energy surging through my nerves and sinews, and triggered me to question what I had thought I knew about how I came to be the man, the husband, and father that I was. It provoked me into taking inventory of the memories of my life.

+ + +

My earliest recollections swirl in the mists of a deep green forest. When I walk up to the forest in my mind, I can see images swirling around the trees, sometimes becoming vivid as they get near the path that leads deeper into the woodland. And if I tread on that twisting path, I can get nearer to these moments, but like skittish birds, they ebb away back into the shadows if I approach them too quickly.

What's clear and visible in one moment shifts and changes, fading from view slowly, vanishing if I look too closely at it. Some distinct moments are not obscured by haze, however. Some moments stand at the edge of these swirling recollections as if they are guideposts or mile markers along the path. These moments are perfectly clear, and I can recall them with lucid detail. I can see the colors, hear the sounds, feel the sensations of these moments. The circumstances around these moments are part of the shadows, but the moments themselves are solid. Like a patient detective, I can take these clear recollections and search for clues to build a case around them.

I lay the scant few photos I have from my childhood in front of me at my desk. My birth certificate and my baptismal record in their plastic document protector sit to one side, and an internet browser is open to a map or Wikipedia. More than a detective now, I feel like a manic conspiracy theorist creating a web of connections using yarn and push pins with the clues, a web meant to trap moments in some sensible arrangement.

+ + +

According to my birth certificate, I was born in Alabama on Brookly Air Force Base in 1966. That it was the place of my birth is the sum total of what I know about Brookly, but I have no recollections of it. My time in Alabama must have been short because images of my time there have faded away.

The earliest moment of my life that I can recall well is of a snowy day. I can see myself walking along what to me felt like a path carved out of the snow. The sides of this path were flanked with sculptures of crystalline white. I can see my arms flopping back and forth covered in heavy, dark blue sleeves. When I focus on this recollection, I get a feeling of wonder. I stopped to look at each snow sculpture as any toddler would have done.

The wonder must have been what I felt as I stopped to gaze at the snow-made brilliantly bright, bluish white doghouse with a dog lying with its head on its paws. I crouched down to look more closely at the dog. In the misty vision of my recollection, the dog is only a shape, generic, colorless. It's just the image of a dog that I see even with my face getting closer as I bent down. While I inspected the dog, my vision went suddenly and violently black. I felt the cold sting of snow on my face as I was briefly blinded, and I heard the laughing of the man, my father, who had just slammed snow into my face.

Oftentimes it's difficult to put times and ages to an early recollection, but in my case my life's timeline is neatly dotted with moves that my father's career in the Navy forced on us. In the case of my earliest moment, I can give it a rough date because there certainly would not have been snow in Alabama where I was born, and the next duty station we had lived at was in Great Lakes, Illinois.

We lived in Illinois from 1966 through 1968, having left Alabama mere months after I was born. There are no photos of our first time in Illinois, just stories from that time: stories that told of a small duplex in Zion, Illinois, not far from the Navy installation on Lake Michigan, and stories that told of the tricks my father, thinking they were funny, used to play on me as a toddler.

When I was older and I was around when my father was regaling new friends, one of the stories he thought would get a laugh from people was the story of smashing snow in my face as a toddler. Depending on the mood of the audience, he would let them know that's not all he did. Another of his favorite tricks was to squirt lemon juice into my mouth while I was in the highchair waiting for my meal. To hear my mother tell it when I was older, he squirted lemon juice into my mouth most days until I stopped reacting to it, and then he switched to little bits of hot cherry peppers just to see how I would handle it.

As an adult I wouldn't feel the sour pucker of the lemon juice, nor would I feel the sharp bite of the hot peppers, but the black cold of the snow slamming into my face would weigh heavily on my mind. Even then, some part of me held to the notion of shelter, of vigilant eyes—though I was learning that such shelter or would not always come from those bound by blood to give it.

+ + +

Life in a career military family is one of constant relocation. The military doesn't like service members setting up dynasties at an installation, so they transfer soldiers and sailors every three years mostly, and occasionally in two. Since my father was a career sailor in the Navy, this kept our family moving. The institution's needs always came first—stable communities and lasting friendships were luxuries the military couldn't afford to let anyone develop.

By 1968, when I was two years old, we had moved to Long Beach, California, in preparation for my father to ship out on his second tour in Vietnam. I don't have direct recollections of this move, but I have photos of this era that anchor the time in my mind.

I can look back on the house we moved into and be reminded of the colors that defined that period of my life. Life in Southern California was a robin egg blue house, a green and orange bird of paradise plant in the yard, and a brownish haze in the sky.

In the 1960s and 70s photos taken with a small format camera were always printed with the date the photo was developed. I can look at these photos of my early life and pinpoint the dates.

In one photo, I can see my father standing in front of that blue house in his khaki uniform with his mother and his mother-in-law flanking him, and I can see that it was taken in May of 1968, before he shipped out to Vietnam. In it, he does not look like the hollowed-out man that I knew later in life. In this photo he is tall and gaunt, smiling. His hands rest on both grandmothers' forearms while their arms cross over his. It's almost as if he felt he should be holding their hands but couldn't bring himself to do it. His mother is a round, soft pale woman who looks uncomfortable getting her picture taken, and his mother-in-law appears angry to have been made to stand there.

Another of the three-by-three-inch photos shows Navy swift boats moored in a river so wide that it had to be the Mekong in Vietnam, and the date on the back says June 1969. The back of the photo has "CCB & Zippo" in my father's handwriting. A CCB was a heavily armed boat designed specifically for combat in the rivers of Vietnam, and the Zippo was an armored river assault boat with flame throwers mounted on the front. As an electrician, my father would have been in Vietnam to do maintenance on these and other river attack boats.

While he was in Vietnam, my mother was left back home like any other Army or Navy wife whose husband was deployed to the war, functioning as a single mother raising her children alone. The military paid my father, but it left my mother to manage a household on an enlisted man's salary while juggling the roles of both parents. For military families like ours, the commissary and base exchange became lifelines—places where a Navy wife could stretch a paycheck, buying groceries at cost and clothing without sales tax. But even with these small mercies, and I would not know it then, money ran lean as winter creeks, and the weight of his absence bore down on everything. Made it all harder. More brittle.

I have fragmented recollections of my mother and me walking in a big building with hard surfaces, highly polished floors, and little decoration. We spent a lot of time on the Navy base. It was where we would have bought groceries, or shopped for clothing, or gone to doctor's appointments. And this trip would have been something official because of the long corridors with the occasional hard, brushed steel chair positioned next to a closed office door.

Along with whatever business my mom was taking care of in that building, at some point we had lunch in a cafeteria. My mother got a tray, some silverware, and led me past the glass streaked with rivulets from the steam table keeping the food warm. She asked the servers for our food, put it on the tray, and slid the tray down the bars in front of the glass. She paid a cashier, and then we went looking for a table in a crowded room. At a square table with a brown formica top, my mother put my food in front of me, and we blessed the meal with a traditional Catholic prayer of grace, the familiar words a small comfort in the uncertainty of military family life. My plate had some sort of sandwich on it along with some french fries. My mother had used the bottle at the table to put ketchup near the fries in a red blob, and I immediately grabbed the saltshaker and put salt on the ketchup, watching the white crystals pile up.

"Stop that," my mother snapped.

"Why? You put salt on yours."

"We don't put salt on ketchup," she responded.

Before I could ask another "Why," a sailor in a Navy blue, winter uniform sat down at the table with us. The room was completely full, and there were no other seats available. He must have asked permission to sit with us, but I didn't hear it. When he sat down, seeing a man in uniform join us at the table, I said to my mother, "Is this my dad?"

The sailor chuckled politely, and my mother said with obvious embarrassment, "No. No, that's not your dad."

+ + +

The house in Long Beach was a single-story house on a block of single-story houses. Across the street was an elementary school with an asphalt playground.

I could watch out the front window of the living room as the children played at recess in the smoggy Southern California air. The living room was small with dark furniture, including a rocking chair with brown cushions on it. The carpet was a dark green, and the wooden trim in the room was dark brown. There was always a haze of cigarette smoke in the room, and if the sun was at the right angle there would be golden sunbeams cutting across the room highlighting the smoke and the dust motes. Near the rocking chair stood a small end table, with an ashtray and a small, square, metal picture frame.

I would often kneel at that table and look at the photo of my father in the frame.

Even though I didn't remember him, I had been told that the man in the frame was my father, so I studied the picture often. If I slid the brown back of the flimsy golden frame off, there were two other photos inside. I could take one of the photos from the back and slip it to the front, and put the frame back together, and I would have a different view of my father. All three of the photos were similar though. One photo was him in a Navy dress uniform on the deck of a ship. Another was of him in a work uniform on a deck of a ship off the coast of Vietnam, and the last was a photo of him with a straw hat, a scarf, and white t-shirt, again on the deck of a ship. Once a day, I would rotate a photo to the front, just to see another view of my father.

+ + +

There was no homecoming, no going to the Navy base and watching the ship come to port, no welcoming band, no streamers or ticker tape. My father had served his second tour in Vietnam in support of attack boats that operated on the rivers in the jungles. He didn't sail over on a ship. To get to Vietnam, he had gotten on an airplane and flown over, and to return he had gotten on another airplane and flown home.

I have no memory of his arrival, of joy, of tears or embraces. As if suddenly a tall, gaunt, chain-smoking man had just appeared in our small house in Long Beach.

While I didn't notice it consciously, we must have simply slipped into a sort of routine. The next clear recollection that stands in my mind occurred soon after my father returned from the war. This incident is that of a car accident.

The year 1970 was a time before seatbelt laws and children's car seats, and my sister and I would often ride in the car standing up in the back seat with our arms resting on the front bench seat, elbows splayed, chins resting on laced fingers, watching the road from our perch.

One day in particular, my sister stood in the back of the car, while I, at the age of four, sat in the passenger seat, without a seatbelt, just within arm's reach of my mother behind the steering wheel. I didn't notice a stop light or a stop sign or see the car my mother struck.

What I saw was my sister flying over the back seat and hitting her head on the rear-view mirror. I didn't see her falling into the front seat of the car and sliding down to the floor. I didn't see that my mother had struck the steering wheel with her chest, but I did feel the sharp impact of the dashboard as I slammed into it.

We must not have been traveling too fast, because I heard the crying of my mother and my sister rather than silence. To me it felt as if no time at all had passed by the time an ambulance arrived and took us to a hospital. But in that moment of impact, in the sudden violence of metal meeting metal, I learned that the world could change in an instant—a lesson that would stay with me long after the bruises faded. I was already learning to watch for danger, to prepare for the next blow, whether it came from a car accident or a mother's or father's hand.

There was no blood, but something in the way they looked brought urgency to the staff when we reached the hospital. My mother and sister were taken quickly to examination rooms, and I was left alone in the waiting area. I was not panicked or frightened. I just sat there in that vast room, legs hanging from the grown-up chair, learning the particular silence that comes when the people who are supposed to stay simply vanish.

Since he had been home from Vietnam for a while, I had grown accustomed to the uniformed man who headed our household. So, when he eventually reached the hospital in uniform, I recognized him coming into the emergency room waiting area as I was sitting in that gray room all by myself. He must have said something to me as he walked past; at the very least, I think, he must have acknowledged me, but he left me there alone, while he went back to the examination rooms to check on my mother and sister.

After some time had passed, time enough to have taken x-rays of my mother's chest and my sister's head, the three of them came into the waiting room together. Despite the reaction when we had arrived, neither my mother nor my sister had been injured severely enough to have been admitted.

They gathered me up from the waiting room, and we went home. For my mother and my sister, there was no lasting damage, but for me, I have never forgotten being abandoned and ignored in that waiting room.

Over the years, wrestling with my memories, I had convinced myself that the military had trained my father to prioritize mission over family, and in my mind years later I forged the idea that in that waiting room, I witnessed what that training wrought. But there was more to it. I learned that institutions and individuals, along with my father, often times served only themselves, and children like me were expendable. Disposable. I did not matter in their calculations, and I never would.

+ + +

During one of his deployments, the ship my father sailed made port in Japan. I was never told of that voyage, nor of any deployment. I know he had been there because he brought back a lacquered box, round and deep, along with a pair of chopsticks I was forbidden to touch. My mother used this box, dark as dried blood with cherry blossoms painted across its surface, to hold our photographs. There was no order to them. They were simply cast into the box like refuse, and the lid sealed shut.

When I was small and my parents were elsewhere, I would take that box from its shelf, sit on the floor, and place it before me. Then I would lift the lid with care, remove the photos one by one, study them briefly, and set them on the floor. I handled them gently so as not to damage what little record we had, sorting them into piles—Navy here, siblings there, Long Beach in one corner, Vietnam in another.

There would be many photos in most categories. Of father and son, there were two. Perhaps three.

I sort through memory the same way now. When no one watches, I take down the box of images I have buried in my mind and open it with the same care. I examine each moment, most often treating them with nothing more than passing curiosity before returning them to their darkness. Other times, I arrange the recollections in their proper categories. This careful cataloging, this need to impose order on chaos, became my first way to survive.

When I examine these early years, I cannot escape how fundamental they were to what passed between my father and me. Or perhaps what never passed at all.

I place these memories in the category father and son. There is room yet in that small pile.

What I could not know then, sitting on that floor with scattered photographs, was that that box would grow heavy with loss. That the categories would multiply and darken. That I would learn the particular weight of abandonment not once but again and again, until it became the language I spoke most fluently.

I could not know that years later I would build my own different box, fill it with better photographs, only to watch death empty it piece by piece.

Or that in the deepest darkness, when even God seemed absent from the frame, something would remain. Some thread that connected the abandoned boy on the floor to the man who would one day understand grace.

But that understanding lay buried beneath years of leaving and being left. Beneath the sound of doors closing and the silence that follows. Beneath the weight of soil and the echo of final words–or the echo of no words spoken.

MICHAEL LAFLEUR

The photographs in my mind are scattered still. But I have learned, at last, how to arrange them. How to see the hand that was always there, even when the frame seemed empty.

CHAPTER THREE

The skies above Southern California were thick with poison in 1970. Any photograph from that time shows the brownish haze that settled over everything like judgment, dulling the world to sepia tones. Even at four, I could taste its bitter presence when the smog lay heaviest. The air itself had weight.

Before I began this excavation of memory, I would have called that poisoned sky normal. I did not recognize the acrid haze that filled my lungs or the silent toxins that filled my days for what they were. I breathed them both without question, a child learning that corruption was simply the nature of air.

Only now do I understand that some poisons work slowly. That they settle into bone and breath and become the very substance of what you think is life. The smog would lift some days, but other toxins proved more permanent. They seeped into the foundation of everything, invisible and patient as cancer.

I was learning to breathe poison and call it normal. Learning that the sky could be brown and still be called sky.

Our house at 6480 Myrtle Avenue in Long Beach could have been plucked off the set of any contemporary movie filmed in the late 1960s, but that house was not the setting for a comedy. The palette, the shape, the features were all as if they were chosen by a set designer in mid-century California. With the smog softening its edges, it looked perpetually faded—dull white aluminum awnings above the front windows, weathered shutters alongside, a neglected flower box with one empty flowerpot under the larger window. The lawn was yellow and brown from lack of care, and the ragged shrubs were dark green in front of the fading robin egg blue exterior walls.

The interior was no better than the outside. Instead of smog, though, the house was filled with lingering cigarette smoke. My father chain smoked Pall Mall filterless. My mother smoked the same brand, though she was a more modest smoker.

Usually there was a smoldering cigarette in an ashtray somewhere in the house, its wisp of white smoke rising up, only to evanesce before it reached the ceiling. I have no recollection that the cigarette smoke gave off a lingering odor, having no experience of being inside without the constant pall of my parents smoking.

Looking back, I realize so much more than just the smoke hung heavy in that house.

+ + +

When my father was gone, my mother would impose rules that carried no logic I could figure out. Some days, the law was exile—I was to remain in the backyard until summoned. Other days it was confinement—I was to stay within the house until she chose to cast me out.

There was no pattern to these decrees, no crime that preceded the punishment. Only the arbitrary will of a woman who seemed to need distance from the child she had carried. I learned to read her moods like weather, watching for the signs that would determine whether I was banished to sun or shadow.

The rules changed with her moods, but the message remained constant: I was something to be managed. Contained. Kept at whatever distance her psyche required on any given day.

When she wanted me inside, my mother would lock the doors—even the screen doors, which had a small, difficult-to-move tab that would slide up into a slot on the handle. The tab was too stiff for my little fingers to press out of the slot, so the lock usually worked to keep me trapped wherever she decided I belonged.

The day before my planned escape, I had figured out a way to open the door without needing to slide the tab down. The screen door used a spring-loaded little bar to catch the barbed end of the door handle. If you pressed the little bar up against the door frame, the handle would free itself.

Finally, the day arrived for my planned breakout. When my mother was out of the kitchen, I pressed the spring all the way to the door jamb and pushed the screen door open.

I don't know how long I was in the backyard, but at some point my mother called me. "Mike! Mike!" I heard her call. "Mike where in the hell are you?" her voice turning angry. "Little mister, you get over here right now!" she shouted when I didn't respond. I pulled on the screen door to try to get back in the house, but since the door was locked and the handle caught on the spring-loaded bar again, I was trapped outside.

I began to get frightened. My mother appeared in the door and yelled, "There you are! Get in here right now!" She unlocked the screen door, swung it open wide, reached down and grabbed my arm, and dragged me into the house. She didn't stop until she got to the tiny bedroom my sister and I shared, threw me on the bed so I landed face down, tore my pants down so my bottom was bare, and started beating me with her open hand.

Sometimes the spankings included counting, as if there were some designated number she had to reach. Other times the spankings continued until she just quit. Most every time she spanked me, she would throw in a threat of eternal damnation: "You are going to hell if you don't start behaving." I sobbed into the pillow after she had stopped and left the room.

By the time I was four, I would have known that if I had a toy out and my mother thought it was no longer time to play with that particular toy, I would be punished for not picking up. At some point, I realized that if I didn't get any toys out, I would not risk getting a beating. Into adulthood, my sister would tell me repeatedly, and tell anyone she introduced me to, that I was a strange child who never played with toys.

The rules were never explained to me, but I began to learn which of my actions would bring wrath. Which sounds I made were too loud, which movements too quick. This knowing helped me avoid some beatings, and more than that, it helped me breathe easier because I was not always waiting for damnation to come from nowhere.

The beatings still happened, but the wild fear began to settle into something I could carry. I had learned the weather of her anger, and that small knowledge was the first power I ever held.

+ + +

In my memory, I don't see much furniture in our room. The only piece I can recall clearly was a small blue chest that when opened revealed the toys I had slowly stopped playing with. The room became more cramped when Billy moved in with us.

Even in normal families, parents don't explain everything to their children before they do it. So in our family, there would have been absolutely no way my parents would have sat down with my sister and me to explain their plans to become foster parents, or that they looked at fostering as a stepping stone to adoption.

One day my father started attaching padding to the corners of furniture and to the edges of walls.

"What are you doing?" I asked.

"I am getting ready for Billy," he replied without stopping.

"Who's Billy?"

"Billy is going to be your brother."

When I asked my mother about it, she explained that Billy was a boy who bruised easily, which is why we were putting padding all over the house. She said Billy had no parents, and that she and my father had agreed to take him into our house. Later I learned that Billy suffered from hemophilia and was in the foster system. My parents had decided they would first foster Billy, then adopt him into our family.

There are two photos of Billy that remain. One shows my sister at age seven in a red jumper dress over a blue blouse, me in a light brown suit and black shoes, bracketing my father who is sitting on the front step in his blue suit, trying to hold a four-year-old Billy upright. Billy, wearing an umber colored jacket with dark brown pants, is bent over, looking as if he is about to dart away. This was definitely a Holy day photo of us ready to go to church.

The other photo is black-and-white and professionally done. My sister and I both have light colored hair, mine in a crew cut and hers in a pixie cut.

Our complexions are light, and even in black-and-white, you can see that our eyes are light in color. We both have formed smiles with our mouths, but our eyes are not smiling. Billy sits in contrast to us, with his black hair and deeply dark eyes and dark skin. On his face is a true smile that starts with his eyes and carries down to the huge grin on his face. He seems to be the only truly happy one in the photo.

Billy is etched into my memory even without the photos. His small stature, his dark features, his occasional bursts of happiness.

My parents treated Billy differently than they treated me. Perhaps it was due to his condition, with their thinking that he was too fragile for the treatment they gave me, but in any conflict between the two of us, my parents would come down on Billy's side. Even so, Billy cried most of the time, no matter how gently my parents handled him. I would hear Billy wailing in the living room, and when I walked in, I would see him being rocked in the brown padded rocking chair, its spring rockers squeaking with each motion, keeping a rhythm that was out of sync with Billy's sobs. Either my mother or my father would be rocking him, something they never did for me.

Billy and I played together as any two boys would. He was even able to get toys out of the small blue chest in our room and play with them without my mother's wrath descending on him. However, he was not allowed outside without my parents watching over him. Their concern that he might fall and bruise himself or start bleeding uncontrollably was too horrifying for them to contemplate.

+ + +

One misty and smoggy morning, while my mother was in the kitchen where there was a small window that opened to the backyard, Billy and I were allowed to go outside, with the stern warning that we were to stay on the concrete patio because the grass was wet with dew. My mother was frightened that Billy would slip in the grass and bruise himself.

Before Billy had come to our house, I had a rusted red tricycle on that patio that I would ride around in circles alone, like a circus bear that nobody cared to watch. After Billy arrived, the trike was gone, so when we were on the patio it was just the two of us with no toys on a slab of cement, the red paint that used to cover it flaking away.

While we were walking around the patio, I spotted in the yard a ball that must have been left out overnight. It couldn't have been more than three feet from the edge of the patio, but with the command that we stay on the patio it might as well have been a mile away.

"Billy. There's a ball right there. You want to play with it, don't you?" I said rather cagily, hoping Billy would take the bait and fetch it.

"No. I can't go there," he whined.

"If you get the ball, we can play here. Mom won't know."

"No… You get it."

I knew if I went to get the ball and my mother found out, I would get beaten. So I said, "You want to play with it."

"But…" he said, shaking his head and looking at the cement.

"Go get it. We'll play catch."

I had successfully talked Billy into venturing out into the yard to get the yellow striped ball lying in the dew-soaked grass, thinking that my mother would not punish him. Billy didn't walk slowly or carefully out into the grass. He ran from the dry, textured patio out onto the wet grass. Within two steps, well short of where the ball was, Billy fell hard, and he started to screech and wail.

When I heard the high shriek of the aluminum screen door, I knew my mother had heard Billy and was coming. The sound cut through the morning like a blade, sharp and final. Knowing what awaited me, the belt and the words that would follow, I wanted to fade into the smoggy morning air so she wouldn't see me standing there.

My mother was outside in an instant, picking Billy up off the ground. She cradled him as she brought him into the house, yelling at me, "Michael Orlin, you get your butt inside the house this moment." That was followed by, "Go to your room and get on your bed!" I knew what came next and started crying in anticipation.

She brought Billy, still crying, into the room and placed him on a bed. With hardly a second's delay, she pushed me so that I had my face down on my pillow, tore my pants down, and slapped my bare bottom repeatedly. This time there was no counting as fury alone dictated the number of slaps I got, each blow punctuated with "You!" Slap. "Are!" Slap. "Going!" Slap. "To!" Slap. "Hell!" Slap.

When she quit, she turned her attention to Billy to try and console him, leaving me to sob into my pillow.

+ + +

Occasionally, a woman would visit our house to check on my parents' care of Billy. They would invite the woman in and shoo my sister and me away to our room, while encouraging Billy to come into the living room. He would fuss and cry about having to go with the adults rather than with the children, as they coaxed him to go to the woman sitting in the rocking chair.

My sister and I would be able to hear discussions in hushed tones coming from the room, but at the time we had no idea that the woman was a social worker evaluating the fostering done by my parents. Billy's crying seemed to grow more frequent as the length of time he was at our house grew, and the visits from the social worker increased as well.

One day, just as suddenly as he had appeared in our house, Billy vanished. My days went back to watching my sister leave for school in the morning, leaning my head on the windowsill as she walked down the step past the ragged shrubs, along the browned, unkempt grass, and out of sight. Then I would wait for my mother to dictate the rules of the day, whether I was to be kept outside, or kept inside, or banished to my room, all the while trying to avoid a beating and banishment to hell.

+ + +

I think of Billy often. The weight of what I caused settles heavier now that I am grown. I pray he found people who could tend him properly, who could give him what our house could not. I pray the joy I glimpsed in that photograph took root and flourished despite us.

I hold no malice toward Billy, but his time among us brought only more ways to transgress, more paths to punishment. More welts, more promises of damnation.

The social worker came to inspect Billy's care but never questioned ours. She did not see the particular stillness my sister and I had learned, or wonder why a four-year-old would not touch the toys placed before him. When something went wrong with Billy, she took him. When something went wrong with us, she left us to endure it.

Even then, I was learning that those charged with protecting children served other masters. That they could witness one variety of suffering and remain blind to another. That some lives carried more weight in their calculations than others.

In that poisoned air, thick as the silence that governed our days, I learned to watch and wait and endure. These lessons would help me well.

CHAPTER FOUR

The smog that poisoned the days would transform at sunset, painting the sky in soft pinks and purples and oranges. The air would cool and carry salt from the nearby ocean, and the palms and Bird of Paradise would sway in the evening wind, their dark shapes cutting against the colored sky.

It was beautiful, this poison made lovely by dying light. The same corruption that burned our lungs by day became something almost sacred when the sun fell toward the water. Even toxin could be transformed by the proper angle of illumination.

On evenings when everything was just right, my mother would step into the kitchen, her hands deft and practiced as she fried golden-brown chicken in a cast-iron skillet.

The scent of seasoned meat and heated oil would overtake the ocean air drifting through our windows. On the stove next to the skillet, a pot of potatoes would boil gently, the smell of starch mingling with the savory aromas. I would watch as she moved to the counter, where she began to mash the steaming potatoes with butter and milk, transforming them into something warm and comforting.

On other days when things fell into place, my mother might carefully measure me with her seamstress's tape, so she could sew a shirt for me. She would pin the pattern to the cloth stretched out over the single table in our house and make small white marks with a piece of chalk. The spool of thread would spin on top of the sewing machine as she quietly and deliberately stitched the pieces together with care. Seemingly without effort, she would make the shirt take shape as she sewed, each seam a small act of creation.

Those acts of caring, those brief flashes of love, served to confuse me when her erratic and unpredictable behavior took over. The same hands that made my shirts would strike without warning. The same voice that hummed while cooking would scream threats of eternal damnation. It seemed to me that her treatment worsened during the times my father was deployed, as if his absence gave her permission to become someone I couldn't recognize.

Sometimes heavy clouds would gather on the horizon, gray as gunmetal, creeping inland from the ocean to devour the light. The air would thicken and turn electric, charged with something that made the skin prickle. Wind would lash the palms and drive chill through the streets, and everything would grow still in that particular way that comes before violence.

When weather arrived like this, slow and deliberate, it would transform our house into something else entirely. The walls would seem to contract, the rooms to darken, as if the storm outside had found its way into the very foundation of where we lived.

Even the light changed, becoming the color of old bruises.

+ + +

My father would rarely talk about his life in the Navy. Other than his orders to new duty stations, which involved uprooting my mother, my sister, and me, and moving to a new military town, everything I knew about his military career I had to piece together using the fragments left in our family's wake.

At the end of 1970 we moved from the little robin egg blue house in Long Beach to a condominium in San Diego. I was nearly five years old by then, and my memories became more numerous and clearer.

The townhouse complex housed military families like ours—fathers deployed for months, mothers managing alone with varying degrees of success, children left to navigate systems designed for different kinds of families.

In my short life, I had never seen a townhouse before. Until we moved to San Diego, my entire world had been a 900-square-foot, free-standing house, with two bedrooms, one bathroom, a concrete patio, and a backyard.

The only neighbors in my little world in Long Beach had been Mr. Holden in his short-sleeved button-up shirts which struggled to contain his well-earned belly. He would occasionally toss my sister and me bits of candy over the backyard fence. His wife, Mrs. Holden, the quintessential grandmotherly figure, would cluck and caution her husband not to give us too much candy and get us into trouble.

The move to San Diego meant being packed into a space dense with other people, with neighbors whose homes shared walls and concrete walkways with ours.

We lived on Pinecone Lane in a building that contained four townhouses. The building looked like a very large house, and it was part of a complex with dozens of identical buildings. Our townhouse was even smaller than our house in Long Beach—just over 800 square feet with two bedrooms and one bathroom. Each building was fronted by small patches of grass that formed a courtyard, with a sprawling network of curving walkways that connected the buildings.

During the day, children would play on the grass between the buildings, but when darkness came the young men would emerge to claim the benches along the sidewalks. They would drink and smoke and their voices would rise until the laughter turned harsh and threatening, all of it carrying through walls thin as paper.

After we moved to the townhouse, my mother grew afraid when the sun went down. Even with my father present those few weeks before he shipped out, she would pace and listen and start at every sound. Her fear moved through the house like smoke, settling into corners.

When my father vanished again, leaving her alone with her terror and leaving us alone with her, the nights became something to endure. Her fear had weight now, filling the rooms like smoke. We learned that darkness brought not just the threat of what prowled outside our windows, but the storms that raged within our walls.

The pattern of her moods followed no logic I could discern, but I began to understand that fear makes its own weather. Most of the violence stayed trapped inside her, but sometimes it would break free like lightning, sudden and scorching, before retreating back into the charged silence.

+ + +

By this time, I had learned to read my mother's moods and avoid most beatings. The technique was to do what she told me to do immediately with no questioning. On most Saturdays, when my mother told me that I needed to be bathed and scrubbed to prepare for church the next day, I did what she ordered and got into the tub. On Sunday mornings, I was expected to comb my hair and put on the suit my mother had sewn for me.

The Catholic church we attended was a short drive from our townhouse, and the three of us would dutifully make the trip. While the Sunday mornings in San Diego were typically sunny with blue skies, the sanctuary of the church was dimly lit and oppressive. The pews and wooden trim were dark brown, almost black wood, and the stained glass so dense that little outside light filtered into the space. The sanctuary held the odor of incense from countless holy days, a dry, acrid smell that seemed permanently embedded in the walls.

Facing the altar, the left and right walls displayed the Stations of the Cross—a series of relief sculptures depicting Jesus on the day of his crucifixion. The sculptures were dark metal with black patina, and they frightened me as a five-year-old. Like most families, we typically sat in the same pew every week, and our pew was positioned directly below Station 5, which depicted Simon of Cyrene helping Jesus carry the cross. It showed a man straining while dragging the cross, led by Jesus who had a halo surrounding his head in the relief image.

For a five-year-old, the services ran forever, and the pew seemed like a torture rack. If I fidgeted, swung my legs, or looked anywhere other than at the altar or pulpit, my mother would grasp and pinch my knee, squeezing hard enough that it hurt. I never cried out at the pain, knowing what would happen when we got home.

At the front of the church stood a votive stand of candles before the altar, and during mass there were many lit candles flickering on the altar itself. Since I couldn't occupy myself in any other way, I used to concentrate on the dancing of the candle flames in the distance. I had convinced myself that I could make the candles flicker and dance differently if I tried hard enough. Sitting perhaps ten rows back from the altar off to one side of the sanctuary, I would gently blow out air from between my lips. I had to do this quietly and subtly, so my mother would not notice. I watched the candles I had targeted, looking for the change in the flame that I believed I had caused. It was a small way of exerting control in a place where I had none.

At the time of service when communion was served, my mother and my sister would briefly leave me alone as they went forward to the altar together. During communion, I wasn't old enough to participate, so I remained in the pew, watching the other families move in orderly lines toward the priest.

The power to cast me into hell that the priest held—a power my mother's zealous theology reminded me of often—made me cautious of how I greeted him after service. Mostly, I would extend my hand for the required handshake with my eyes firmly directed to the dark floor just in front of my toes.

The little boy I was found church an uncomfortable, oppressive experience, and I would have found it this way even if I had not been seated next to my mother. But the church, like the school I would soon attend, seemed designed for families different from ours.

+ + +

In the fall of 1971, I started kindergarten at William Penn Elementary School. There was no excited anticipation on the first day of school, no loving preparation for the grand adventure that awaited. I was gathered up, put into the car, driven to the school, and unceremoniously dropped off at the door of the kindergarten classroom.

After learning that one way of avoiding a beating was to not play with toys, I had spent my time before kindergarten occupied with other pursuits. It must have been my sister who helped me learn the alphabet and introduced me to books, and by the time I showed up on that first day of kindergarten, I already knew how to read. The little books with one- or two-word sentences under line-drawn images were no challenge for me. We were presented with stacks of these books with yellow, blue, and green covers, and I tore through them within days.

This presented a problem for my teacher, because within the first week, I had finished the kindergarten reading curriculum and soon after finished the math curriculum as well.

Other teachers were brought in to assess my progress and figure out a way to keep me busy. The solution was to give me the first-grade curriculum, which I was to do on my own while sitting at a desk in the back of the room. I raced through that as well. By the time the school year was over, I had finished the second-grade materials and was starting on third grade.

The teachers who assessed my reading and gave me advanced work never asked why a five-year-old had learned to read so early, or why I seemed more comfortable working alone than playing with other children. They never asked why I walked home by myself each day, or why my mother never came to school events. Their solution was academic—more worksheets, harder books—but they never looked at the child completing the work.

Our short, half-day sessions included a recess, where the kids were sent out onto an asphalt playground dotted with sandboxes, red monkey bars, and swing sets with black rubber seats. But I spent my recesses walking around, mostly trying to avoid other kids. Sometimes I would dig in one of the sandboxes, moving the dry warm sand aside to expose the damp, musky-smelling earth beneath. One of the reasons for my reluctance to be with other kids during unstructured time was that I had no idea how to play; after all, I was punished at home for playing.

Kindergarten became a pattern: my mother dropping me off, the teachers puzzling over what to do with me, my sitting alone doing advanced curriculum, and my wandering around at recess trying not to interact with other kids. That pattern guaranteed I wouldn't be forced to do something I didn't understand, but it also guaranteed my isolation.

+ + +

One day this routine changed abruptly. As I was leaving for school, my mother took a piece of green yarn and threaded our front door key onto it. She tied a knot to keep it secure and placed it around my neck.

"What's that for?" I asked.

"You're walking home from school today, and it's the key to the door. You can let yourself in."

"You're not going to be here?"

"No," she replied, "I have someplace to be."

My mother was a stay-at-home mother, so it wasn't work that kept her from being home, and she never told me where she was on those early afternoons when I came home from school alone.

The school was several blocks from our townhouse, and I walked those blocks at midday by myself, a five-year-old navigating busy San Diego streets with cars and strangers. I probably made the journey more treacherous in my mind than it was, but when I got safely to our door, I was relieved as I slid the key into the lock and turned it to let myself in.

Once inside the empty townhouse, since I didn't want to create a mess and stir my mother's wrath, I would find a book and read until she came back or until my sister came home from school two or three hours later. Nobody at school asked why I had a key around my neck, or why I walked home alone, or what I did in the empty house until evening.

Over time I got used to the walk home and pushing open the door to an empty living room. One day I returned, pulled the yarn up from beneath my shirt, put the key into the lock, and turned it, but I was unable to push the door open. I was puzzled. It was as if something was blocking the door from the inside. After many tries, I began to panic. I could think of nothing to do but sit on one of the benches that dotted the courtyard in front of our building.

That's where my sister found me when she came home from school. I had been sitting all alone for the two hours it took for her school day to be done.

When she saw me, she asked, "What are you doing out here?"

"I can't get into the house."

She laughed at me and said, "Come on. I'll let us in."

She took her key out and tried just as unsuccessfully as I had to push open the door. The key turned, but something was definitely blocking our entry. She gave up quickly.

"We'll just wait for Mom to show up," she said.

The next few hours passed slowly. When school is in session in Southern California, the sun sets around 5 PM, and by the time the sun was setting that day, my sister and I were getting hungry. She had not eaten since lunch at school, and I had not eaten since breakfast, because the kindergarten day ended before lunch was served.

We had not seen my mother return, but we tried the door again. It would still unlock, but we couldn't budge it open. My sister, who at eight years old had already learned to manage situations like this, decided to go to the one neighbor we knew, Mrs. Hansen, and ask if she could help us get inside.

Mrs. Hansen was a slightly heavy woman with blond hair that seemed to be piled on top of her head, leaving her ears visible. She wore big colorful plastic jewelry—chunky necklaces that matched the chunky earrings that dangled down. Her dresses were usually flowery, colorful, and loud. Her voice, which matched her dresses, used to make me cringe when she spoke.

When my sister told Mrs. Hansen what was happening, she responded loudly with, "Well, let's just go over there and see about getting that door open!"

I followed my sister, who followed Mrs. Hansen, back to our door.

When the key worked but the door wouldn't open, Mrs. Hansen shouted in her sing-song voice, "Yoo hoo! Mary! Can you open the door?"

She knocked loudly. "Mary! Open the door!"

When there was no response, Mrs. Hansen, like a mother hen, clucked at us and waved us back to her townhouse. She fed us dinner along with Mr. Hansen, made us spots of piled blankets to sleep on in her living room, and we spent the night in our neighbor's house.

Mrs. Hansen never called anyone to ask where our mother was or why two children were locked out of their home. She simply did what needed to be done and asked no questions that might have required official answers.

The next morning, wearing the same clothes we had worn the day before, my sister and I walked to school together. When midday came and kindergarten was finished, I left the school not knowing what I was going to do if the door wouldn't open again. When I reached our townhouse, it was not even closed. Behind the screen door, I could see that the front door was wide open into the living room.

Mrs. Hansen must have seen me coming because I had barely touched the screen door when I heard her footsteps. Without warning, she took my hand and led me back down the stairs, away from whatever waited inside. But at the top of those stairs I caught sight of a priest kneeling before my mother, who sat on the edge of her bed like he was the penitent. His black suit clinging to him, and the afternoon light cutting through a small window to fall across them both.

The scene burned itself into memory—my mother's hands folded in her lap, the priest's bowed head as he spoke words in a language I did not know, the terrible stillness that had settled over our house like dust. Mrs. Hansen's grip tightened as she pulled me toward safety I had not known I needed.

I spent those hours at her house until my sister came home from school. When Mrs. Hansen led us back, the priest was gone and my mother stood in the kitchen preparing dinner as if nothing had torn apart the fabric of our Tuesday afternoon.

After that day, I returned to the rhythm of survival—school, empty house, the careful dance of avoiding punishment. Nobody spoke of what had happened during those two days. Not Mrs. Hansen, not my sister, not my mother. The priest who had knelt in her bedroom vanished from mention as completely as he had vanished from our house.

I was learning that the people meant to protect me were often the ones who posed a danger, and that some questions would only bring more pain. But I was also learning something else—that even in a house where madness could descend without warning, there were those who would reach out their hand when the darkness came.

The lesson would serve me in the years ahead, when I would need to know the difference between sanctuary and trap.

CHAPTER FIVE

When my father sailed with the Navy, the crews would fashion a book to mark each deployment—photographs and records of ports visited, ceremonies witnessed, the chronicle of months spent on distant waters. In early summer 1972, my father brought to our house a book from the USS Ticonderoga, and within its pages I discovered he had been present for the recovery of Apollo 16, had watched the capsule fall from space into the Pacific like a burnt star returning to earth.

This would be his final voyage. My mother had made certain of that.

I never learned whether his presence in our house contained my mother's darkness or merely concealed it from our view. I knew only that when he was home, the beatings came less often and we ate at regular hours, though our meals remained silent as prayers in an empty church.

Soon after his return, word came that we would move again. This time to a training base in the heart of the country—Great Lakes Naval Station on the shore of Lake Michigan, where I had been a child too small to remember. My father would serve as instructor now, teaching other men the skills he had learned on the water.

My sister remembered Illinois and warned me it was not like California. She spoke of trees that turned the color of fire in autumn, of leaves that fell like snow, of winter that brought true snow that buried the world in white. When she described it, something stirred in my memory—the taste of cold air, the weight of silence that snow brings. I felt unease at the thought of my father and snow together again, as if my body remembered what my mind could not.

But those two years at Great Lakes would prove the most peaceable of my childhood, marked only by small storms instead of the great tempests that had come before and would come again.

+ + +

The Navy sent someone from a shipping company to our townhouse on Pinecone Lane. They inventoried our possessions—putting little red stickers with numbers on the few bits of furniture we had, recording the numbers on a clipboard.

Our belongings fit on a single page.

The next day came the boxes and the movers.

Our tiny townhouse was crowded with men packing our stuff into boxes, and I wandered around watching them take large thin sheets of paper and wrap our cups, plates, and bowls and shove them in boxes. My few clothes and small things filled only two boxes. When everything was packed, they loaded our stuff onto a semi-trailer. The entire time these strangers were in our house, there was no yelling from my father, nor threats from my mother, and my sister and I just acted like curious kids.

+ + +

We moved into the minimalist housing that the Navy provided for families of sailors who were stationed at Great Lakes. The housing was meant to be strictly utilitarian. The houses were not upscale in the least.

In perfect military symmetry, our street was a series of uniform duplexes that formed pairs that stood at attention in opposition to each other across the street. Each house had a driveway leading up to a carport that had a divider in its middle, each side meant for the residents of either side of the duplex. Other than a grass lawn there was no landscaping.

It was a spartan neighborhood.

The military has policies, procedures, and standards that must be met and maintained. This doesn't only apply to personnel; it also applies to weapons, equipment, and even family housing. If the Navy policy states that a sailor with a family of four is provisioned housing that includes three bedrooms and a carport, then the sailor's family will be given access to a three-bedroom house.

It doesn't matter what the mother or the father would choose if left to their own wishes.

+ + +

When I stepped through the front door of our side of the duplex, it was as if I stepped into a palace, with the living room recently painted brilliant white and having a vaulted ceiling that whispered tales of grandeur to me. It was the nicest house I had ever been in.

My father told me, "Go upstairs. Your room is the first door at the top of the stairs."

"Come on, Bonnie. Let's go see our room!"

"No, Bonnie's room is on the left side of the hallway. Your room is on the right, just up there," my father corrected.

"I get my own room?"

The Navy must have partially furnished the room, because there was already a small, white, unassuming desk, a bedside table to match the desk, and a twin-sized bed waiting for sheets and blankets. Once the movers arrived, my few clothes and small things were placed in my room, and from somewhere a small, black, AM radio showed up on my nightstand.

As I settled into the room, I spent my days wondering when life was going to fall apart and go back to the way it had been before.

+ + +

St. Mary's, the Catholic school my parents enrolled my sister and me in, was a thirty-minute bus ride from our house. The grass, bushes, and trees formed a deep green tapestry along the route, in contrast to what I was used to in the semi-arid hills of Southern California.

Unlike the novelty of the green landscape, the first days of first grade started much as they did in kindergarten.

Mrs. Brown handed out our first set of reading curriculum, and I raced through it, and I raced through the other subjects with ease. Soon Mrs. Brown didn't know what to do with me.

I was sent to other staff at the school for evaluations and sessions that felt like interrogations, with three teachers on one side of a long table and me on the other getting peppered with paragraphs and problems which I answered with ease.

Eventually, the teachers settled on the work I would do during my time at St. Mary's, and a new rhythm began. I would start the day with the entire class for the Pledge of Allegiance and morning prayer, and then I would be shunted off to the side to work on my accelerated curriculum all alone. That was my day at school.

After the school day and the bus ride home, my days were not much different than they had been in San Diego. I would get to the front door, take my key out from under my shirt, and open the door to get in. My mother would not be there. As I found out much later, she had found an on-base charity shop to volunteer in—not from generosity, but because the small stipend helped with our tight budget, and it gave her somewhere to go during the long days while my father worked and my sister and I were at school.

On the rare occasion that I created a mess, strewing paper or leaving open books around, my mother would still shout her threats of infernal flames, cloaking it in the guise of discipline. Since we had moved to Great Lakes, the beatings rarely accompanied the threats, but the cruelty of the way she wielded her maternal authority made me keep my distance from her.

+ + +

My father's routine started well before sunrise each day, and by the time I was supposed to be up and getting ready for school, he would have been gone. In the dark mornings, I would hear him coughing as he got up from bed and walk downstairs to the little kitchen. I'd hear the chair scrape the floor as he pulled it out to sit in it in the dark. I could see the kitchen from my room if I got into the right spot in the doorway.

Downstairs, he never turned the lights on, so he would sit in darkness, except for the moments when he would light his cigarettes. His Zippo lighter would make a sonorous clink as he flipped the lid open, and as his thumb would spin the wheel of the lighter, tiny sparks would fly and ignite the wick. An amber flame would dance as he pulled the lighter toward his face to the tip of the cigarette that hung from his lips. That brief moment of illumination would be over in an instant as he snapped the lid shut. The lid issuing a click with the ring of finality. My father's face along with the kitchen would be plunged back into darkness.

Watching him through the doorway crack, I studied this ritual of masculine solitude. In my mind, other fathers on base would gather in groups outside the training buildings, talking and laughing before their shifts. But my father performed his morning preparations alone, in darkness, as if the day ahead required some private steeling that couldn't be shared with anyone.

By the time my mother was up, and I knew it was okay for me to leave my room, my father would be away at work.

+ + +

In September, while the hot, humid air from Lake Michigan still pressed down on our military neighborhood, my mother and father brought home a little grey kitten with tiny blue marbles for eyes. While it had free roam of the house, my door was shut when I went to bed, so it must have slept with my sister, I couldn't imagine it being cuddled by my mother or father. Although the cat was all but helpless, my mother or father would shoo it out of the house most days, and it was left to fend for itself. On some nights it was locked out of the house.

On a Thursday morning, late in September, I came down out of my room to get ready for school. When I got to the bottom of the stairs, I found my father still at home and my mother in the kitchen with him. "Something is wrong today," I thought to myself.

The ashtray in the middle of the kitchen table had recently been emptied of cigarette butts and ashes, and there were two cigarettes resting on its edge, with their tendrils of smoke twisting and looping upward. Neither my mother nor my father had any particular expression on their faces.

"Morning," I ventured tentatively.

My dad grunted, "Morning."

"The cat's dead," he said.

I tried to take my emotional cues from my mother and father, but I felt my throat tighten, "The kitten?"

"Yeah, it crawled up under the hood of the car, and when I started the car to go to work, I killed it."

I looked at my mother, who showed no sign of emotion, and I thought that if I cried, she would not approve, and I knew what happened when I did things she didn't approve of. I shoved the lump in my throat down and started to get my breakfast ready.

I never learned what they did with the dead kitten, because soon after breakfast I was out the door bound for the bus stop. As we rode toward St. Mary's, the sky was turning the color of old pewter, promising what was to come.

When I reached home, my mother was gone. I climbed to my room, turned on the small radio, and sat at my desk with my schoolwork spread before me.

The music died in a burst of static like breaking glass. When it returned, thunder cracked overhead, shaking the house down to its bones, rattling the windows and my small desk. Having grown up where rain seldom fell, at that time I had learned to fear the violence that sky could bring. My sister was home, but at ten she was no help against what gathered above us. I would face this storm as I faced all storms—alone.

The first wave had passed by the time my mother returned. She came home as she always did, just before my father, carrying cans of SpaghettiOs to stretch what money we had. When my father arrived, we gathered at the white table where that morning they had contemplated the kitten's death. The Formica surface bore brown scars where cigarettes had fallen and burned their mark into our daily bread.

We said grace and began to eat in our familiar silence.

Then the gray sky turned the green color of bile, and the wind began to howl. Through the kitchen window I watched a dark cloud churn like something alive, its surface boiling with malice. The screen door between us and the storm began to rattle as if something outside wanted in. The air was being pulled from our lungs.

Sirens wailed, but above them came a sound my father would later call the noise of a freight train bearing down on our small lives.

We fled to the unfinished basement beneath the house and crouched in a corner away from the ground-level windows. There, in that concrete hole, I prayed with a desperation I had never known. Not the empty words they taught at St. Mary's, but something real torn from my chest.

I asked God to spare us, to hold our house together, to let me see another day. In that darkness, with the world tearing itself apart above us, I reached not for the wrathful judge my mother served, but for the father the nuns described—one who might hear a frightened child and answer.

Time stopped while the tornado fed on our neighborhood. When the freight train sound finally died and the sirens fell silent, we emerged to see what remained of the world we had known.

My father was the first to venture out of the basement. He came back in a few moments and told us we could come up. As I cautiously came up the basement stairs, I saw the SpaghettiOs in our bowls just where we had left them. I saw the windows in our living room perfectly intact, and I saw that our roof was still attached to the house.

When I looked across the street at the duplex that mirrored ours, I saw its roof had been completely torn off and had disappeared behind the house. And when we went to look out the back windows, the house that was immediately behind us had lost its roof, too, but the tornado had swept up the debris from the roof and deposited it somewhere else, because it wasn't in our backyard.

The tornado had touched down on the house behind us, lifted up over our house, and touched down again on the house directly across from us.

My mother and father never spoke of the kitten again, just like they never spoke of Billy.

+ + +

On Sundays we attended mass at the chapel that was nestled among the housing on the base. The chapel was shared with other Christian denominations, so it didn't have all of the sacred artifacts our old church did. Just like the houses it was set among, the interior of the chapel was austere yet functional. It even had a confessional at its back.

First confession is a Catholic sacrament, or special ceremony or ritual, where a believer confesses their sins to a priest for the first time. It is meant to be an important step in the Catholic faith journey. Rome teaches that this confession via a priest is the way to receive forgiveness of sins through the grace of God.

In the Catholic Church there is a lengthy process of preparation for the sacraments that someone is expected to participate in, and my preparation happened both at St. Mary's and at that little chapel near our house. At St. Mary's I was taught the basics of the Catholic faith. I learned about the Eucharist, the meaning of mass, and how important it was to participate in the sacraments.

It was during these classes at St. Mary's that I began to realize that my mother's interpretation of our relationship with God was different than the Church's interpretation was. In my mother's theology, if good works earned merit and reward, then necessarily lack of good works earned hellfire and damnation. Having grown up learning my mother's doctrine, which had no room for grace, I had a hard time fully understanding the true nature of God.

In my mind God was angry and constantly looking for fault, and even the slightest deviation from what my mother deemed right and good could reap his wrath. If I believed the fifth commandment, "Honor your father and mother," then of course if I did something my mother did not like I was sinning. Of course, I was going to hell when she didn't agree with what I was doing.

To prepare for the actual act of first confession, I was taught the prayers and rituals of the Our Father, the Hail Mary, and the Act of Contrition by the priest on the Navy base as part of a preparatory class.

That confessional at the back of the chapel on base was where I performed my first confession. When pushed by my mother toward the confessional door, I opened it, and sat on the hard wooden bench at the back of the dark space that was no bigger than a closet. My back was to the rear wall, and I was facing the door I had just come through. To my left was a latticed opening with a deep red velvet curtain on the back side of the lattice. My classes had taught me what to expect, and they had taught me the ritual, but to sit in the box to be confronted directly by a priest—a man who was supposed to have a direct line of communication to God, a man who, according to my mother, could confirm that hell was my destination for eternity—induced a terror I had never felt before.

When the curtain slid to the side, I could see a faint silhouette of the priest. This was the first time I had been alone with a man who wasn't my father, the first time I had to answer to a male authority who might judge me differently than my mother did. Just as I was taught to do, I started by making the sign of the cross and saying, "Bless me, Father, for I have sinned.

This is my first confession." I was supposed to list my infractions at that point, but in my fear, I froze.

"Ahem, bless you son," he muttered, "but what are the sins you need to confess."

Even though I had listed the sins I would confess as preparation for that moment, I couldn't think of anything that I had done, and I thought, "Wouldn't God already know what I had done?" I thought about the Ten Commandments. I hadn't murdered. I hadn't committed adultery. I didn't even know our neighbors, so I didn't want their stuff. The only thing I could think of was the Fifth Commandment. But how could I explain to this priest that in my house, sin wasn't about God's commandments—it was about my mother's changing moods? How could I tell him that what made her angry on Tuesday might be perfectly acceptable on Wednesday? Finally, I blurted out, "I didn't finish my vegetables without getting yelled at, and I forgot to make my bed."

The priest cleared his throat and began his part of the ritual. He told me to say ten Hail Mary's as my contrition, and he finished by saying, "Go, and sin no more."

In my world, a sin was whatever infraction my mother felt offended by at the time, so the priest's admonition to sin no more was a difficult thing for me to understand. After all, in my house, a sin could change based on my mother's caprice. But sitting in that dark confessional, listening to this man's gentle voice offering forgiveness for such small things, I began to sense that maybe the God my teachers described was different from the one my mother invoked. Maybe there was a God who didn't change the rules without warning.

Rather than feel reconciliation, which is what confession was supposed to do, I felt a new burden placed on me. I was going to hell for sure, because

I knew I could never not offend my mother. But somewhere beneath that familiar fear, a small seed of hope had been planted—the possibility that God's love might be more constant than my mother's anger.

+ + +

And so the two years went, my father leaving for work before sunrise, my sister and I leaving for school on the bus, and my mother leaving the house after all of us. All of us returning to the house later in the day.

In the winter of 1973, my father came home and told us we were going to be stationed in Naples, Italy. I didn't feel giddy anticipation at moving to a foreign country. I didn't feel much at all.

"Where will I go to school?" I asked.

"The Navy base has a school. You and Bonnie'll go there," my father replied.

"Unless we can find a Catholic school. There's got to be a Catholic school in Italy," my mother slipped in, her brows tightening and a faint furrow forming. Clearly, my mother was not excited about the chance to move to Italy, the chance to see another part of the world.

Even though my father's orders to Italy came months before we would be moving, in typical military fashion, there were logistical things that had to happen before we left the US. Most of what needed to be done I only heard mention of. The only preparation that I participated in was medical. All of us had to have a physical to ensure we had no serious medical issues that would need care while overseas, and we all had to get a series of vaccinations.

The vaccination schedule required multiple visits to the base hospital over several weeks. Each shot was documented on a yellow card that we had to carry, and missing any appointment would mean starting the series over. The military's vaccination bureaucracy was rigid—no exceptions, no variations from the prescribed timeline.

After my mother took my sister and me to the base hospital for our first vaccines, she fell ill. Her sickness became a matter of contention between my parents. From my room at the top of the stairs, I could hear their voices carry from the kitchen table below—clipped words exchanged like blows in the gathering dark. My mother and father had never seemed bound by affection, but something had shifted between them now, opening a chasm that grew wider each day.

Within weeks, without warning, my father announced that we would not be going to Naples. As a man grown I would learn the truth—that my mother had refused to continue the vaccine series after falling sick from the first round. This meant we could not be stationed in Italy. My father was forced to surrender his orders and request new assignment, a professional wound that would never heal.

The weight of this decision settled over our house like the thick air that rolled off Lake Michigan in summer. My father's jaw would set hard when he looked at her, and she would turn away as if his gaze burned. Even I could sense that refusing military orders was no small transgression, that it would mark my father for the remainder of his service.

The dreams of Italy died in our kitchen that summer, and with them died something else—whatever small hope had remained that we might become the family the Navy expected us to be.

+ + +

My father's new orders were sending us back to San Diego.

The day he told us, I sat at my desk while snow fell beyond my window like ash from some distant fire. I had watched autumn set the trees ablaze in red and gold, felt winter's snow grow hard as stone beneath my feet, seen spring call forth green life from what had seemed dead. For the first time in my short years, I had witnessed the world die and resurrect itself, and I knew I would mourn the leaving.

I would mourn my own room, too. And the God I had found in the chapel—not the vengeful judge my mother served, but one who heard the prayers of children without demanding payment in fear. Even the tornado that had tried to erase our small lives could not undo what Great Lakes had given me: the knowledge that peace was possible.

But I felt no joy at the thought of returning to the place where my mother's madness had flourished, where everything had been sharper and more dangerous. As I placed my few possessions into boxes once more, I wondered if the quiet man who sat in darkness each dawn—the one whose career now bore the scar of my mother's refusal—would have the strength, or even the desire, to shield us from whatever waited in the California sun.

The seasons had taught me that all things must end, but they had not taught me whether what comes after is better or worse than what came before.

CHAPTER SIX

I carried no fond memories of San Diego. It meant the worst of my childhood was returning like a fever that breaks only to come back stronger. I could not look at the mild climate, the strange plants, or the endless beaches and feel anything but dread. I knew that when my father disappeared again, my mother would surrender to whatever darkness lived within her. And now something else had changed. My parents had become adversaries.

His duty was aboard a ship in dry dock, wounded and waiting for repair. The refurbishment required shakedown cruises—short voyages of a few weeks to test what had been mended—but these trips were not the only reason my father vanished from our house. Our return to San Diego seemed to drive my parents toward opposite horizons. As the distance between them grew, they moved like strangers who happened to share the same address.

Neither seemed to remember that my sister and I existed, much less what we hoped for or feared or needed. We had become invisible passengers on a vessel that was taking on water, and no one was manning the lifeboats.

+ + +

We moved into a house at 2770 Landscape Drive in San Diego. Where the house in Long Beach was robin egg blue, a color that shouted Southern California, this house was millennial pink, which also shouted California. It sat on the corner of Landscape and Plateau, just under ten miles from the Naval base. It was chosen because it was meant to be a short commute for my father, while being in a nice neighborhood. My mother's wishes obviously weighed heavily on the choice of the house, because it was only two blocks from St. Michael's Church and Catholic school, where we were all supposed to attend mass, and where my sister and I would go to school.

To me, at the age of ten, it seemed a modest house. It wasn't as nice as our duplex in Illinois, but when we moved in, it had enough bedrooms for the four of us. Over the short time that we lived there it would end up having more than enough room for us.

Like all California houses built in the 1950s and 60s, the garage was the prominent feature in the front, and somewhere along the way, an addition was put on the house that paralleled the garage giving the house a small courtyard that hemmed in the front door. This courtyard had two huge bougainvillea vines on the wall of the garage and the wall of the addition. With each passing day the bougainvillea would shed its blossoms as if they were tears. The papery thin blossoms would float down and pile up in the courtyard, their slowly browning mass adding to the debris already accumulating.

Those vines are burned into memory because the mess they made became mine to clean. Every morning I would emerge to find the concrete scattered with papery pink petals, like confetti from some celebration I had not been invited to. Every morning I would sweep them into the dustpan and toss them into the trash.

This ritual of cleaning what could not stay clean, of imposing order on what would only return to chaos by the next day.

The shedding bougainvillea is but one reason I have no love for that house. It taught me that beauty and burden often had the same face, that what others admired from a distance became, up close, just another chore for small hands to manage.

When we first moved into the house, I had one of the three bedrooms. My sister had another, and my parents shared the master bedroom when my dad was not out to sea or on duty. The addition to the front of the house, the part that paralleled the garage, had a cathedral ceiling, with dark brown beams that angled up from the walls to the peak of the equally dark brown ceiling. On the dark wood paneled wall opposite the courtyard, it had one small window above head level, which let very little light in, so the room was perpetually dark.

The weekend my father went to the lumber yard to get building supplies would change the room, and it would change where I slept.

My father never invited me to work with him, nor did he teach me how to safely handle tools, but I was allowed to watch him work, as long as I didn't talk to him. In silence I watched him frame up a partial wall whose top stopped just at the point where the ceiling began to slope up from the exterior walls of the room. He framed an opening for a doorway. Before the sheetrock was applied to the frame, the space looked like a small prison cell.

With the door installed and wallpaper applied to the finished walls, the new "room" became my bedroom, a space that was little more than a closet. Perhaps it was a bit bigger than I recall because my twin-sized bed fit in this small room, but it had no room for any other furniture. There wasn't even room for a nightstand.

I had no idea why I was kicked out of a bedroom and into this closet, but I knew that something in our family was changing. Since the wall to my little living space was completely open underneath the vaulted ceiling, when I was in my room, I could hear clearly all of the conversations in living room and kitchen, which more often than not turned into shouting. When my father was home, it was my mother and father shouting at each other. When he was away, it was my mother and my sister shouting. I was never part of these fights. I kept to myself mostly in my little space, lying on my bed and staring up at the dark wood ceiling that seemed to press down on me.

+ + +

My father had always been distant and aloof, coming into our lives mostly with brief flashes of intense anger. Mostly he was a mysterious man with an unhappy, dark face who only rarely took notice of me. The move had changed this. In the house on Landscape Drive, he became someone who sat brooding at the table, a heavy presence that was only relieved when his work took him to sea on brief two- or three-week trips. If it hadn't been for the constant fighting between my mother and my sister, those trips would have been a relief.

Life turned into intense periods where two different worlds of emotion and anger crashed into each other. When my father was home, my mother and father would argue about things I couldn't understand about each other and their marriage. When my father was away, my mother and my

THE CLOUD GROWS THIN

sister would argue about the sort of life my sister was supposed to lead. Most of the fights were beyond my understanding. But I could feel the constant back and forth of tensions in that house.

When my father wasn't home, my sister would argue with my mom about things I couldn't understand. But there was one fight I really understood. It started on a Saturday morning when my sister came out of her room for breakfast.

"What is that all over your face?" my mother said. Her voice was already sharp, the way it got before things went bad.

I looked up from my cereal bowl. My sister had red circles on her cheeks that looked like someone had rubbed them with a crayon.

"It's rouge, and it's not all over my face," my sister said. She was trying to sound calm, but I could hear something tight in her voice.

"Rouge? Rouge!" My mother's voice got louder. "Who told you to put rouge on your face?"

"No one told me to put it on. I read that it adds color and brightness."

My mother sucked her breath in between her teeth, which was never a good sign. "Where did you get it?"

"I bought it."

"With what money?"

My sister didn't answer right away. I kept eating my cereal, but I was watching them both out of the corner of my eye.

"Girls don't wear rouge," my mother said. Her voice was getting that growling quality that meant someone was about to get in trouble. "Rouge is for old women." She paused, and then continued, "If I wanted you to wear makeup, I would have had you wear blush."

"What's the difference?" my sister asked.

That was the wrong thing to say.

"Don't you get smart with me, young lady. You go wash that garbage off your face right now."

"I'm not washing it off."

"You most certainly are."

"No, I'm not."

The argument descended into screaming. My sister retreated to her room and slammed the door with such force that the house seemed to shudder. My mother stood in the kitchen, breathing hard, her hands balled into fists at her sides like a fighter who had won nothing.

For reasons I could not fathom, the color of my sister's cheeks had become cause for war. The arguments between them escalated with the speed of summer storms—from disagreement to shouting to something darker. What had been words became fists, and what had been discipline became something else entirely.

The first time I witnessed my mother take the belt to my sister, I was sitting on the floor before our small television. We had acquired it from somewhere—nothing fancy, just a box that brought distant voices into our silence. The odd addition to our house had three steps that spanned the width of the room, and the TV sat perched on the top step like a witness.

From that vantage point, I watched my mother cross a line she had never crossed before. The belt sang through the air with a sound I would come to know well, and my sister's cries joined the chorus of violence that was becoming the music of our household.

I was sitting crossed legged on the floor of the addition watching cartoons. At the time, San Diego would have had only five channels to pick from, and I was probably watching the independent channel because it showed cartoons in the afternoon.

I heard an argument starting up between my mother and my sister. They were down the hallway that led to the bedrooms. My sister's room was the last room down the hallway, and I could tell their argument had started down there because I heard my sister's door slam.

The voices got louder, and I heard footsteps coming down the hallway. I crawled up the stairs, staying low, and crept toward the hallway. I could see my sister stomping toward the living room, her face red and angry.

Behind her came my mother, and I saw something that made my stomach drop. My mother had a belt in her hand, but it wasn't hanging down the way it usually did when she carried it for spankings. The leather strap was wrapped around her hand, and the buckle was dangling at the end, swinging back and forth as she walked.

I backed down the stairs quickly, but I couldn't stop watching.

When both my mother and sister reached the living room, my mother raised the belt high over her head. The buckle caught the light from the window. My sister saw it coming and threw her hands up to protect her face.

"Don't you ever talk back to me," my mother said, and she swung the belt down hard.

My sister screamed—not the angry scream from their arguments, but a different kind of scream, high and sharp and full of pain. I buried my face in the green shag carpeting and pressed my hands over my ears, but I could still hear the sound of the buckle hitting her and my sister crying.

When it was quiet, I looked up. My sister was on the floor, curled up in a ball, and my mother was standing over her, breathing hard. The belt was still in her hand.

"Now go to your room," my mother said, "and think about how you're going to behave from now on."

My sister got up slowly and walked back down the hallway. She was holding her arm against her side, and I could see red marks on her face where the buckle had hit her.

After that day, when I heard the loud talking change to shouting, I knew to duck my head and take cover, eyes looking down at that green shag carpeting as I hurried off to hide in my tiny room. I had been taught at Catholic school that if I ever felt unsafe, I could pray for protection. When the violence was going on, I would hide in my little space all alone, and I would pray that I would not be caught up in the storm, just as I had done during the tornado in Illinois.

But the belt buckle wasn't the worst thing that happened to my sister in that house.

+ + +

Getting hit with the belt had not stopped my sister's fighting. The two seemed to be constantly at war by this time. Like all the fights, other than the one about makeup, I had no clue what caused them. I just knew that every few days there would be shouting, and doors slamming, and sometimes the sound of the belt.

Then one day, after arguing with my sister for what seemed like hours, my mother did something I had never seen her do before. She called two friends and asked them to come over to our house.

The first woman to show up was someone I recognized from church. She was shorter than my mother and had black hair and dark eyes. She always wore dark dresses and had a serious expression, even when she was talking to other adults after mass.

The second woman that arrived was a family friend from outside of church whose house was the only other house in San Diego that I had been to. This friend was similar in build to my mother and had fiery, artificially colored red hair. She smoked cigarettes and laughed loudly and always seemed to be in a good mood, which made it strange to see her looking so serious when she came to our house that day.

By the time the two friends showed up, my sister had long ago slammed the door to her room shut and stayed there. The three women sat in the living room talking in angry hushed tones for a few minutes. I couldn't hear what they were saying, but I could tell from their voices that they were planning something. They kept looking down the hallway toward my sister's room, and the church lady kept nodding her head and saying things like "absolutely" and "that's right."

Then, like people who had decided on war, they suddenly stood up and marched down the hallway. There were no locks on the bedroom doors in this house, so the three of them charged into my sister's room with nothing to stop them.

The yelling started immediately, but this time it was different. Instead of just my mother and my sister, there were four voices—three angry adult women and one frightened teenage girl.

I heard my sister scream, "Get out! Get out of my room!" but the other voices just got louder.

I sneaked down the hallway to see what was going on. The door to my sister's room was wide open, and I could see inside. The two women were holding my sister on her bed, face down. The church lady had her arms pinned down, and the red-haired woman was holding her legs. My sister was thrashing and kicking, trying to get free, but they were both bigger and stronger than she was.

My mother was standing at the foot of the bed with a belt in her hand—not the regular belt, but a wider one, and she had it doubled over so the buckle end was in her hand and the leather loop was hanging down.

"Hold her still," my mother said.

"We've got her," the red-haired woman said. "She's not going anywhere."

My sister was crying now, not just angry crying but scared crying. "Please don't," she kept saying. "Please don't. I'm sorry. I'm sorry."

But my mother raised the belt high over her head and brought it down hard across my sister's back. The sound was different from when she hit her with the buckle end—this was a loud slapping sound that seemed to echo in the room. My sister screamed, and her whole body jerked, but the two women held her down.

My mother hit her again, and again. Each time the belt came down, my sister's screams got louder and more desperate. I could see red marks appearing on her back where the belt was hitting her, even through her shirt.

I couldn't watch anymore. I ran back down the hallway as fast as I could and dove into my little room, pulling the door shut behind me. I threw myself on my bed and buried my head under my pillow, but I could still hear my sister screaming and the sound of the belt hitting her, over and over.

It seemed to go on forever, but it probably only lasted a few minutes. When it finally stopped, I could hear the women talking in low voices, and then I heard footsteps coming back down the hallway. I stayed under my pillow until I heard the front door close twice, and then I heard my mother's footsteps going back to the kitchen.

After that day, when I heard the loud talking change to shouting, I knew to duck my head and take cover and get to my tiny room as fast as I could. I would lie on my bed and pray that I would not be caught up in whatever was happening. I would whisper the same desperate words over and over:

"Please God, don't let her come for me. Please don't let her hurt me. Please make her forget I'm here."

In that house, my mother still said cruel things to me, but I never got beaten with a belt buckle, and I never had two women hold me down while my mother hit me with a doubled-over belt.

+ + +

I didn't know if my father ever learned about what my mother did to my sister, but he was gone whenever it happened. Even though the hitting and the cruel words stopped when my father was home, there was still a heavy feeling that hung over the house when he was around.

Mostly, he sat at the round pedestal table that served as our dining room table, with both his elbows resting on the tabletop as he chain-smoked filterless Pall Mall cigarettes. A pendant light with a green glass shade hung directly above it, and if I peeked out of my room after the sun had gone down, I could see the smoke from a cigarette curling up into the light, and my dad in half shadow and half-light at the table.

My mother and my father were rarely in the same room at that time, and when they were, there was usually loud talking, leading to shouting. If it ever got worse, which it often did, I buried my head under my pillow in my tiny room, no matter what time of day it was.

By this point, I had learned to avoid both of my parents most of the time, but sometimes I couldn't avoid them. On a school morning one day, I was on my way to the kitchen to get my breakfast. I realized that I had to pass him at the table as he sat smoking, and my heart started pounding. I tried to walk quietly, hoping he wouldn't notice me, but as I got close to the table, he looked up.

"Hey, Buddy. Good morning."

The word "Buddy" stopped me in my tracks. He had never called me that before. I looked at his face in the morning light coming through the kitchen window. His eyes were red and puffy, and he looked like he hadn't slept.

"Morning," I replied, still not sure if I should keep walking or stay.

"Sorry if I kept you up last night," he said. His voice sounded different than usual - softer, but also sadder.

"Uh, you didn't keep me up." That wasn't entirely true. I had heard voices late into the night, but I couldn't make out what they were saying through the walls of my little room.

He took a long drag from his cigarette and blew the smoke toward the ceiling. "You had to have heard me. I was sitting here crying most of the night."

I didn't know what to say to that. I had never heard my father admit to crying before. I wasn't even sure I had ever seen him cry.

"You were crying?" I asked.

"Yeah." He rubbed his eyes with the back of his free hand. "Your mom and I aren't getting along."

I stood there, not knowing what to say. I could see the ashtray on the table was full of cigarette butts, more than usual. There were also coffee cups—two of them—which meant my mother had been up with him at some point during the night.

"Oh," was all I could manage.

I got a bowl out of the cupboard, filled it with cereal, and poured milk on it. Since my father was at the table, I couldn't sit down to eat, so I stood at the kitchen counter by the sink with my cereal bowl.

As I ate, I kept glancing over at him. He was staring down at the table, smoking his cigarette, and I could see that his hands were shaking slightly.

I had never seen my father look so small before. He was still the same size, but something about the way he was sitting, the way his shoulders were hunched over, made him seem smaller.

"You know," he said, without looking at me, "sometimes grown-ups don't know how to fix things."

I stopped eating and looked at him. "What things?"

"Things between them. Things that get broken." He stubbed out his cigarette in the ashtray. "I don't want you to think it's your fault, or your sister's fault. It's not."

I didn't know what to say to that either. It had never occurred to me that it might be my fault, but now that he mentioned it, I wondered if maybe it was.

"Is Mom sick again?" I asked.

He looked at me then, really looked at me, and I saw something in his eyes that I had never seen before. It might have been fear.

"Yeah," he said. "I think she is."

I finished my cereal and put the bowl in the sink. I got my books from the counter where I had left them the night before.

"I have to go to school," I said.

"Yeah, okay." He lit another cigarette. "Have a good day, Buddy."

There was that word again. As I walked toward the front door, I thought about why he was calling me that. I thought about him sitting at the table crying, and about the way his hands had been shaking. I thought about him saying that grown-ups don't know how to fix things.

I made sure not to let the screen door slam on the way out, because a loud noise like that would set my father off, and rather than get yelled at as I was heading to school, I wanted to remember him calling me "Buddy" and the way he looked so small sitting at that table.

That was the first time I really understood that my parents' marriage was ending, even though no one had said those words.

Soon after that morning, I noticed that my dad was spending less and less time in that house on Landscape Drive. At first, he would only be gone for three or four days at a time, coming home with his seabag holding his dirty clothes. I knew his ship was not going out on cruises, because the trips were too short. No one told me he was living on the ship in port, but as the time he was away grew longer, I figured it out when the only time I would see him was when my mom took me to the Navy base and dropped me off with him for a few hours at a time.

Toward the end of 1976, my father had moved out of the house for good.

+ + +

That morning when my father called me "Buddy" burned itself into memory. He was trying to draw me toward him somehow, but I had no desire to be drawn. I barely knew this man who sat smoking in the shadows like some ghost haunting the edges of our lives.

As 1976 died and my father departed for good, I was ten years old and alone in a house where the shouting had ceased but the silence carried its own menace. The quiet was not peace—it was the stillness that comes before something breaks, the held breath before the blow falls.

I had learned to navigate the storms of my mother's rage, but this new silence was uncharted territory. In the absence of his cigarette smoke and morning darkness, the house seemed larger and more hollow, as if his leaving had taken something structural with it.

What remained was my mother and my sister and me, and the knowledge that whatever protection his presence had provided—however small—was gone.

CHAPTER SEVEN

By late 1976, my father's contract with the Navy was bleeding toward its end, and since he had refused the orders to Italy, there would be no reprieve. His career was finished. The Navy had assigned him to the USS Norton Sound, docked in Port Hueneme some two hundred miles north—a vessel that served as testing ground for weapons that might never see war. To serve aboard her was to be exiled to the margins of military purpose, a place where broken careers went to die quietly.

The Norton Sound was not a ship of the line but a floating laboratory for experiments the brass deemed necessary but not urgent. Assignment there carried the particular shame reserved for men who had somehow disappointed their superiors, who had chosen family concerns over naval imperatives.

By the time he received these final orders, my father had already moved from our house to quarters aboard his ship in San Diego. When he transferred to the Norton Sound, I felt no absence where his presence had been. He had become a stranger long before he became a ghost.

+ + +

On a spring day, near the end of the school week, I came into the house after walking back from St. Michael's. I could tell my mother was home, because the radio in the house was tuned to the easy listening music station. I dropped my books off in my little room, changed out of the white short-sleeve, button up shirt and the salt and pepper pants that were my school uniform, and went to look for my mother.

I found her in the back yard picking dead blossoms off one of her pink and white Martha Washington geraniums she cared for. She was bent over the plant, a cigarette hanging from between her lips, gently pushing the stems around, so she could find a blossom that needed to be pruned. Her hands moved carefully around the flowers.

When she noticed that I was outside with her, she didn't greet me or look up. She took the cigarette out from between her lips with her free hand and said, "You're going to see your dad this weekend."

"On Friday?" I asked.

"Yeah. I am going to take you to the bus station, and you are going to ride the bus up there."

A chill went down my spine. "Bonnie's going too?"

"No, your sister is staying here. You're going to go by yourself."

I had ridden the Greyhound to see my father once before with my sister, who was fifteen then. There was no direct route, so the journey to Port Hueneme required a transfer at the Greyhound station in downtown Los Angeles, which sat in the heart of what men called Skid Row like it was where hope went to die.

When school ended that Friday, my stomach twisted itself into knots as I walked home. My mother barked orders the moment I crossed the threshold—change clothes, hurry to the station. A bus ticket in those days was handwritten paper, small sheets for each leg of the journey. She pressed four tickets into my palm—two outbound, two for return—and sent me into the world alone.

The ninety-minute ride to Los Angeles passed in silent prayer and growing dread. My mother had never laid eyes on the station where she was sending me to navigate alone, but this would not have stopped her even if she had witnessed what waited there.

When we pulled into the station as evening fell, I followed the other passengers into the waiting area—a vast cavern with white floors stained black where countless cigarettes had been ground into the tile. The air hung thick with diesel fumes and stale smoke and the smell of human waste. I approached the ticket counter like a penitent seeking mercy, asked about my connection, then found a seat where I could watch the clock and pray that no stranger would mark me as prey.

When they called for the bus to Port Hueneme, I walked through the doors and onto the dark loading platform. I waited my turn in line with the other pilgrims bound for destinations unknown, handed the driver my proper ticket like an offering, and climbed aboard into whatever darkness awaited.

When the bus pulled into Port Hueneme, a few sailors got off the bus along with me. I had to wait alone for my father to show up at the depot. That first weekend, I stayed on board the ship, sleeping in one of the cabins that was usually used by one of the ship's officers, but that was the only time I stayed on the Norton Sound.

At first, my trips up were on random weekends, but they became more and more frequent, and every time I would ride the Greyhound bus. Early on, my father started taking me to a house owned by the Aherns.

Bill Ahern was a thirty-year Navy veteran, who was on the verge of forced retirement, and Mary was his wife. My father would pick me up from the bus station and drive over to the Ahern's house. He would come inside, start drinking beer with Bill, and Mary would show me to the spare room that they were letting me sleep in.

When I woke up, my father wouldn't be at the house, but most Saturday's he would come over in the early afternoon and stay until evening. One of those Saturday afternoons, my father brought two baseball mitts with him. The Ahern's house was in a development with small, well-kept, single-story houses that were meant to be retirement homes. The dark green, stucco house had a front yard with perfect grass, but it had no yard in the back of the house.

"Let's play catch," my father offered on that Saturday.

Since there was no backyard, and the grass in front was so perfect, we went to the sidewalk, where my father handed me the baseball mitt. He walked backwards away from me tossing the ball into his own mitt.

"You ready? Put your mitt up," he ordered.

"Yeah. I'm ready."

He threw the ball lightly at me, and I was able to open the mitt and catch the ball, using two hands as I was taught at school. I threw the ball back to him, but it went to his left side and he had to take a step to catch it. We had a few back-and-forth tosses, and then my father said, "I'm gonna throw it harder now."

"No. I don't think I can catch it," I pleaded.

"Nah, you'll catch it."

He threw the ball faster than he had been throwing, but I couldn't get the mitt open in time.

It hit the side of the mitt, bounced off, and hit me in the face.

My cheek stung and I could feel tears coming. I didn't want to cry in front of my father, but I did.

"Give me the mitt, and let's go inside," he said.

That was the last time my father and I played catch.

The weekends at the Aherns' eventually turned into a week-long experiment. During a week my father was supposed to have me, he left me with Bill and Mary. At the end of the week, when my dad came to get me, Mary told him that it wasn't going to work. I was standing there when she said it. I never stayed at the Aherns' again, and my father was forced to rent an apartment.

+ + +

On a Friday afternoon, when my mother was driving me to the Greyhound station downtown, so I would have to stay at the apartment my father rented, I asked, "Why do I have to go on the bus all the time?"

Driving her little green, four-door, Toyota down to the bus station, my mother replied, "You want to see your father." It was not a question.

"I guess, but I don't like the bus."

"You want to get to know your father. And you have to go see him to get to know him."

"But do I have to go all the time?"

"You are going to see your father." Keeping her eyes on the road, and hands tightly gripping the wheel, the tone she used let me know that the conversation was over.

Ever since my father had rented the apartment, he would pick me up from the bus station, and we would go straight to the apartment in silence.

The only furniture in the apartment was a kitchen table with chrome legs and a chrome metal band that ran around it just beneath the tabletop, and a bed in the one room at the top of the white stairs.

My father slept in the room on the bed, and I slept on the floor in the living room in a sleeping bag on a thin foam pad that was covered in slippery vinyl which I would slide off of during the night, ending up on the dirty green carpet.

One morning, having slid off the foam pad, I woke in the sleeping bag on the carpet. My legs were itching, and when I unzipped the bag to look at the red spots on my legs, I saw fleas hopping out of the bag and into the carpet.

On Sundays we wouldn't go to mass, and I could feel something missing. At home with my mother, we had stopped going to church too. There was comfort in the routine of Catholic mass, in the prayers to start the day at school, and in confession on Saturdays. But my mother's strict rules about behavior during mass were confusing. Even though I wasn't sure how I felt about mass, when we stopped going to church, something felt empty. I would continue to pray, but they were my own prayers mostly, sometimes mixed with some prayers that I had learned during school.

Then my father would put me in the car on Sunday afternoon, and we would drive to the bus station, as always in silence. And I would make the return trip to San Diego.

+ + +

St. Michael's school was built like a horseshoe with an asphalt courtyard that all the rooms opened into. This meant that when our class along with the other classes were heading out for recess, or our class was going to the library as a group, we would be outside. This also meant that if someone was moving across the campus, or going from one room to another, anyone outside could see them.

I started to see my mother show up at our school most days. During her time there, she would dart in and out of rooms, and spend a lot of time in the library. When my class was in the library, she would be in the room, but she would not talk to me, other than to say, "Hello."

After a while, she became a regular part of my day at school. Each morning, I would get up, get dressed in my white and grey uniform, pour cereal and milk into a bowl, eat it, and walk to school, and sometime after we said the Pledge of Allegiance and our morning prayer, my mother would show up on the school grounds.

I had three teachers while at St. Michael's, and of those three, two were women who used to be Catholic nuns but had left the orders. I learned this because my mother started spending time outside of school with these women. She spent time with other teachers from the school as well, including my sister's teachers, who had also been nuns before.

On several occasions, my mother took me along when she went to these women's houses. I usually sat at the table with my mother and my teacher as they smoked cigarettes and drank white wine and talked about things I had no interest in listening to.

During this same time, my sister spent less and less of her time at home. Some days she wouldn't return from school until late in the evening, and other days she wouldn't return home until the next day. My sister may have won the fight between them, because my mother stopped trying to beat her, and so my sister started coming and going from the house as she pleased—not as my mother pleased.

On a morning that my sister had not returned the previous evening, I woke up, left my bedroom, and started walking toward the bathroom when

I heard voices from down the hallway. There was someone else in what had been my mother and father's room. As I was leaving the bathroom, the door to the bedroom opened, and out stepped the woman who had been my fourth-grade teacher the previous year.

"Mike! Good morning. How are you?"

"Uh, hi, Ms. C."

I stood frozen. I was surprised that someone other than my mother had come out of that room, but also surprised to see the person who came out was the woman who had been my teacher the previous year. She was tying the belt of a terry cloth bathrobe that she must have brought with her, and she didn't seem to be wearing clothes under the robe.

"It's nice to see you this morning, Mike."

I looked down at the floor, and said, "Nice to see you, too."

I hurried back down to my little space at the far end of the house and changed into clothes. I didn't eat breakfast that morning, but I rushed to get out of the house.

+ + +

Sometimes, my sister and I would walk to school together. We would never walk home at the same time, but even with the school year almost over for the summer, she would walk to school with me once in a while.

"Why does Dad never come home?" I asked one day.

"They're getting a divorce."

"A divorce? What's that?"

"It's when two people don't want to be married anymore," she explained, "Then they get a divorce."

"So, what happens to us?"

"I'll be living with Dad. I don't know what's going to happen to you."

My sister was comfortable calling my father "Dad" even though he was not her father. My father had adopted her, but my mother had my sister with a man neither I nor my sister had ever met. My mother married my father when my sister was still a baby, so he was the only father she had ever known. When my sister told me about the divorce and that she knew who she would live with, it was all new to me. I was the only one who didn't know what was happening.

After my mother found out that I knew that she and my father were getting divorced, she would tell me that I should see my father more often—that I should get to know him better.

Sitting at the kitchen table under the green light, after just finishing our evening meal, I asked, "Where will I live when you get divorced?"

"You want to live with your father. We've talked about this."

"I don't know," I said, not wanting to tell her I didn't like sleeping on the floor with fleas.

"No. You would rather stay with him."

I really didn't know who I wanted to live with. My mother had stopped hitting me, but my father had never really hit me either.

While the school year was ending, the divorce case was working its way to the judge, who would decide who I would live with.

Near the end of school, I took another trip to Port Hueneme to stay with my father. The bus station where I got off was a small square building with a waiting room that was surrounded by glass on three sides, with the back of the waiting area next to the ticket desk. When the bus pulled into the station, it stopped at the side of the building, and since my father was usually not there, I would enter the waiting area from a side door.

That night my father pulled up to the bus station in a car I had never seen before. It was a large four-door car with a bench seat in back and a bench seat up front. As I got into the car, the cigarette lighter popped out letting him know it was hot. He took the red glowing end of the lighter and brought it to the cigarette that was hanging from his lips. After he inhaled a long drag of smoke, he blew it out and said, "We have to make a stop before we go home."

"Where?"

"You'll see," he responded as he moved the lever on the steering column up, to put the big car in reverse.

We drove in silence to what I recognized as being the turn to the Navy base entrance, but he turned the opposite way down a road that was lined with small shops, restaurants, and bars. He parked the car on the street, and we got out. We walked half a block to just in front of one of the bars, which had a red door with a round window in the middle near the top. I could see colors from neon lights through the window, even though it was too high for me to see through directly, and I could hear country music.

When we got into the bar, he walked me to a table where a woman with dark hair and dark eyes was seated. She looked like she belonged in a restaurant from the 1950s. I would spend the next seven years of my life living with this woman.

When the divorce was finalized, I was placed on the bus from San Diego to Port Hueneme one final time. The judge had decreed that I was to live with a man I barely knew and—as I would discover—a woman and her sons who were strangers entirely, all of us bound together by legal document rather than blood or choice.

CHAPTER EIGHT

By early summer of 1977, my father's Naval career was in its final months, dying its final death, and the court had granted him sole custody of my sister and me. We had moved into the apartment in Port Hueneme with this man who was meant to be our father, and my sister claimed the room with the bed. At some point before our arrival, he had acquired a brown couch for the living room. He would sleep on that couch, my sister on the bed, and I would make my nest on the floor like some animal learning to be domesticated.

His twenty years in the Navy had trained him to rise before the sun, and he was always awake when darkness still held the world. The first thing he would do was light a cigarette as he walked to the small kitchen separated from the living room by a half wall. He used a small aluminum percolator to make his coffee, and I could hear the dull metallic sounds of him taking the pot apart, filling it with water and grounds. After pouring his coffee, the only sound that would break the silence of him sitting at that table would be the harsh coughing fits the cigarette smoke brought on.

When my father went to work, my sister at fifteen and I at eleven were left alone in that complex like feral children turned loose. The place was strange territory where people left their apartment doors wide open and neighbors walked into each other's spaces without invitation. Even my sister began leaving our door open. "It's not like we have anything to steal," she would say.

With its mix of the impoverished and sailors between deployments, substance abuse flourished in the complex like weeds in untended ground. I grew comfortable wandering into neighbors' apartments when I saw their doors open, and it was on one such day that I entered our next-door neighbors' place and was taught how to smoke marijuana.

The young woman was in her living room painting on an easel, and when she saw me, she greeted me, "Hi, Mike. What are you doing today?"

"Nothing really."

"Where's Bonnie?"

"I don't know. She took off a while ago."

She went back to painting, and I sat on her couch. The apartment had the same green shag carpeting my father's apartment did, and sitting in the living room didn't feel much different from sitting in my dad's apartment. She had a coffee table in front of her couch, though, and on the table was a round cookie tin.

"Are those cookies?" I asked hopefully.

"No, that's where I keep my stash."

"Your stash? Of what?"

She chuckled and said, "My marijuana."

I knew what marijuana was because my sister had started smoking before we left San Diego, and she spent most of her days in the apartment complex finding ways to get high.

"Do you want to try a bowl?" the woman asked.

"I guess so," I answered.

As she continued to paint, she talked me through the process of taking the pipe, cleaning it, and then packing the bowl with dried green flakes. I had seen my sister light a bowl, so I put the pipe to my lips as she would have done, and I struck the lighter and lit the bowl as I inhaled.

The acrid smoke hit my lungs, and I went into a coughing fit. The woman laughed and told me, "You are going to have practice some more, so you can handle your hits, little man." I spent the next few months of the summer diligently practicing.

+ + +

It turned out that the woman I had met in the bar that night my father picked me up from the bus station, lived in the apartment complex—along with her three sons. Jean had black shoulder-length hair that she feathered back from her face in the style that was popular then. She had a way of smoking that made the cigarette look like it was an extension of her hand, and when she laughed, which was seldom, her voice had a raspy quality from years of smoking.

During our days unsupervised in the apartment complex, my sister got to know the middle son, Dan, who was her same age, and they become romantically involved. This made for an awkward situation when my father moved us out of his apartment and into Jean's, with my father sharing a bedroom with her, my sister getting a room to herself, and me sleeping on the floor in the sleeping bag while the other three boys slept on their beds.

Soon after moving us into Jean's apartment, my father came home from the Navy base and made me and the son who was my age, Sean, go find my sister and Dan. He said he had an announcement to make. The living room in the apartment was furnished with the detritus of a broken marriage: a green couch, an overstuffed red velour chair, and a brown dining room table and mismatched chairs.

When everyone was gathered and seated, my father cleared his throat and said, "We have something that you all should know."

The silence stretched between his words like a held breath before he continued. "We are moving to Wyoming, and Jean and I are going to be married."

"F___ that," said Sid, the oldest boy. He was past eighteen and would not be moved like cargo with the rest of us.

My father's face turned the color of drying blood, and tremors began in his hands. The vein at his temple—the one that served as warning of the violence to come—stood out like rope beneath his skin. He looked to Jean, and she made some small gesture of restraint, a plea that worked this time but might not work the next.

To Sid he said, "You don't have to come with us, but the other four are going."

The words fell like a judgment of a prison sentence, from which there would be no appeal.

+ + +

We drove the thousand miles from Port Hueneme to Lander, Wyoming in the great Cadillac my father had used to collect me that first night—a 1968 Sedan Seville that Jean had claimed from her divorce like spoils of war. It was just large enough to contain the six of us. The car reeked of cigarettes and the vinyl seats would crack and protest when you settled into them. My father and Jean traded the wheel every few hours when fatigue or stiffness claimed the driver.

We did not stop for the night. When my father drove, Jean would stretch across the passenger seat with her feet on the dashboard, smoking and watching the world pass beyond the glass. When Jean took the wheel, my father would recline his seat and attempt sleep, though mostly he sat with eyes closed, opening them occasionally to study her driving as if calculating some risk only he could see. In the back seat, the four of us shifted like restless animals, seeking positions where flesh would not touch flesh, but in such confinement it was impossible. We reached Lander as the sun died behind the mountains.

We arrived with no place to live. The six of us spent a week in a tent made for four at a barren campground on the town's edge. The campground was nothing more than a dirt lot with electrical hookups for the RVs and a few picnic tables scattered like bones across the hardpan. There was a small building with bathrooms and showers, but the water ran cold as mountain streams.

Each morning my father and Jean would drive into town hunting shelter, leaving the four of us to wander among the sagebrush that stretched to every horizon. We would walk for hours through that gray-green expanse, following worn trails and searching for arrowheads or anything that might prove this desolation held meaning, but mostly there was only the endless sage and the sound of wind moving through it like some ancient language we could not decode.

In an alley off 7th Street, between Cliff and Cascade, they found a pink trailer squatting between two other ruins, and that became our new home.

+ + +

Lander sat at the feet of the Wind River Range, and the high altitude sun burned with a merciless brightness that had baked the trailer's paint until it looked like flesh that had suffered too long under that pitiless sky—faded and cracked and peeling like a wound that would not heal. The interior was paneled in dark brown wood, with carpet so dirty and matted it felt like the pelt of some diseased animal beneath my feet.

The trailer had two bedrooms—the larger for my two stepbrothers and me, the smaller for my sister. My father and Jean would claim the living room with its double bed, while my sister had a twin bed to herself. We boys made our beds on the floor in sleeping bags, like soldiers bivouacked in territory that would never be home.

Since we had just moved to town, my sister and older stepbrother were not able to find any marijuana, so they decided to try other ways of getting high. There was a small neighborhood store on the corner of 8th and Cliff, called Olsons Market, two blocks from the alley we lived in. It carried a small assortment of food staples and sundries. In the sundries section of the store they had a small display of hardware items, like screws, batteries, tape, and glue.

They even carried modeling glue, which was used for building plastic scale models, such as cars or airplanes. Modeling glue at the time contained toluene. Toluene is a solvent that, when inhaled in concentrated amounts, can lead to a hallucinatory high.

The first time I shoplifted was at Olson's Market. My older stepbrother had convinced me and my younger stepbrother to go get some glue, so we could "huff" it. My younger stepbrother distracted the owner of the store by asking a question about a brand of candy on the other side of the store, while I stole tubes of glue. The four of us spent the last few weeks before school started getting high on glue. When the glue was gone, we found other solvents, like lighter fluid, to use.

+ + +

Before Lander, we had not lived in luxury, but in that high desert town I learned what destitution meant. My father had counted on his Navy retirement to sustain us, but the divorce settlement had given my mother half his monthly pension despite her not having custody of my sister and me. With Jean unable to find work in Lander and my father's job paying wages that would not feed a family, we quickly descended into poverty.

On the first day of school—my sixth grade year—I owned two shirts and one pair of pants. The pants were jeans, the shirts solid-colored cotton with raglan sleeves. I wore one shirt the first day, the other the second, then returned to the first on the third day. The clothes grew soiled quickly, and with no one to teach me the rituals of cleanliness, my grooming deteriorated. Within days I had become the object of ridicule at my new school, marked as surely as if I bore some visible stigma.

The only bright spot was academics. That first week of school, I was sent to a room where two people tried to assess my learning levels. I was given a reading test that progressively got harder the more questions that I answered. I got no question wrong on the test. The people giving me the test were shocked and impressed, saying I could read at a college level, but I was sent back to my sixth-grade classroom as if nothing had happened. Possibly due to my advanced reading skills, my school days were filled with boredom in the classroom, and torment at lunch and recess.

That fall we would still huff glue when nothing else could be found, but my stepbrother had discovered a source for marijuana, and when he and my sister allowed it, I would smoke with them. In my heart I knew what we were doing carried the weight of transgression. It was not merely that the law forbade it—in my core I could feel that it violated something fundamental, some order that preceded all human statute.

By late fall I had grown sick with self-disgust and felt the burn of shame each time I drew smoke into my lungs. I felt corrupted from within, the filth inside matching the grime I wore on my skin. I remembered the times I had prayed when fear overtook me as a child, and what we were doing now, the way it made me feel in my spirit, had begun to frighten me in ways I could not name.

At night, before sleep claimed me, I began to recite the Lord's Prayer like a man drowning who calls out to whatever might save him.

+ + +

Over Christmas, my younger stepbrother, who was twelve and a year older than me, had gotten a toy typewriter as a gift for reasons no one could explain. One day after school resumed, my older stepbrother announced he was going to the library to type a paper. My younger stepbrother, who had just huffed glue, began pleading with him to type the paper on his toy machine instead. When told no, the boy closest in age to me collapsed into weeping that would not cease.

He sobbed without stop for more than an hour, his body wracked with a grief that seemed to come from some deeper well than disappointment. The glue had stripped away whatever defenses that twelve-year-old boy might have possessed, leaving him raw and inconsolable over a typewriter that could barely form letters on paper.

Watching this spectacle, I made a decision that would alter the course of my days. I would never get high again. That night I went to bed and spoke my own prayer, asking God to help me keep the promise I had made to myself and to whatever watched over children who were learning to save themselves.

+ + +

In the summer of 1978, my sister vanished.

From even before the start of our time in Lander, my father and Jean had never really interacted with me directly. Their interaction was always to the group of us. After I stopped chasing the next high with my stepbrothers and my sister, they went from treating me as part of their clan, to pushing me to be an outsider. I would tread at the boundaries of their territory, where the sounds of their daily life would faintly reach my ears, but I was not included in their plans, schemes, or activities.

Since no one spoke to me most of the time, I had to ask my father directly what had happened when I noticed my sister had not come back to the trailer after a night out.

"Where's Bonnie?"

"I don't know. She probably ran away."

"Ran away? To where?"

"I don't know," was his curt response.

"Are you calling the police?"

"No. The police aren't getting involved."

"Then are we going to go looking for her? We have to do something," I pleaded.

Two days before I learned of her running away was the last time I saw my sister in Lander. She had abandoned me, leaving me in the broken, rotten trailer full of strangers, including my father.

+ + +

I was ambivalent when junior high school started in the fall of 1978. I would be entering the 7th grade, and I would be back among the classmates that had bullied and tormented me about my dirty clothes and, over time, about everything else. However, I knew that junior high included extracurricular activities, and I could use the time spent practicing and playing sports as a way to avoid going to that trailer.

At our school, you could participate in four sports over the course the year, so I played football and basketball. I wrestled, and I threw the discus and ran track. Five days a week, I would stay after school to practice these sports. This meant that rather than be at the trailer at 3:30, if I took my time after practice was over, it might be almost 6 o'clock when I got to the trailer full of strangers.

Even though I had never played organized sports, I had a knack for each of the sports I played. My first taste of success happened in wrestling that first year. Wrestling practice was held in the school's gymnasium, which smelled like floor wax and sweat. The wrestling mats were old and worn, with tape covering the tears, but when I stepped onto them for the first time, something clicked. Coach Miller, a short, stocky man who had wrestled in high school twenty years earlier, taught me the basic positions and moves. Within a few weeks, I was beating kids who had been wrestling since elementary school.

At the conference wrestling tournament at the end of the season, I won the championship for my weight class, and our team won the overall championship. I was the best 145-pound wrestler in our conference. The tournament was held in our gymnasium, packed with parents and families cheering for their kids. When they called my name for the championship match, I walked to the center of the mat alone. When I pinned my opponent in the third period to win, I looked into the stands and saw empty seats where my family should have been. At the end-of-the-year award ceremony, I was given the honor of presenting the team's championship trophy to the school because I was an individual champion. Again, I walked into the school gymnasium alone.

I had joined the wrestling team, made sure I attended practice, got to the school on travel days when we had a meet, and, on the day the gymnasium was filled with the families of students getting awards, I walked into the school gymnasium—all of this alone. This would turn out to be the pattern for the rest of my time in Lander.

+ + +

My sister, as it would come to pass, had fled from that trailer, from the strangers who shared our roof, from Lander, from my father... and from me. My father made no effort to find her, and for nearly a year none of us—not he, not my mother, not I—knew whether she lived or had vanished from the earth entirely.

One day in 1979, the Lander police came to our door bearing news. They said my sister had been found at a truck stop in Cheyenne, Wyoming, where she was being held by law enforcement. Rather than bring her back to our trailer, my father arranged for them to fly her to California, back to my mother.

Soon after her return to San Diego, my mother petitioned the courts and had my sister declared a ward of the state. She was delivered into the custody of California's Child Welfare Services, another child swallowed by the institutions that were meant to protect what they could not understand.

CHAPTER NINE

Life at the edge of the wilderness that stretched into the Wind River Range was harsh beyond measure. The landscape of the valley was semi-arid and unforgiving—what some would call godforsaken, though perhaps God seemed to have simply turned his face away and not abandoned it.

Most days dawned clear with skies so blue and boundless they seemed like pools of liquid sapphire stretched tight above the earth. The air held no moisture, so dry that when rain clouds gathered at the valley's far end, you could watch the water fall from heaven and die in the air before it ever kissed the ground.

On some days, dark clouds would mass like armies at the mountain's edge, creeping steadily over the peaks with the patience of predators. The air would thicken and grow heavy with menace. Lightning would strike the mountainsides in brief, violent bursts of white fire, and the valley would shake with the deep voice of thunder rolling between the peaks. When the storm finally pushed beyond the mountains and turned toward the valley, the wind would howl and lash the trees into a wild dance of submission.

Then the storm would break free and surge forward with terrible speed, racing to claim Lander. Lightning would fork across the sky in brilliant, jagged scars, illuminating the town even in daylight with the color of judgment. When a bolt reached down to touch the earth, its fury was sudden and absolute.

The weather was not the only thing in our lives that could turn violent without warning.

+ + +

I had started to develop an expectation that we would never live anywhere permanently. We had moved four times between 1977 and 1979. In 1979, we had moved to different trailer on the far, northern edge of town, near the corner of Jefferson Street and Riverview Drive—a part of town that had very few trees and sat at the edge of the expanses of sage brush that spread across the valley away from the mountains. Since my days were spent mostly figuring out ways to not have to be near the trailer, I usually got home well after dark, just in time to sleep, and I left soon after waking each morning.

One morning before I had made my escape for the day, I found my father and my stepmother sitting at the kitchen table, smoking and drinking coffee.

"Hey, Buddy. Good morning," my father greeted me.

"Morning," I replied, hoping my suspicion was not evident in my tone of voice. He only called me "Buddy" when he wanted something from me.

"I have an idea that I was telling Jean about, and I want to see what you think."

"Okay."

He and my stepmother sat beside each other on one side of the table, a dark green glass ashtray positioned between them like an altar where cigarettes smoldered, their smoke rising in thin spirals toward the ceiling. Between them as well, but closer to the table's center, sat a frosted glass piggy bank.

My father pointed to the piggy bank and said, "When that piggy bank is full, I am going to build a lighthouse."

"A lighthouse? In California?"

"No, here, in the sage brush. I've always wanted to build a light house in the desert, but Wyoming is close enough."

"Okay..."

"When we build the lighthouse, you'll get your own bedroom. You, Dan, and Sid can put your change in the piggy bank. We will, too, and as soon as it's full, I'll get the plans drawn up by an architect."

Starting that day, I spent my afternoons picking up aluminum cans I found in ditches and taking them to the recycling center to get the few coins they would be worth. I walked the alleys of the town looking for bottles that could be returned to the grocery store in exchange for their deposits. I offered to help neighbors clean their yards, mow their grass, and do odd jobs. I took all of the money I made and shoved it into that piggy bank. After several weeks, the piggy bank was full.

The piggy bank was always in the center of the kitchen table, and since he spent his mornings sitting at that table getting the initial doses of caffeine and nicotine that jump started his days, he would have noticed it.

When I pointed out that the piggy bank was full, he said, "Yeah, I saw that." He took the piggy bank to the bedroom he shared with my stepmother, and I never saw it again. I never got my own bedroom in the lighthouse.

It was another lesson in not believing my father's promises, though I hadn't yet learned to stop hoping.

+ + +

In the late summer of 1980, we moved to a house with three bedrooms at 170 Popo Agie Street. The house was built on the site of an old homestead, and in the alley was the original cabin. Originally a single-story house built on a slab, somewhere along the way it had been raised up, and a basement dug beneath it. The basement had two bedrooms; by the time we moved into the house, my older stepbrother, Dan, who had been living with us, had left the house. This meant that I had a room to myself, and at 14 I had a bed at last.

Since we had moved to Lander, my father had mostly ignored me, spending time with my older stepbrother. My father had bought a used motorcycle, and they spent evenings and weekends in the garage restoring it. My father taught him how to drive, and the truck that my father had bought—the one he explicitly told me I would never be allowed to drive—was my stepbrother's informal driver's ed vehicle.

But as high school approached, my father started paying attention to me and the things I was doing, and it wasn't the sort of attention a boy in his early teenaged years needed. Our first few years in Lander, while my father's presence was heavy and dark, he wasn't prone to fits of rage. This changed as we moved to the house on Popo Agie.

That small, raised house had a tiny yard in the front with patchy grass that, if watered, would occasionally grow long, lush, and green. It was a spot of grass that occasionally needed mowing. The house came with a lawn mower, and I had learned how make sure it had fuel in it and how to start it. Whenever I noticed the grass had grown higher than the neighbors' on either side of us, I would go out and mow the yard. I knew nothing of how to care for a lawn, but I had seen the other people who lived on our street mow their yards, so I assumed I could follow their example without going too far wrong. Back and forth, back and forth, kicking cut grass out the side of the mower and scenting the air with the sweet, wet, earthy odor.

One day as I was finishing mowing the yard, as I pushed the lawn mower to the driveway to put it into the garage, my father burst out the front door.

"What the hell do you think you are doing!" he yelled as he came down the steps in front of the house.

"I am putting the lawnmower away."

"The hell you are. Get back here right now!" he ordered, "You missed a bunch of spots!"

I looked at the grass and said, "I don't see anything."

"It's right there," he pointed.

"Where? I don't see it."

He stalked over, grabbed the back of my head by the hair, and pushed me to the lawn, where he saw a spot of unmown grass.

"Do you see it now?" he asked as he pushed my head down.

"No," I lied. I did see a small patch of grass that I had missed when I had turned the mower back around.

My father lifted my head back up, let go of my hair, pulled back his right hand and punched me in the side of my face. I felt the jolt of that first blow and saw an explosion of bright white. This sensation was followed by a shock of disorientation as he continued to hit me. In my confusion, I couldn't keep track of how many times or where exactly he hit me. It could have been one or a dozen times. When he finished hitting me, I went back to the lawn mower, started it up, and mowed the lawn again, making sure that all the missed spots were shorn down. As soon as I was done mowing, I left the house.

Hours later, when I finally returned home, I had to walk past the living room where my father had been sitting. It was obvious he had been in that spot for a while, due to the number of cigarettes in the ash tray, and the beer cans on the end table. He was crying as I walked past. That was the first time my father beat me. To that point, he had been angry and prone to yelling, but he had never been physically violent before.

After this, when he disliked something I did or said, there was usually a physical reaction. Even small infractions, like saying I didn't like a certain food, or that I didn't want to take the trash out would earn a slap from him. Sometimes, long after I had gotten away from him after he beat me, I would come home and again see him crying.

My prayers at night changed from pleas for protection to cries for deliverance, and I began asking God what sin I had committed to merit such punishment, what transgression had earned me this exile from grace. Yet even as I questioned, some deeper voice whispered that perhaps this suffering was not punishment at all, but some larger design I could not comprehend—that grace might come not despite the darkness, but through it.

+ + +

In the spring of 1981, after basketball had ended and school resumed from Christmas break, my father announced he had taken work with the US Geological Survey aboard a research vessel doing exploratory work at sea. He would return to the waters that had always claimed him, but I would remain in Lander. The job would keep him away from the house on Popo Agie for six months at a stretch.

On a cold February morning, my father walked out and abandoned me to whatever mercy my stepmother might possess, leaving me with her and one stepbrother under our roof, and two other stepbrothers loose in the town who would prove to be instruments of constant torment.

The house changed after his departure—not safer, but emptied of one particular menace. The heavy tension that had pressed down on every room when he was present lifted like smoke, though new terrors rushed in to fill the space he had vacated. Without his presence to contain them, the other dangers in my life seemed to swell and multiply, as if his leaving had removed some dam that had held back darker waters.

+ + +

I had taken advantage of every opportunity to work out that came about from the athletics program at our school: summer strength training, group runs, and pickup games during open gym. I used these as an excuse to stay away from the house.

By the time football season started, I was large enough, strong enough, fast enough, and fit enough, to start to excel. When I had made the varsity squad Friday nights were my favorite night. I would get to the gym early in the evening, suit up, and be ready to play before any of the rest of the team would be there. After the game, I wouldn't linger on the field like the other players, because I had no family or family friends to linger with and talk to. I would shower and be dressed, ready to leave, before most of the team was finished talking to their family.

And it was not just in sports that I led this solitary existence; I was alone in most of my high school activities and events. No one went to parent teacher conferences on my behalf. No one came to the art show that my drawing of a hawk was in. No one was with me at the awards banquets.

Occasionally I would encounter Mrs. W____ at school events or about town. She was a large woman with graying hair and gentle blue eyes, mother to a boy who shared most of my classes and played alongside me in whatever sports the season demanded.

"Mike," she would say each time our paths crossed, "I hope you are doing well. I am praying for you."

Her words carried a weight I had not felt elsewhere. When no one else marked my existence, Mrs. W____ bore witness to my struggle and offered what she could—prayer to a God I was learning to trust more than the people who were meant to care for me.

+ + +

From somewhere I found the self-discipline to study and get most of my homework done. All in all, I was doing pretty well at school. My younger stepbrother had dropped out of school by the time I was 15, and he would not be around the house most evenings. My stepmother had found a job that required her to be at work from 3pm to 11pm, so I would come back to a house that had no one in it nearly every school day.

It was my habit at the time to try to do my homework with the TV on, while I was sitting a rocking chair in the living room of our small, dingy house. One evening in early 1982, during one of my father's rare two-week visits home, I found him, likely a little drunk, sleeping on the couch in the living room where I did my homework. Along with the beer cans, there was an ash tray with a smoldering cigarette on the walnut brown coffee table next to the couch.

I settled at my desk to begin my homework and turned on the television. That night the movie Scanners was playing. I cannot recall its premise, but I remember the villains possessed the ability to make heads explode through thought alone—some manner of telekinetic weapon. As a youth of sixteen grown numb to violence, I was not disturbed by the sight of obviously fake heads bursting apart. I may have found the absurdity of it amusing.

My father did not share my casual regard. When the noise of a particular scene startled him from his stupor, he turned toward the television just as a skull erupted in gore.

"Turn that off!" he commanded.

"Why? It's funny," I replied.

"Turn that f___ng thing off now!"

Then he began to shake and weep. I did not know what to do or say or what was happening before my eyes. In that moment I understood that something was broken in my father. If I had believed he was merely unwilling to play the role of loving, protecting father, I knew then that something had rendered him incapable of playing any role at all.

I turned off the television and retreated to my room, leaving him trembling on the couch. The sound of his weeping followed me down the hall like an accusation I could not answer.

+ + +

Several months later, on an evening when I was alone again, sitting in the rocking chair with my homework spread before me, the doorbell shattered the silence, followed immediately by heavy pounding on the door like fists of judgment. I rose, turned on the outside light, and opened the door to whatever waited beyond.

As the door swung inward, I found myself facing several sheriffs, two with hands resting on their weapons like gunfighters prepared for violence. They stood arrayed before me like harbingers of some reckoning I had not foreseen.

The sheriff nearest the door spoke with the authority of one who carried the weight of law behind his words. "I have a warrant for Sean Williams."

"He's not here. I'm the only one here."

"Do you know where he is?"

"No, I haven't seen him for weeks," I said, telling him the complete truth. "What's the warrant for?" I asked.

"He's wanted for distribution of narcotics. If you see him, please call us. Here's my card."

I didn't tell my stepmother or my stepbrother that the sheriff was looking for him, but my stepbrother was arrested, tried, and convicted within a few months. It was just another piece of chaos in our fractured household, another reminder that normal families didn't have police showing up at their doors.

+ + +

In January, Lander, perched on the eastern slope of the Rockies, would feel the breath of the Chinooks—dry, warm winds that raced down from the peaks into the valley like messengers from some distant country. These winds could transform the world in their path with sudden violence. They would devour snow in mere hours, leaving behind pools of meltwater scattered across grass and pavement like the remnants of some great thaw. When the winds finally died, winter would reclaim its territory, and the cold January air would return to freeze the pools into treacherous mirrors.

In the late winter of 1983, I was away overnight at the state basketball tournament. The oldest stepbrother—the one who had not followed us to Lander initially—had come to live with his wife in the small cabin that squatted in the alley behind our house like some afterthought to our misery.

THE CLOUD GROWS THIN

When I returned that Saturday afternoon, I found the sidewalk in front of our house scarred with divots of broken concrete, each crater surrounded by ice. It appeared someone had tried to break the frozen pools but had succeeded only in wounding the pavement beneath.

I walked into the house, and my stepbrother's wife was in the living room folding clothes and watching TV.

"What the hell happened to the sidewalk?" I asked her, "My dad's going to be pissed when he sees that."

She immediately said, "Sid was trying to get the ice off." She stopped folding the clothes and left the house.

I had put the stuff I had taken with me on the overnight trip into my room, made myself a sandwich, and sat in the rocking chair where I typically watched TV.

I heard the backdoor open and slam shut, followed by pounding footsteps coming up the few stairs that led to the kitchen from the back. When I turned to look at the kitchen, I saw Sid walking toward me carrying a shotgun. As he came into the living room, he pointed the shotgun at my head, and I turned to look at the TV.

"Who the f___ do you think you are, talking to my wife like that?" he bellowed.

I did not respond but looked forward and began to pray. *God, please don't let me die. Please help me. I don't know what I did wrong, but please don't let this happen.*

"I asked you a question!"

I stared straight ahead, continuing my silent prayer.

After a few silent seconds, he said, "Don't ever talk to my wife like that again."

I heard him leave with the slamming of the back door. I sat in that chair for a long time after he left, my hands shaking, not sure if he might come back.

+ + +

I had my suspicions that Mrs. W____ had a sense of what my life at our house was like, but I had never told anyone anything about my life. At school the Monday following Sid's threat, I finally risked telling people. The first person I talked to was a girl named Sarah who was mostly gentle and friendly to me. Sarah came from the type of family that seemed to be what I would have called normal. They spent time together, went to church together, and took foreign holiday trips together.

As I went to my first class at school on Monday, Sarah was the first person I talked to.

"Hey, I have to tell you something that happened this weekend."

Probably expecting something mundane, maybe about having watched a movie, Sarah replied, "What did you do?"

"I didn't do anything. My stepbrother had a shotgun pointed at me, and he said he was going to kill me," I told her.

"What?" Her eyes widened as she asked, "What happened?"

I recounted what he had done, and she said, "You need to talk to Mrs. Lee, right now!"

I took Sarah's advice and left the classroom.

I went to the counselor's office where Mrs. Lee, the school's social worker, sat a desk that separated her from the damaged children who found their way to her door. Mrs. Lee listened with patience as I recounted what had happened. After a moment's silence, she delivered her verdict: "I'm sorry that happened to you, Mike. You'll have to be careful when you are home. If anything like this happens again, you make sure to come see me."

THE CLOUD GROWS THIN

It was as if I had walked from the building and a winter's worth of snow had avalanched from the roof to crush my shoulders. I felt the weight of facing that house alone settle upon me once more, and worse, I felt the brief hope that someone might intervene die like a flame starved of air.

In that moment I understood with terrible clarity that I would have to engineer my own escape. I would have to find my way out of that house, out of Lander, out of the life that was slowly killing me, because no soul on earth was coming to deliver me from it.

The truth struck me like lightning: I was utterly alone, and if I meant to survive, I would have to become my own salvation. Yet somewhere in that desolation, Mrs. W____'s voice persisted like an echo in a canyon: "I am praying for you." Her prayers had not rescued me from this moment, but they had preserved something within me—some ember that refused to be extinguished, some conviction that I was worth the saving.

I thought if no one would deliver me, I would deliver myself. And perhaps, in ways I could not yet comprehend, her prayers were already working in me, preparing me for deliverance I could not yet imagine—that what felt like abandonment might be the very means by which grace would find me.

CHAPTER TEN

In February 1983, just weeks after my stepbrother had held me at gunpoint, I turned seventeen. I remained too young to flee the house legally, still held by the laws that governed minors, but old enough to begin planning my deliverance in earnest. As I walked through the school lobby on my way to class one day, I spotted a military recruiter seated at a table like some agent of an earthly providence.

When I had first thought of my escape, I had imagined a college degree would serve as my passage to freedom, and the military had never entered my calculations. But on that day, with all that had transpired weighing on my mind, I found myself thinking, "Why not speak to this guy?"

After introductions and small talk, I told the recruiter my plans. "I'm gonna go to college when I graduate, so I don't really want to do four years."

"Oh, you can go to college while you're in. We only need you to meet once a month and two weeks in the summer. It's not like active duty. It's part time," he explained cheerfully, "And college, well, once you make it through basic training, you'll get $2000 a year for tuition."

"It's part time?" I asked. "I thought when you joined you had to do four years."

"That's active duty. I am with the National Guard. You know where the armory is up near the Chevy dealer on 789?"

"Yeah, where the army trucks and tanks are?"

"Those aren't tanks. Those are cannons. And yeah, that's the place. That's the National Guard armory."

After talking with the recruiter some more over the course of a few weeks, I learned that I would be able to escape my house for the summer, have a part time job when I returned, and have most of my college tuition paid for. The decision was easy. At seventeen, I signed up with the Army National Guard and got ready to ship out to Army Basic Training in May.

+ + +

The previous two years, I had competed on the track and field team as a discus thrower. That year, though, I began training with the long-distance runners when I was not hurling the iron and wood disc through space. I also started doing pushups at every opportunity. Soon I was in the finest physical condition of my young life.

But no amount of physical preparation could prepare me for the emotional burden of departure. The night before I would leave, I lay in my narrow bed listening to the familiar chorus of our house—the steady hum of the refrigerator, the settling complaints of thin walls, the distant murmur of late-night television. Everything I had known, however brutal, was about to vanish. I was trading the familiar torment for complete uncertainty, and despite my yearning for escape, dread moved through my chest like ice water in my veins.

I thought of the families I had seen at school, parents who ferried their children to practice and attended conferences about their progress. What would it feel like to have someone notice your absence, to have a mother weep when you departed for the military instead of one who would exhale with relief had she known? I buried those thoughts and fixed my mind on what lay ahead. Whatever awaited me in that distant place had to be better than what I was leaving behind.

On the 16th of May, I joined a group of eight recruits at the airport in the next town over. As we waited to board, I watched the other guys say goodbye to their families. Parents hugged their sons, mothers wiped away tears, fathers offered last-minute advice. I stood alone with my small duffel bag, watching these scenes of love and connection that felt as foreign to me as a movie about life on another planet.

We flew to Denver, where we met up with a dozen more recruits from the Wyoming National Guard and boarded a flight to Oklahoma City bound for Fort Sill, Oklahoma.

+ + +

The training the Army put recruits through started even before they arrived at the base. The travel day and flight arrival were planned so that the recruits arrived at the base late in the evening after a long journey. Our plane landed in Oklahoma City in the late afternoon, but we were made to wait in several parallel lines in a secluded part of the airport, waiting for recruits from other states to arrive. By the time everyone who would be starting basic combat training with us got there, we had been standing for nearly two hours.

Lander, perched at its high altitude with its arid breath, had been cool and pleasant when we departed. Stepping from the air-conditioned terminal into the Oklahoma evening was like opening the door to hell's own furnace—thick with humidity, the sultry air wrapping us like a shroud of damp wool. The heat pressed against my flesh, heavy and inescapable as judgment. I would come to learn that the most oppressive heat can yield the most fertile growth. For that, this place would prove ideal ground for discovery.

As the sun began its descent behind the trees and buildings, we filed onto the coach buses that waited. No one spoke of how long the journey would be, so as we pulled onto the interstate, I felt the familiar flutter of fear in my gut. Just as I had done on those bus rides to see my father, I began to pray. "God, I do not know what I am doing. I do not know if I have the strength for what is coming. But please, help me make it."

As the sky at the horizon turned the color of fresh blood, streams of smoke began racing upward into the darkness, and when the smoke dissipated, brilliant golden lights burst into view like fallen stars. The lights descended so slowly and drifted with such grace that I could not fathom their nature.

I watched those mysterious lights with a yearning I had never known—not for the lights themselves, but for home. Like most souls on the threshold of transformation, I wanted to return to Lander, not to my house of torment, but to the comfort of familiar ground. I wanted to be ordinary, to possess a family like those who had delivered the other recruits to the airport with tears and embraces.

When the longing faded as the illumination flares I had been watching faded into darkness, I understood that the path I had chosen would remake me entirely.

+ + +

The bus pulled up to the reception center at the base when it was completely dark, and the hour must have been close to 9 pm. The scene outside the bus was just like the movies I had watched trying to get ready for what I would be going through in basic training. There were dozens of drill sergeants and other soldiers waiting for the buses, and as soon as the doors opened a drill sergeant came on and yelled, "Get your goat smelling behinds off my bus right now! Get out there and find a yellow line to stand behind!"

Without pausing he continued, "Why are you maggots still on my bus!"

As I got off the bus two soldiers flanked me on either side and yelled at me to find a yellow line to stand behind. Each line had a number painted in black on it, which I could barely see in the orange glow from the light poles. When everyone was standing behind a yellow line, it turned out that we were almost in formation.

A drill sergeant stood in front of the formation and gave us concise instructions on what was going to happen in the next couple of hours.

"You will enter the barracks behind you, find a bunk and place your personal items on that bunk. Then you will walk back and take your place at the line you are now standing at. After that you will go to the dining hall and eat a meal. Following the meal, it will be lights out in the barracks. You have thirty seconds to get into those barracks and get back out here in formation. If you do not make it back here in thirty seconds, you will wish you were never born."

He had taken not a breath during his tirade.

To this point he had been addressing us in a loud, clear voice. Suddenly, he switched to his drill sergeant voice and yelled, "Do I make myself clear? Now move it! Your thirty seconds starts now!"

The soldiers and drill sergeants started yelling at us as we tried to make it into the barracks.

After the meal, we were brought back to the barracks. We were directed to get into our bunks and warned that we needed to sleep. Although my heart pounded so hard in my chest that I wondered how I'd ever rest, I fell asleep soon after my head hit the pillow.

It seemed to me that I had just closed my eyes, when the fluorescent lights flashed on, the banging of a lid on a galvanized trash can shattered the silence, and the barking and yelling of the drill sergeants started.

My basic training had begun. We spent the first few days at the reception center where we filled out forms, got vaccinations, and were issued our uniforms. When the administrative tasks were done, we were piled into an olive drab bus and were taken to the training barracks.

+ + +

I had thought the welcome we received at the reception station was stressful, but I knew nothing about stress until I got to what was called the battery area. In artillery a battery is an organizational unit, like a platoon or company, and the battery area was comprised of the barracks, latrines, chow hall, and parade ground for our training unit.

The training drill sergeants were lined up and waiting for us as our buses arrived. Just as before, they barked and yelled at us, but this time we had an idea of what a formation was and formed up as they shouted at us. Once we were in formation and the shouting had stopped, our drill sergeant, the one who would be guiding us through the rest of our training, explained to us what was expected.

"You will enter the barracks, find a bunk, and set your duffle bag on the floor in front of the locker. Then you will return to this formation. Do you understand!" he shouted.

We mumbled, "Yes, staff sergeant."

"Move!"

The barracks were wooden two-story structures raised during the Second World War, designed as temporary shelter but now meticulously maintained and perfectly clean. They would serve as my house for the next twelve weeks. I shouldered my duffle bag and began walking toward the entrance.

From the corner of my vision, I glimpsed a massive figure bearing down on me from the right, but I did not turn to look and continued my advance. Suddenly, another camouflaged form was charging from the left. Before I could comprehend what was unfolding, more drill sergeants had materialized before me, surrounding me in a chorus of commands.

"Recruit! What is your malfunction!"

"You were ordered into the barracks! Why are you not in the barracks?"

"You carry that bag like you're on vacation! This is not a vacation!"

One survival skill I had mastered in childhood was avoiding direct eye contact with those who sought to break me. When my mother would rage in my face, I would fix my gaze just behind her head, creating the illusion of meeting her eyes while protecting myself from her fury. I used this technique now with the drill sergeants. Looking past them allowed me to maintain my bearing without lowering my gaze or turning away—either of which would signal weakness and certainly prolong their assault.

When they had yelled at me the proper amount, one of them shouted, "Get in the grass, and give me twenty!"

I dropped my duffle bag and jogged off the gravel parade ground and onto a patch of grass and started doing pushups. After twenty, a drill sergeant said, "Now get your duffle bag, and get your goat smelling butt in that barracks!"

That was my first shark attack. The goal of basic combat training during my time there was to break down the individual recruit and build them back up as part of a cohesive team. The shark attack was one of the tools they used.

Sometimes, the drill sergeants would use the shark attacks on someone they thought they could completely break and get to drop out of basic training, and they could use the attacks to break someone who looked as though they would have a problem with authority.

From that first day, several times a day I would be surrounded by drill sergeants yelling at me in a confusing cacophony of conflicting orders. I would stand at parade rest, looking just beyond their heads, and not react at all. My jaw didn't clench. My fists didn't ball up. My breathing didn't change. I'd been through this before, and I knew how to endure it. I watched others suffer the shark attack, thanking God that that moment wasn't my turn for another feeding frenzy. Our barracks lost two people who could not handle the stress of the basic training. They had washed out.

Since one of the goals of basic was to breakdown individuality, our uniforms didn't have name tapes on them, so the drill sergeants had a list of pet names they would call recruits. During those shark attacks I was called, "Maggot," "Worm," "Turd," and if they were feeling nice, "Recruit." Regardless of the names they called us, toward the end of the first two weeks, as a unit we had learned to follow orders, how to get into formation and begun to learn how to march.

One day our drill sergeant directed us to get all of our uniform tops, and he marched us to a building that had rows of sewing machines. The machines were used to sew "US Army" over one pocket and our last name over the other pocket of our uniform tops. By making it this far in training, we had earned our names back.

+ + +

The days at basic started at 5 am with calisthenics and running, followed by personal grooming, and then breakfast. After those were finished real training would start.

On the day we were going to the rifle range for the first time, a milestone day in basic training, I was standing in line at the armory waiting to be issued my rifle for the day.

I could hear the drill sergeants barking their way up the line from the back, correcting a recruit's posture or getting him to adjust his uniform, and I knew a shark attack was looming. As they got to me, they yelled at me to get out of line and stand at parade rest in front of them, and then the yelling started. I stood rigid, with my chin level and endured it.

Suddenly, louder than the other drill sergeants, one yelled, "Private LaFleur! How old are you, son?"

"Seventeen, staff sergeant!" At the age of seventeen I was six foot two inches tall, as tall as I would ever be. I had not lived an easy life, and it must have shown on my face.

"Seventeen?" he paused and then continued, "Son, that's a hard seventeen years. Did you get the number of the truck that hit you?"

"No, staff sergeant!"

When I answered, the yelling stopped.

"Make a hole!" the drill sergeant barked, "Let LaFleur back in line where he was!"

That was the final shark attack I would endure. Something had shifted in the bearing of the drill sergeants, and I felt a transformation within myself. I knew I would navigate the remainder of basic training; more than that, I was beginning to understand that I could endure the chaos and turbulence that life would bring.

That morning the sun rose like a great red eye opening above the horizon, promising heat that would test our limits. It would be a day of trial by fire, but I knew I would survive it.

+ + +

The drill sergeants had a tradition of teaching a chant or a song to their battery. This chant or song was shouted by the recruits before they sat down for any classroom training. Our chant was: "When the going gets tough, the tough get going! Drive on drill sergeant, drive on!" After that we sang the jingle from the Army recruiting commercial at the time, "Be all that you can be, in the Army!"

Most of the rest of basic training was a jumble of dark mornings, pushups, oppressive heat, loud noises, the smell of cordite, not enough sleep, hunger, and singing "Be all that you can be, in the Army!" multiple times a day. Still, I had grown in confidence that I would be able to make it through basic training and artillery training, but there was one hurdle that I was dreading, and I didn't know if I could overcome it—the challenge course.

The challenge course is an obstacle course that is designed to mimic conditions soldiers might face in combat. It is meant to test physical, mental, and emotional resilience. At basic training, I had told no one of my one irrational fear. I was afraid of heights, a fear so strong that my legs could begin to shake and go weak if I were to stand on a chair. A climb up a ladder could make my arms and grip go soft. I only heard rumors of the obstacles on the challenge course: wall climbs, low crawls, balance beams, monkey bars. All of these would be easy. The thought of the pole climb, though, caused me deep anxiety.

When the trucks dropped us off at the challenge course, we got into formation near the start of the course, and although we were supposed to fall into formation at the position of attention, in which you were supposed to stare straight ahead, I couldn't help but move my head slightly to look at the obstacles. Just over the tops of the trees, I could see what looked like a telephone pole about 50 feet high, with climbing spikes jutting from its sides. That was my nightmare. If I failed to climb that pole and finish the obstacle, I would be kicked out of basic training, and my plan to escape my house would have failed.

The fear that gripped me was the same terror I'd felt when my father or mother would rage through the house—that paralyzing certainty that I was too small, too weak, too nothing to survive what was coming. But this time was different. This time, I had a choice. I could let fear win and go back to that house, back to the threats and violence and helplessness. Or I could find a way to climb that pole.

Because there are so many trainees that have to go through the obstacles, they broke us up into squads in order to have different starting points on the course. This kept us from having to wait to start.

My squad got the pole as our starting obstacle. We ran over to wait in line, and I ended up being the fourth person from the front of the line. In my mind, in the short time it took us to run over from the formation, the pole had grown 20 feet higher.

The trainees in front of me navigated the obstacle with no problems. I watched with my knees getting that shaking sensation when they wanted to go weak, as the guys from my platoon used the climbing spikes to scale the pole whose top was attached to a vertical frame. When they were at the top, they hoisted their bodies over the eight-inch-by-eight-inch horizontal bar that was the top of the frame and climbed down a set of horizontal braces until they reached a mostly open platform that was thirty feet above the ground. They crossed the platform, and then used a cargo net at the far end to get back down to the ground.

When it was my turn, I ran to the base of the pole. I felt sick to my stomach, and my vision suddenly became narrow and focused. All I could see was the pole and the first climbing spike.

"God, please," I prayed silently, the words desperate and quick. "Don't let me fall. Don't let me fail."

And then, in that moment of pure terror, something shifted. A calm descended over me like warm water, washing away the panic and leaving behind a clarity I had never experienced. It wasn't the absence of fear—the fear was still there, real and sharp. But underneath it was something stronger: a quiet certainty that I was not alone in this moment.

With crystal clarity I realized that I didn't have to climb the entire pole at once. The peace that filled me whispered a simple truth: I only had to do the next right thing. At that moment, the only thing I had to do was reach out my hand and grab the spike that was in front of me, and that's what I did. The moment was over. I had grabbed the spike. I had done what I had to do. Success.

The next moment, the only thing I had to do was reach out my other hand and grab the other spike, and I did it. Again, success. And that was it, hand-over-hand, foot-above-foot, I climbed the pole, went over the top bar, and climbed back down. Each movement was deliberate, guided by that same quiet voice that said, "This spike. This step. This breath."

In the sum of those moments, with each grab of the spike, with each step I took, I was changed. The rest of the challenge course was full of obstacles, and as I touched the ground, I knew with total confidence that I would be able to conquer any obstacle I was to face. Not because I was suddenly fearless, but because I had learned the secret: impossible things become possible when you break them down into individual moments of courage.

+ + +

Days after the challenge course, the drill sergeants began addressing us as soldiers rather than trainees. Tests remained ahead of us, but I had prepared for seven weeks to meet whatever they demanded. I was ready. Those of us who had endured the full crucible of training had been forged from raw civilian flesh into something harder—soldiers tempered by fire and discipline.

After graduation from basic training and field artillery school, I returned to Lander transformed. I was no longer the frightened boy who had fled that place, but something new wrought from what I had been.

CHAPTER ELEVEN

Fort Sill sprawled across the Great Plains where the horizon stretched endless in all directions, and the mornings blazed orange with a great red sun visible from the moment it breached the edge of the world. Lander nestled in the foothills of the Rockies, cradled in a valley and hemmed by mountains that concealed the horizon from view. After twelve weeks of absence, the contrast upon my return struck me like the difference between warfare and childhood.

When the clouds descended over the peaks and the aspens scattered through the foothills began their transformation to gold, other seniors—guided by families who knew the way forward—started speaking of the ACT college entrance examination.

By the time I returned, football season was about to start, and I was granted a starting position despite having missed most of summer practice.

Even as I settled into the familiar rhythms of school and sport, my mind turned toward what lay ahead, which meant college.

I had no idea what it took to get into college, and I had not heard of this test, so I went to the same counseling office that had turned me away when I had been threatened, to see if they could help me once again.

They were skeptical, but polite, and told me that there was a fee to take the test. I was making money in the National Guard, and I had saved all my pay from basic training, and I let them know it wasn't a problem.

I never knew why the counselors were reluctant, but they only begrudgingly helped me apply to take the test in October; the next test wouldn't be until the following year, after the college application deadlines. I would have to score well if I were to get accepted to a university.

I showed up to the test with my three number two pencils and sat to take the exam. After it was over, I had weeks before my results would be known.

One day in November, I was notified by one of my teachers that the guidance counselors wanted to see me. I walked into the office, "You guys wanted to see me?"

"Yeah. Hi, Mike. Thanks for stopping in," Mr. Davis greeted, "We got your ACT scores, and we'd like to go over them with you."

I was prepared to be told I didn't do well. I hadn't taken the prep courses my classmates had, and I hadn't studied. I had gone into the test not knowing how it worked, so I must have done poorly.

Sitting at across the table from me, Mr. Davis said, "You're score is a 29. This is a really good score, Mike. You are in the top 10% of all test takers. You could get in to almost any competitive university or college." He went on to explain the test results further, but I had stopped paying attention.

I went from excited about my high score, to realizing I had no idea how to know what college to go to. The pride that had swelled in my chest when he announced my score quickly deflated as the weight of actually choosing a school settled over me. With no one to help guide me and no money other than the tuition bonus I would get from the National Guard, I was at a loss for what to do.

I went to the guidance counselors to see if they could help me choose a school to attend, but they offered no advice. The only universities I knew of where the Ivy League schools, and when I mentioned those, the counselor, said, "No one from Lander has made it in to the Ivy League," and they offered no alternatives.

In spring, right before the application deadline, I applied to what I thought would be the safest choice—the University of Wyoming. I could afford the tuition and the room and board, and I could drive down in the car I had bought with my National Guard money, I reasoned on my own.

+ + +

My father was gone most of my last year in high school. On Senior Day at football, when parents escorted their sons onto the field to be recognized by the crowd, I walked to the fifty-yard line to be announced by myself.

At graduation, I drove myself to the gymnasium, and there was no family cheering when I received my diploma; however, after the ceremony Mrs. W____ invited me over to her house to have cake with her son and their family.

That summer brought National Guard camp, and I volunteered for what they called the advance party. This meant I could depart my house and remain at the training site immediately following graduation. I returned to 170 Popo Agie only two or three times after that. I was free of that place, but I felt that I was truly alone.

+ + +

Driving along I-80 toward Laramie from Lander, some thirty miles out, I crested the final hill before descending to the High Plains that stretched to the eastern edge of the world. The view beyond the Snowy Range was harsher and more unforgiving than anything I had left behind. Where Lander Valley had been dotted with sagebrush and cottonwoods that followed the creek beds, the expanse before me was stripped bare. Only short prairie grass, already browning, dared to cling to ground that looked as if it could sustain nothing.

I had survived basic training, had been forged into something stronger, but the empty plains that spread before me promised a different kind of trial. Here there would be no drill sergeants to guide me, no clear objectives to meet, no brotherhood of fellow soldiers. Just the vast indifference of open country and whatever tests awaited a young man truly alone for the first time.

The landscape stretched endlessly ahead, empty as a prayer spoken into silence—though perhaps silence, too, could be a form of answer.

I pulled into the parking lot of the high-rise dorms, took what few belongings I had, and moved into the room I would share with a classmate from Lander. The cardboard boxes and duffel bag that held everything I owned felt insignificant as I watched other families unload entire cars worth of belongings, complete with matching bedding sets and mini-refrigerators their parents had carefully selected.

Just like all the other first year students I wandered around the campus the first day of classes trying to act like I was not lost, but I was truly lost. As I drifted around the campus, there were clusters of students in each other's orbits, laughing, talking, sharing experiences. I moved among them in a silent fog of isolation. I saw them as normal people, with normal families, living normal lives. I felt like a spectator in a universe in which I might never belong. I managed to find my way to my first class.

Presently, I found myself into the largest classroom I had ever seen. There were over one-hundred seats with desktops that folded over the chairs. The seats sloped down to a large open floor with a huge island with a slate top in the middle, and four movable chalk boards behind.

When the calculus professor walked in, he set his notes down on the island, and introduced himself. I feared the choices I had made that led me to this moment were about to backfire on me. I was a mediocre math student at best, but, since I had no help or guidance from anyone, I had convinced myself that I should study engineering, which would require higher math. Even though I had taken calculus in high school, I was not prepared for university level calculus, especially taught by a man whose accent I couldn't understand. I was behind in the course from that very first day.

Walking into the room for next class, which was English composition, I was taken aback by how intimate and small this space was than my first class. This class was an honors course, and the setting was a small room with deep brown wooden wainscoting and trim, like something out of a movie about a university class. In its center there were three long deep brown wooden tables set in a horseshoe arrangement, and at these tables there was only room for nine students and the professor. I looked around the room at the other eight handpicked students at the tables, and immediately I felt like an outsider. The alienation I felt when wandering around looking for my classrooms earlier that day rushed back, an alienation so deep that I felt didn't belong there.

+ + +

Winter descended early upon the High Plains, and soon after the school year started, bitter winds began to scour the campus with merciless speed and darkness settled over the land like a judgment that would not lift.

I fell behind in calculus more and more as the weeks went by, and with each week I cared less and less that I was faltering. In composition I never fell behind, but I never put in the effort to truly excel. During the discussions in class, listening to the stories of the other student's lives, I began to feel embarrassed about where I had come from, and I talked less and less in the discussions.

As the semester progressed, the only class that I looked forward to, and the only class that I put true work into was Russian. In the afternoons, I would diligently study my vocabulary words, memorizing them with ease, practice the conjugation of the verbs, and work on the noun declensions. Since I had never studied a foreign language, I had no idea before I started the class that I had a gift for learning them. But as it turned out, my Russian class was the sole bright spot in a season that was turning progressively darker.

+ + +

Wandering the campus one day, I discovered a vending machine that popped corn the old way, with heating elements and oil, not the sterile microwave packets. Some evenings I would walk to that mostly abandoned building alone, forcing myself through the settling darkness and the bitter winds that by this time of year drove snow like buckshot against my face. For solace, I would buy a bag of popcorn.

My thoughts during the trudge over dwelt mostly on the pointlessness of it all, and while waiting for the corn to pop, I would contemplate the futility of my existence here, fearing that I did not belong at the university, that I was an impostor in every class save Russian.

I could not fathom what any of it was for. The hot popcorn offered brief respite from my black thoughts, but as I finished eating, the questions would return like wolves circling in darkness. Why was I in school? Why was I so different from everyone else? Why had I been given such a brutal childhood? Why was I alive at all?

Like a vessel torn from its moorings in rough seas, I felt myself drifting without anchor or compass, tossed by forces I could not control or understand. Though I knew I could endure any trial—had learned that lesson well—I was now questioning whether endurance itself had any meaning.

When the last kernel was gone, I would cast the empty bag into the trash, lean against the door that the wind held shut like some malevolent guardian, and push through into the storm that waited beyond.

+ + +

When finals came, I was utterly unprepared for the calculus exam. If I was passing the course at that point, it would have been by the thinnest of margins. Passing would have hinged on acing the exam.

As the professor passed out the exam sheets and gave us our instructions, I looked down at the problems in front of me and my heart sank in my chest. I knew immediately that I would be unable to solve any equation on the test and sat almost motionless in my seat completely dejected. After staring at the paper for several minutes, to the sound of other students' pencils scratching on paper, I picked up my test and pencils as quietly as I could and walked to the table in the center of the floor. I dropped the test face down in front of the professor who gave me a puzzled look as I left the room. I had failed calculus.

Worse than that, I knew that the plan I had made to escape my house and Lander was falling apart.

+ + +

The dormitory at the university closed for part of the winter break, but it would reopen a couple of weeks before classes restarted. My plan was to go back to Lander for as short a period as I could. I told myself that It would have been better if I had found somewhere else to go, but no other place existed for me then.

I had a sometimes friend in Lander whose home situation was no better than mine, and we had spent a lot of time in each other's company. And during the holidays, when most people were home enjoying time with their families, Kenny and I would spend time together driving around doing not much of anything, except drinking.

In December and January, Lander would suffer what the locals called temperature inversions—atmospheric traps that held bitter, subzero cold in the valley like a bowl collecting poison. During such an inversion on a moonless night when few souls dared venture into the killing air, Kenny and I set out to drink beer and wander the back roads without purpose or destination. We stopped far from any lights in the mountain foothills to relieve ourselves.

I had been dwelling in particularly dark thoughts in the days prior, and while we stood outside the truck breathing vapor into the frozen air, I said to Kenny, "I don't understand it. Why does everything suck?"

"What sucks?" Kenny shrugged, zipping up his jacket against the cold.

"Everything. The weather. Lander. School. Life. It all sucks."

"I don't know. I guess it sucks." He kicked at a clump of frozen dirt.

"I can't handle it anymore," I said, and drove my fist into the large exterior mirror on the passenger side of Kenny's truck.

As I pulled back my hand from the shattered frame, a shard of glass still embedded in the housing opened the back of my hand like a mouth, severing the tendon that controlled my little finger. Kenny pressed a rag onto my hand to stanch the flow, but the blood would not stop.

Since Kenny had been drinking while driving, we both knew the danger we faced. Finally, I convinced him to drive toward the hospital, where he could leave me several blocks away and I would make my way to the emergency room alone.

I went back to the dormitory in Laramie when they reopened wearing a cast on my right hand to keep me from tearing the stitches out of my repaired tendon. Also, I found out that I had failed two classes and passed two classes.

Even with my "A" in Russian, my grade point average was below 2.0, and I was on academic probation, meaning that if I didn't get my GPA up the next semester, I would be kicked out of the university.

+ + +

From the moment I had chosen the University of Wyoming, I had begun to dig a pit around myself, and each poor decision during the semester had deepened the excavation. I began to look at my childhood and felt the weight of shame—that I did not deserve deliverance from what I had been given. As the new semester approached, the walls of that pit grew slick and insurmountable, while the bottom filled with the decay of abandoned hopes, their corruption rising like miasma to choke whatever breath remained in me.

It seemed pointless to attempt escape. Some voice in the depths whispered that I should surrender to the darkness gathering below, that I should cease my struggle and let the earth claim what had always belonged to it. The voice spoke of rest, of an end to the clawing and fighting that had marked every day of my existence.

On a Thursday evening as I staggered back from a bar, I saw a television in a common space that had been left on. The eighties were a time when TV stations did not broadcast 24 hours a day, so the station on the TV I saw was announcing the end of its broadcast day with a prerecorded message before the test pattern filled the screen.

In the dark room, lit only by the flickering glow of the television, I stood and watched as the message ended and a video began with the opening notes of the national anthem. The screen filled with images of Marines storming beaches, naval vessels cutting through heavy seas, tanks trailing dust clouds as they advanced down empty roads, and an F-16 climbing above mountain peaks like some metal bird seeking heaven.

In my drunken state, something stirred within me that had been buried beneath months of failure. Even though I was stumbling through darkness at that moment, I knew I possessed the strength to climb out of the pit I had dug. I had survived worse than this, and though I could not see it then, the same hand that had carried me through every abandonment was still at work—not because of anything I had done to earn such grace, but because grace itself chooses whom it will redeem. What felt like my decision to rise was perhaps something deeper, a call that had been pursuing me long before I knew to listen for it.

The next day, I went to the Army recruiting office to see about going on active duty. When I told the Army recruiter that I wanted to go active, I also told him that I didn't want to stay in the field artillery.

"You can't do that," he said. "We've spent too much money training you. You'll have to stay artillery."

"Really? I can't change to something else?"

"Nope." He gestured toward his desk. "Come over to the desk, take a seat, and we'll look at getting you shipped out."

I said, "No, thanks," as I walked out of his office.

The image of the F-16 from the night before was in my mind as I walked into the Air Force recruiter's office. I had come up with a new plan.

CHAPTER TWELVE

When I entered the Air Force recruiter's office, the reception was cordial but measured.

"What can I do for you?" came the greeting.

"I am in the Army National Guard, and I want to go active duty," I said. "I spoke with the Army recruiter, and he told me I would have to remain in my MOS. I do not want to do that."

"What is your MOS?" the Air Force sergeant in his blue uniform asked.

"13B, field artillery."

"Well, I can see why you would not want to do that full time," he said, laughing. "Have a seat. Let us see what we can figure out."

I did not tell him I was failing out of the university—that my academic probation was really academic collapse, that I was drowning in the same despair that had consumed me in high school. I did tell him I was currently enrolled, studying Russian among other subjects.

When I mentioned Russian, he leaned closer to his desk.

"Russian, did you say? How is that going for you?"

"I am getting A's."

When he heard that, his demeanor shifted entirely—from caution to hunger. I would learn later that linguists were among the most difficult positions to fill in the Air Force, and recruiters received substantial bonuses when they signed one up. Soon I had taken an entrance exam and scored high enough to be scheduled for a language aptitude test. Based on my performance on the aptitude test, I could choose any language the Air Force offered. I made the decision, without guidance as always, to study Polish—perhaps because it resembled Russian, or perhaps because the language school for Polish was in Monterey, California, while the Russian school was in San Antonio, Texas. The temperate climate of Northern California compared to the brutal heat of Texas settled the matter.

+ + +

During the summer break, my mother had relocated from San Diego to Fort Collins, Colorado—another restless migration in her pattern of seeking geographic cures for ailments that traveled with her. When school ended and I had officially withdrawn, I moved in with her for little more than two months before I would ship out to the Air Force. Those weeks felt suspended, like dwelling in some liminal space between one existence and another.

On the afternoon of August 14, 1985, I boarded what would be my final Greyhound, with my mother delivering me to the depot as she had so many times before. Unlike the journeys of the past that had always carried return tickets, this passage was singular. This bus would carry me from Fort Collins to Denver, and when I reached the depot, I understood that I would never return to dwell in Wyoming or in that house in Lander again.

As I stood waiting to board at the depot, I gazed out over the plains stretching eastward, where dawn had broken hours before. The day was uncommonly still, and I could taste the diesel fumes as I walked toward the door, each step carrying me further from the shadows, like some deliberate march toward a life I was attempting to forge for myself, trying to break free from the chaos that had marked my first eighteen years. But I carried more than a duffel bag onto that bus—I carried questions about God, about purpose, about whether existence held anything beyond the mere survival that had consumed me thus far.

The following day, August 15, I traveled to San Antonio for abbreviated basic training, having already endured the Army's version. I would remain in San Antonio only long enough to be issued Air Force uniforms, complete a physical fitness test, and attend to paperwork.

+ + +

The Monterey peninsula thrust out into the Pacific like an ancient blade, cleaving the waters where the continent made its last stand against the void. At the northern edge of the city, the Presidio climbed westward from the bay into the hills before turning south, following the coastline like a watchtower keeping vigil over sacred ground.

The days at the Presidio moved with their own rhythm—bright and clear at dawn, then each afternoon the fog would advance up the western slopes like the breath of some vast unseen presence. Its fingers would probe through pine and cypress, threading over the ridge to descend and wrap the Presidio in gray silence. But come morning the fog would retreat, burned away by the sun's relentless work, driven back to the waters that had spawned it.

I had dwelt so long in storm that I had forgotten weather could change. Here, at the world's edge, I began to sense what I had not known before—

not the absence of storm, but the knowledge that a storm need not be permanent. The fog came each day with the certainty of judgment, but it departed with equal certainty. And in that rhythm, that compact between shadow and light, I glimpsed the truth that even the deepest winter must yield its dominion to spring.

The Presidio was home to the Defense Language Institute, where I was to study for the next year. When I was assigned my spot in a Polish language class, the Air Force had based my slotting on an assumption that I would be attending their entire six-week basic training, even though I had been excused for most of it. This meant that for four weeks, I was idle waiting for my class to start.

While I had been assigned temporary work performing menial tasks in the unit's administration, I remained adrift during those weeks. The routine I had anticipated—the structure I believed would deliver me—was absent, and I could feel myself descending once more into the pit I had clawed my way out of. Some mornings I could not rise from my bunk until the final possible moment. Some evenings I would walk the perimeter of the base alone, questioning whether I had committed yet another error in judgment.

The military's rigid framework, which I had trusted would provide order, instead revealed its own species of institutional neglect—not malicious, but mechanically indifferent in the way of systems that grind forward without regard for the sufferings of those caught within their gears.

The day my language course started, everything changed. As I walked down the steep hillside toward the shimmering expanse of Monterey Bay, I moved through the dissipating fog as if casting off the dead skin of what I had been, each step taking me toward the sunlit expanse and a horizon bright with promise. Soon I settled into the most satisfying rhythm of my existence—one that felt ordained rather than inflicted.

In the morning, often just after the sun started to rise, I would get out of my bunk, pull on the jeans and t-shirt that I had thrown onto the floor before going to bed, and go to the dining hall, its floors freshly scrubbed with pine oil. Like a hound after its prey, I walked through the lingering fog following my nose toward the bacon and coffee. Breakfast was followed by getting into my uniform, heading down to formation, where Air Force sergeants told us the forgettable things that sergeants tell their airmen. Then I headed down the hill to class.

The immersion course was designed to drive the acquisition of Polish into the head with relentless efficiency. The days were filled with instruction, drills, laboratories, and conversation, and I flourished within this regimen. Each day I felt mastery growing within me—not merely of the language, but of things I had not known I possessed. For the first time in my existence, academic achievement felt as natural as breathing, like uncovering some buried capacity that had lain dormant beneath years of failure. I had never experienced such fulfillment, such complete communion with the act of learning.

Afternoons, after class was done for the day, were filled with mandated, organized physical training, which meant some calisthenics and jogging. Beyond that, I added to the exercise, by training for a marathon with a fellow student. The repetitive pounding of our feet on the coastal roads became a meditation, each mile rebuilding not just my body but my sense that I could endure, that I could push through barriers I had thought were permanent. After dinner in the dining hall, my evenings were spent with hours of homework at my desk.

As I gained fluency in the language, I began to find time to read whatever books caught my interest in the post library. One day, as I climbed the hill from class, a well-dressed man stationed at the crossroads of two post roads pressed a copy of the New Testament into my hands. When I reached my room, I cast it onto my desk as I prepared for physical training.

But that small book seemed to possess its own weight.

When I sat down to complete my studies that evening, there it lay. I lifted it, turned through several pages, and found myself reading of a man who bore the punishment meant for others, whose death ransomed souls that had no power to ransom themselves.

The language was archaic, formal, yet something in those accounts drew me forward. I placed it in my desk drawer, but in the weeks that followed, I found myself retrieving it with increasing frequency, pulled toward passages I could not fully comprehend but which seemed to address some void in my existence—something beyond linguistic mastery, beyond physical conditioning, beyond the institutional acceptance I was finally tasting.

+ + +

At Monterey, I began to feel like some creature that had been caged in a roadside menagerie, penned in quarters without light or enough food, now released into the wild country I was born to roam. My physical strength was returning, my limbs extending and flexing like an animal remembering what it was made for. My mind ranged across vast territories, claiming dominion over ground I had never known I could possess, exploring with the fierce hunger of something long starved. Emotionally, I began to cast off the deadness of captivity, emerging with instincts sharp and spirit unbroken.

I even started writing letters to both my mother and my father. My mother was living in San Diego at the time, and my father was on a ship docked in Redwood Shores, California. I didn't understand my intentions when deciding to write to the two people who had abandoned me. When I dropped each envelope I sealed, addressed, and stamped into the mailbox, it felt like casting a bottle into the vast, indifferent bay, with no hope of reply. The act of writing to them became an inexplicable, mysterious ritual—perhaps an attempt to construct the family connections that had never naturally existed.

Eventually my mother would reply to my letters, but my father would not. I would end up calling my mother from a payphone on the Presidio occasionally, and I managed to call my father once during my time there. His voice sounded strange and distant, not just across the phone line but across the years of absence, and I realized that whatever relationship we might have would have to be built from nothing if it were to be built at all.

+ + +

By late summer of 1986, it was as if the fog had abandoned the Presidio entirely. The days blazed with a piercing brightness, and when I stood at the right vantage on that hillside, I could see beyond the mouth of Monterey Bay toward horizons I was only beginning to understand. My orders came for Hahn Air Base in what was then West Germany. I would endure temporary training assignments along the way, but by February of 1987, I would be overseas, carrying my newly forged skills into the Cold War, in a country divided by ideology. The same Cold War that my father had fought in Vietnam..

The passage from California to Germany would represent more than a change of station. In California, I had discovered I could master what was set before me, could achieve what was demanded, could bind myself to something greater than mere survival. But as I prepared to depart Monterey, a question began to take shape in the depths of my mind: What purpose did all this serve? Toward what end was I building?

+ + +

The sky over the Hunsrück in February hung like a vast shroud of grey that released its burden of snow in spirals through the bare bones of beech and the dark spears of spruce. The slate roofs of the village houses mirrored the color of the heavens above them, as if earth and sky had conspired to drain all warmth from the world. The country I entered was alien, hushed, unforgiving, and locked beneath cold and the ancient crust of winter.

Beneath the grey mantle lay the promise of spring waiting beyond the coming thaw—and beneath my growing mastery lay something else in wait, something that would soon make its presence known.

My unit's barracks at Hahn Air Base was a squat looking three-story building covered in brown stucco, which sat in a row of other squat brown barracks. By now, having been in the military, both the Army and Air Force, for a few years, I was used to dull uniformity. However, I was in for one surprise.

The barracks on Hahn Air Base were overcrowded, and through a combination of bureaucratic confusion and my own naivety, I was duped into signing an agreement that waived my right to the regulation-mandated minimum living space. I was assigned a room with two other airmen in space designed for two. The institutional efficiency that had saved me was already showing its limitations—the same system that had given me purpose could just as easily treat me as a problem to be managed.

Although I couldn't have known it at the time, I was arriving in Germany right at the final movement of the symphony that was the Cold War. I landed right at the crescendo of the massing of forces. It felt like a place where young men would face questions of life and death, purpose and meaning, like my father had faced in Vietnam

When I got to the work site for my first duty day, I walked into the orderly room, which is where all the administrative work is done, including processing orders, managing duty rosters, and other clerical work, including personnel records.

"Hey, Airman LaFleur. How was the trip over?" the sergeant asked as I walked into the orderly room.

"Pretty good, Sergeant. I think I may have jet lag though." Which was no lie.

"Yeah, it happens," he returned in a tone friendlier than I had expected. "Did they put you in a room with two other guys?"

"Yeah," I answered, wanting to complain but not daring to.

"You don't have to stay there, if you don't want to."

"What do you mean?"

"As soon as you have been cleared to sit missions, you can request to move off base," he explained. "You can find a room or an apartment in one of the villages. They can't make you live in an overcrowded barracks."

Since my job as a linguist was in intelligence, my work was top secret, and after I got done with the orderly room, I was taken to the secured part of the facility. It turned out that I had some on-the-job training, and then some testing and some live evaluations to complete, and as soon as those were done, I would be not only able to move off base, but I would also be able to start traveling, with the additional perk of being eligible for tuition-free college classes. I set my mind to completing my onboarding as quickly as possible. After four weeks of hard work, I believed myself ready.

After I passed my final check that would certify me as being able to work missions autonomously, the snow had fallen off the spruce, the leaves of the beech trees had begun to bud, and the grey frost was completely gone. I ended up finding a studio apartment in a converted garage that was attached to Frau Schultz's house in the village of Kappel, just a few kilometers from my work site.

Frau Schultz was a widow in her seventies when she became my landlord, though I never thought of her that way. It was clear—even though my apartment had its own outside entry and was not directly connected to her house—that I was Frau Schultz's guest. She expected me to behave as a guest and not a tenant, and I found myself oddly grateful for her maternal oversight, a benevolent authority I had never experienced.

This arrangement had its perks along with its peculiarities. I would often come home from work to find that Frau Schultz had let herself into my apartment to open the blinds and windows to let fresh air in, and I would just as often find a baked treat, like apple strudel, on my little dining table for one. Her small kindnesses were revelations—proof that care could exist without conditions, that someone might tend to another's well-being simply because it was right.

+ + +

That first summer in Germany, I enrolled in classes through the University of Maryland, which ran courses out of Heidelberg, sending instructors and professors to bases such as Hahn to teach college classes. The classes went year-round, so I started work on an associate's degree. By my planning, if I used the college credits I had already earned studying Polish at the Defense Language Institute, I would be able to finish my degree before my contract with the Air Force was up.

That same summer, a sergeant in the maintenance division of our unit found me walking to my workspace.

"Hey, did you play football?" asked the man, who towered over my 6'2" height and whom I would come to know as Tiny.

"Yeah, in high school."

"Did you ever think about playing rugby?"

I hadn't, but something in his tone suggested this wasn't really a question. Within a week, I found myself at my first rugby practice, joining the only rugby team in the US forces in Europe made up entirely of Air Force members.

The rugby pitch became another manner of schooling—a place where I learned of a different breed of masculine strength than what I had witnessed in my upbringing. Not the masculinity of conquest and brutality I had known at home, but something more intricate: the masculinity of brotherhood, of physical force harnessed for common purpose, of men bearing one another through suffering and victory.

On Saturday afternoons, caked in mud and grass, surrounded by teammates who were becoming something close to kinsmen, I began to understand what my father might have discovered among his fellow sailors and soldiers, what bond he might have lost when he returned to a world that could not fathom what he had endured.

But even encircled by this brotherhood, even mastering my duties and my studies, I felt something working at me—a restlessness that bore no relation to my circumstances and everything to do with deeper questions I could not yet give voice to.

With my intelligence job, my little apartment in the village, my college coursework, and the rugby team, the foundation was laid upon which the rest of my Air Force career, and my new life, would be built. Although I was starting to feel like a new person, I could tell something was still missing—

something that all the institutional belonging and personal achievement couldn't fill.

+ + +

The nature of the missions I worked meant that I did not keep a fixed schedule. Some days starting my shift at 5 am, and other days starting at 5 pm—or any variety of hours around the clock. On the days I started in the afternoon, I began visiting the library on base in the morning.

Where the other buildings on base were strictly utilitarian, the library seemed to be the exception, with floor-to-ceiling windows on the entrance side that spanned the front of the building. On the days the sun shone brightly in the Hunsrück, it would stream into the little library. It didn't have an extensive selection of books at any one time, but the neat little rows of towering shelves had a rotating collection, and even with the rotating in and out, the library had the musty, woody, faintly sweet smell of old books.

One day as I was heading to the desk to check out the books I had gathered, I saw a copy of *The Razor's Edge* by W. Somerset Maugham, and I grabbed it and added it to the stack of books I was taking home. As I read the book, I came to recognize that the restlessness entering my life—a life outwardly marked by satisfaction in work, school, and leisure—was the beginning of an existential crisis. In Larry Darrel, I saw a reflection of my own profound yearning for spiritual fulfillment and the meaning of life.

All the institutional success in the world couldn't answer the fundamental questions that were beginning to surface with increasing urgency: What was the point of all this competence and belonging if there was nothing beyond it? What was I working toward besides more work, more achievement, more empty accomplishment? The questions felt like a physical ache, a hunger that couldn't be satisfied with food or success or even human connection.

Since I couldn't drop everything and begin traveling the world looking for spiritual enlightenment, I dived into books—books on Shintoism, Buddhism, Nepalese mysticism, Native American spiritualism. I read hungrily, desperately, but none of them helped me in my crisis. The ancient wisdom felt distant, culturally disconnected from my experience of American military life in Cold War Germany.

I would occasionally take out the small New Testament I had gotten in Monterey and attempt to decipher its contents. Sometimes I would encounter brief illuminations—moments when the words seemed to address directly the questions I could not yet voice, followed by vast stretches of bewilderment and cultural confusion. The language was sometimes ceremonial, ancient, yet beneath its surface I sensed something vital, something that might hold answers if I could only learn the proper way to approach the questions.

+ + +

My work site was comprised of a bunch of interconnected buildings whose entrances were sealed by doors with combination locks. To get to the innermost sections, I would have to know the passcode for three or four doors. The ready room was in the center of the buildings, and so one day I was mildly surprised, after punching in the final code to open the door, to see a chaplain sitting at one of the tables.

He was a man I had seen on base numerous times, since the chapel stood next to the barracks where I had first been sent. I never could have conceived that the Air Force would put the effort to grant a chaplain top-secret clearance, which was the only way he could have entered that room.

As he sat alone, both elbows resting upon the table, reading the Stars and Stripes, I felt a weight descend upon me, nearly physical in its force—a compulsion that urged me to approach him. This was my opportunity—

perhaps the only one I would get—to voice the questions that had been gathering within me. I could ask him about the spiritual hunger that was consuming me, about whether faith could dwell alongside the rational, analytical mind I thought I was gaining through my intelligence work. I could ask him if it were possible to discover God in such a place, surrounded by the instruments of war, or if religion was merely another institutional apparatus designed to govern men like me.

The questions pressed against my throat like words demanding I speak. It was as if some unseen hand was urging me forward, guiding me toward him. But as I drew near the table, something else restrained me—fear, perhaps, or the deeply embedded distrust of religious authority that had been carved into me by a childhood. Perhaps it was the fear that he would offer me the same conditional, guilt-laden version of faith my mother had dispensed, or perhaps simply that I was not prepared to voice questions I could barely understand myself.

When I came within speaking distance, "Hello, sir," was all that emerged from my mouth as I passed by, carrying my spiritual questions with me like classified intelligence I was forbidden to divulge.

Later, driving back through the village streets to my room, I wondered if that moment had been a test I had failed, or if God understood that I was not yet ready, that the hunger itself was part of the preparation, that sometimes we must bear our questions longer before we are ready to receive the answers, if the answers would even come.

+ + +

In the spring of 1989, my enlistment in the Air Force was drawing toward its end. I had earned my Associate Degree in General Studies, which meant that if a college accepted my credits I would require only two years to complete my bachelor's. To figure out where I would go after my discharge, I began searching for universities and colleges.

I had devised a plan to choose which school would serve my needs. Since those were the days before the internet existed, I would send letters of inquiry to schools telling of my interest in applying. If their response returned with "Dear Prospective Student" or some other impersonal greeting, I would discard the application packet; however, if they addressed me by name, I would apply. Another requirement I imposed was that any school on my preliminary list would have to accept all of my transfer credits, or I would not consider them.

By early summer, my choice lay between Maine, Wisconsin, Colorado, and Oregon. Again, without guidance or counsel from any soul, I chose Colorado, because I had learned to ski during my time in Germany, and I thought it would be nice to remain near slopes while I pursued my studies.

At the end of July, I flew to Patterson Air Force Base in New Jersey to begin my discharge. While I still felt something was absent from my existence—that spiritual dimension I had been seeking without success—I was no longer consumed by despair. I had the sense I was finally proceeding toward something, even if I did not yet fully understand my destination.

CHAPTER THIRTEEN

When I was figuring out where to continue my education after leaving the Air Force, I studied a topographical map in the library at Hahn Airbase. As I sat at the table with the great book spread before me, I traced my finger from Denver to Grand Junction along I-80, which carved its path through the Rocky Mountains. Names I recognized from skiing magazines drew my attention: Keystone, Breckenridge, Beaver Creek, Snowmass, Aspen. World-class ski terrain.

I persuaded myself that if I chose Mesa State College in Grand Junction, I would be able to ski through the winter months. Over the course of my final two years in the Air Force, I had managed to save most of my pay. I had enough money to purchase a used car, rent an apartment for at least six months, and cover my tuition for the first year.

On the eastern side of the Rockies, in what is called the Front Range, I acquired an old blue Saab 900 with enough mileage to make me question whether it would survive the two mountain passes that approached 10,000 feet in elevation on the route to Grand Junction.

In late August, I loaded everything I had accumulated in Germany into the vehicle, filled the tank with fuel, and headed over the foothills into the mountains toward the Western Slope and Grand Junction.

On a mental checklist, I marked off the ski resorts as I passed them, the valleys below the slopes still verdant and bordered by aspens in the late summer. When I passed the exit to the final resorts on my list—Snowmass and Aspen—the terrain began to transform.

I was on the western side of the Rockies, which received less snow than the eastern slopes. Ninety miles from Grand Junction I began passing towns with names foreign to me: Silt, Antler, Rifle, Parachute—settlements in high desert even more barren than where I had lived in Wyoming.

The landscape continued to evolve as I descended from the mountains near a town called Palisade. The horizon opened before me, and my heart fell as I gazed out over the desert that stretched across the Grand Valley. I had expected to find myself in the heart of ski country.

That afternoon, I pitched my tent at the KOA campground, and as I sat at the picnic table planning my apartment search for the following morning, my initial disappointment began to weaken.

The mountains still rose dramatically in the distance, and there was something forthright about this high desert country that I had not anticipated.

In the cooling desert evening, surrounded by towering cottonwoods, I looked upon a sky that was the deepest blue I had ever witnessed, with not a single cloud visible from horizon to horizon.

As I composed brief letters to my mother and father announcing that I was in Grand Junction to complete my degree, the western sky transformed to glowing crimson as the sun died. Watching that metamorphosis, I felt peace settle upon me and a burden lift from my shoulders. I grew content with where I found myself.

+ + +

I found an apartment on Bunting Avenue to the east of the college, less than a full block from the campus, and I moved in days before classes started. On the first day of class when I walked from my apartment, I wasn't gripped by nerves, and I didn't feel knots in my stomach; rather, I was surrounded by a sense of almost palpable importance, as if each step I took toward the campus guided me from the ordinary to the momentous.

Mesa State required that all students take at a science class, and I had signed up for Astronomy 101. This was my first class. The midmorning sun was glaringly bright as I walked past the deep green grass of the lawns. The overnight sprinklers had recently shut off, so in the places still in morning shadow the grass and pavement still glistened with moisture.

I had walked the campus the day before, looking for my classrooms, so I wouldn't have to search that first day. I had found the auditorium in Wubben Hall where astronomy was held, just near the main entrance to the building.

Now, as I walked into the lobby, students were milling around waiting for the class that was still in session to get out. Faint sounds of a choir doing vocal exercises drifted down the hall. The waiting students clustered into small groups chatting and laughing together, and I stood at the periphery of the small gatherings.

Unlike my first experience with college, I wasn't bothered by being an outsider. I was five years older than most of the students, had lived for just under three years in a foreign country, and I was a veteran; I was different than they were, and I was perfectly content with that.

Minutes before astronomy was to start, I glanced over to the entrance to the building and noticed a shy looking young woman with pink glasses and curly blonde hair walk in. As she entered, my thoughts turned into a daydream: I was walking into a room full of people. It must have been some sort of party, because people were happily milling about, drinks and food at hand. At my side, as I entered the room, was my wife. In my vision, it was this young woman I'd just watched come into the building that was walking next to me. Then the dream faded.

I had come up with a theory about where to sit in a college classroom to maximize my grade. I didn't want to be in the first row, because that would make it seem that I was too eager. And I certainly didn't want to sit the back row, because that would make it seem I was uninterested or excessively shy. The perfect spot was three or four rows back, directly centered between the left and the right of the room, and that is where I sat. The auditorium seats had small desktops that folded down beside the armrests when not in use.

As I sat down in the perfect spot, I pulled the desk up and tried to fold it down, so I could use it to take notes, but it resisted. The seat was broken, so I slid over two seats. This would become my regular spot.

Over the next few days, I found myself anticipating astronomy class, eager for another glimpse of the woman who had caught my attention on the first day. This expectant anxiety about the woman was both surprising and slightly unsettling. I had spent the last six years of my life trying to get away from what some would call my family. I didn't see what I had been born into as a family at all. I saw a family as something I didn't deserve to have. So, naturally, when returning to school, a romantic connection was far down on my list of ambitions if it was on the list at all.

In the second week of class, some people had shuffled around, so that the seating pattern had changed slightly. I, however, still sat in the seat I had picked out the first day. The woman whom I would come to find out was named Christina, walked down the row I was in, and tried to sit in the seat with the broken desk, which was two seats to my left.

"Hey, that seat's broken," I told Christina.

"What?"

"The desktop doesn't work. This one's not broken though," I said pointing to the seat next to me.

Over the next few classes, Christina started sitting in the desk next to me. We would chat for a few minutes before class started, and though I hadn't asked, I could tell she was not a traditional student, just as I was not a traditional student.

I had been thinking about asking her to dinner for several days, rehearsing different approaches in my mind as I walked to class. Without warning, before class one day, the question came out more boldly than I had planned: "Are you brave?"

"Uh, sometimes. Why?" she responded.

"I'd like to invite you over to my apartment for dinner. I'd invite you out to a restaurant, but I haven't gotten my GI Bill money, yet."

When she came to my apartment for dinner, I served Christina a bowl of soup I had made from a one-dollar bag of Manischewitz Bean Soup Mix. Years later, she would confess that she hated beans at that point in her life, but she ate every spoonful.

+ + +

During those hushed evenings in my studio apartment in Grand Junction, surrounded by recreation magazines and camping supply catalogs, I had conceived what appeared to be a perfect design: study outdoor recreation and become a US Forest Ranger.

For someone who anticipated spending his existence in solitude, the career choice made sense. Yes, I had crafted some friendships while in Germany, but friendships do not endure forever, I believed. They would eventually abandon me, just as my sister, my mother, and my father had done, or so I convinced myself.

Since I would always be alone, I reasoned I could become a ranger, and if I performed everything correctly, I could become one of those rangers who dwelt in a fire watch tower perched at the summit of a mountain in the wilderness.

That vision of solitude had guided me to Mesa State's Outdoor Recreation program, where I was enrolled in an introduction to outdoor recreation course, first aid, and wilderness survival, along with astronomy.

As the days passed and the season began to turn toward autumn, the temperature in Grand Junction began to drop, and the sky transformed to an even clearer, deeper blue. At that time, a storm was beyond imagination.

+ + +

After the first weeks of class were complete, and I had settled into a routine, I decided I would find a part-time job. The college had a bulletin board in the administration building that had jobs posted by local businesses, and on the first day looking at it, I found a job I thought I should apply for.

I drove to downtown Grand Junction to an industrial neighborhood just on the edge of the business district and found a parking spot on the street in front of a light red brick building. The building was fronted by ceiling-to-knee level window panels separated by aluminum braces. Even though it was fewer than thirty years old, it was a museum piece from the

1960s. Through the windows, I could see the rows of benches made from blonde wood that filled the open floor space, and I could see the ticket desk at the far end. I had decided to take a job at the Greyhound bus depot.

When I accepted the position and started to work, I did it mostly because the hours fit well with my schedule. I could get twenty hours of work a week, with no interference with my class schedule. At the time, I hadn't considered how this place might connect to my past.

Grand Junction was a crossroads of east and west along I-80 and north and south along the Western Slope of the Rocky Mountains, and it made for a good transfer spot for passengers to change buses. My work schedule was mostly in the early mornings from 4:30 am to 7:00 am, when a few buses from all directions came to the depot.

My role in those mornings was mostly transferring luggage and helping people find their next bus. After the morning rush, the depot would close until early afternoon. There would be another rush of buses at 3 pm, and the days I didn't have class, I would go the depot at 1 pm to open it. I would be the only staff until nearly 3 pm when the buses would come.

It was during these quiet afternoon hours, alone behind that ticket desk and looking out at the benches slowly filling up with people, that the memories began to surface. Some of the passengers looked desperate in ways that felt familiar.

I started to remember my own time on buses between San Diego and Port Hueneme, the weight of carrying everything I owned in a single bag, the feeling of being in transit with nowhere that felt like home.

After a handful of days had passed, I started to dread the afternoons at the depot, and I began to think I had made yet another mistake in taking the job. It wasn't long before this was confirmed.

One afternoon, I noticed that an older man in a dark suit, with a trilby hat, was bothering people as they sat on the benches, many of whom I felt sure were waiting to continue running away from whatever was behind them. I wasn't sure what he was doing, but as he stood over them, I could tell he was making them uncomfortable because they pleaded with him to go away. Finally, I approached him and led him to the door saying, "You're going to have to stay outside if you can't leave people alone."

"Boss, I'm sorry. I won't bother no one," was his response, his breath reeking of alcohol.

"You're not coming back in," I said firmly.

He stayed outside for a little while, but soon he was back in lurching over passengers on the benches. As I rushed around the edge of the counter, I yelled, "Hey! Leave them alone!" The man started cowering, putting his hands over his head to shield himself from the beating he thought I was going to deliver.

As I got closer, I could see the urine dribbling down from inside his suit pant leg. The Salvation Army was on a laminated list of numbers taped under the phone. I called and within a few minutes they came and took the elderly man away saying they would get him showered, give him some new clothes, feed him, and bring him back in time to catch his bus.

While he was away, I started thinking about the times I spent in the depot in Los Angeles, surrounded by desperate and damaged people, about how I was one of those desperate and damaged people even as a little boy. When he came back to the depot in time for the bus he had been waiting for, I watched him walk in and decided that I couldn't handle working at the depot. I was trying to push my past as far behind me as I could, and working at the depot was a constant reminder of it.

+ + +

Christina and I continued to see each other outside of astronomy most every day. She also had an apartment on Bunting Avenue two blocks east of mine, so we would pass each other most mornings, as she returned from class, and I headed to class.

In late October, the heat of the desert summer had given way, but the skies were still always clear and cloudless. Even without the threat of the heat or the absence of any threat of rain, it felt a little vulnerable to stand there. There were few trees along Bunting Avenue, and the parking lot of the Kinko's Copies was especially barren.

On a Friday morning, Christina and I ran into each other in that parking lot, and we stopped to talk. Christina's hands were trembling, and she was having a difficult time looking me in the eye. Her face turned red when she asked, "Do you want to come to church with me on Sunday?"

"Church? Where?"

"It's a Lutheran church toward the airport."

"Is that like Catholic?" I asked suspiciously.

"Maybe a little, but I don't think so."

On the following Sunday morning, October 29th, I walked to Christina's apartment so she could drive me to church. The building was a small, white stucco structure surrounded by a modest parking lot. The sanctuary was bright white, with light-colored wooden pews arranged in three sections forming an angular horseshoe that opened toward the altar.

It was far removed from the dark, oppressive atmosphere I had known in the Catholic churches of my youth. I had no notion of what to expect, so I began to steel myself to be told how I had continued down the road to perdition, especially having abandoned the Catholic Church for more than ten years.

We found a pew and sat. The service was foreign to me, but not entirely so. The liturgy resembled Catholic mass closely enough that I was not completely lost, but the sermon was unlike anything I had ever heard.

The pastor began by explaining that this was Reformation Sunday, the significance of which seemed clear to all other attendees and of which I had no understanding. The pastor spoke of religious concepts I had never encountered before. He mentioned faith and scripture, which at the time I believed I comprehended, but he also spoke of grace. I had heard of grace in school and church as a child, but never in the manner this pastor explained it.

At that moment in that sanctuary, I heard something that cut through every assumption I had carried about God and punishment and what I deserved. The pastor spoke of grace as if it were something real, something that could reach into the darkness where I had lived and pull me toward light I had never imagined possible.

That Sunday sitting beside Christina, something fundamental shifted in my understanding. The God I had feared—the one who kept ledgers of my failures and waited to pronounce judgment—began to fade. In his place emerged the possibility of a Father who might actually want me, not because I had earned it, but because that was his nature.

Walking from that small white church into the clear Colorado afternoon, I felt something I had never known before: the possibility that I might actually be worthy of love.

CHAPTER FOURTEEN

Christina lived in a lower-level apartment that was more austere than even mine. Her living room stood empty save for a single chair without legs, its curved bottom resting directly upon the floor. The bionic chair was two-toned—brown on the bottom and sides, while the back and seat were golden. In the small dining space, she possessed a vintage oak table that had been meticulously restored, its surface and legs radiating the red oak stain that brought forth the dark grain. The table commanded attention because of its beauty, not merely because it and its two chairs comprised the only furniture in the room.

We had started attending church together each Sunday, and afterward I would go to Christina's apartment where she would use a small aluminum stovetop espresso maker to brew us coffee. She did not believe in skim milk, and she truly did not believe in whole milk either. She would transform the coffee from deep, opaque sable to a swirl of sepia tones by pouring from a carton labeled "extra rich."

We would sit at that small oak table as the coffee settled into a warm caramel that resembled softly worn leather, and talk of school.

"I think I am going to change majors," I said one Sunday.

"Really? Why?"

"Dr. Harrison told me that the only way to make sure I could be hired by the Forest Service as a ranger is to attend the federal law enforcement academy," I explained. "I do not want to be a cop."

"Yes, I do not want you to be a cop."

My heart quickened at hearing these words from her.

After our coffee was finished, I walked the two blocks to my apartment to collect my books and head to the campus library where I studied and worked on my assignments. That afternoon, I could think of nothing but Christina, and at night I lay in my bed with the lights out, staring at the ceiling trying to figure out how I could buy her engagement ring.

During the week sometimes, we would visit each other's apartments to simply to see one another.

The week that followed that conversation about my major, after class one day, I walked down to Christina's apartment. The front door stood open, and I could see through the screen door as she sat in the solitary bionic chair, low to the ground, in the center of her living room. Around her was spread the contents of the local newspaper, the top layer composed of glossy advertisement inserts.

As I entered, I asked, "What are you checking out? Why are you looking at advertisements?"

When I got closer, I could see the advertisements were for jewelry stores.

She turned crimson.

"I was looking at rings," she confessed.

I laughed. "That's hilarious, because I have been trying to figure out how to buy you a ring all week."

That Friday, we went to the jeweler at the mall. She chose a bridal set, and I paid with some of the money I had saved from the Air Force.

+ + +

Over Christmas break, I decided to share my news with the friends I'd left behind in high school. Kenny had been my closest friend back then—we'd spent hours driving around and talking about what we'd do after graduation. He'd stayed in town, working odd jobs, and was always the one who could gather the group together.

I called Kenny and told him that I had some news that I wanted to share with him, and I asked if he could gather a few of our friends to his house, so I could tell them, too. When the Saturday came, I called Kenny again.

"Hey, Kenny. I met this girl at Mesa State, and I asked her to marry me," I paused, listening to silence, "She said, 'Yes,' and we are going to have the wedding in May."

"Oh, cool," was his reply.

"So will you be my best man?"

"Yeah, sure, I can do that."

I told the others, one by one, my news, and I asked each of them if they would serve as ushers or stand with me in some capacity. When I asked them to take part in my wedding, I was met mostly with silence.

The most I received from any of them was "Congratulations. I will see if I can make it."

Their words left me empty as a dry well. I had anticipated celebration, perhaps some eagerness about getting together once more. Instead, I felt as if I were speaking to men I had never known.

Soon after the engagement, I wrote to my mother and my father and invited them to my wedding. My mother was effusive when she called in response to my letter.

"Oh, Michael I am so happy for you!"

It made no sense to me that she would express such joy, given how little interest she had shown in my existence up to this point. I thought to myself, "Why does this matter to her now?"

"I always knew the day would come when a girl would take you away from me."

My initial bewilderment turned to distrust. I let the distrust fade with time and allowed myself to entertain a cautious hope that her reaction might signal a change in her disposition, or a transformation in what passed between us.

To my surprise my father wrote back and said that he would attend the wedding.

+ + +

In May of 1990, on the day of our wedding rehearsal, Kenny and his brother appeared at the little red brick chapel across the street from the campus of the University of Colorado in Boulder, but none of the others I had invited came. Tradition dictated that the groom's family host a rehearsal dinner the evening before the wedding, which meant that I was to host, and since I had no money for a restaurant, I ordered pizza from the best pizzeria in Boulder.

It was past nine o'clock when we finished cleaning the gathering hall at the chapel after we had eaten, and I walked out into the twilit parking lot, into the cool, still evening, and looked down both Folsom Street and Colorado Avenue, searching for any cars heading toward the chapel.

Christina left with her bridesmaid to their hotel after her parents had gone home. Kenny and Joe headed to the hotel where we were staying, and I stood beside my used Saab 900, still clinging to hope.

But I was not watching for my friends. I was watching for a man who had written that he would attend his son's wedding, who had given his word after years of absence and broken promises. I was watching for my father, who had said he would be there when it mattered most.

Eventually, I too headed to the hotel, carrying the weight of his silence and absence like a stone in my chest.

The next morning, I drove to where our reception was to be held, hid my car in case someone wanted to decorate it with the newlywed regalia, and walked to the chapel.

I stood outside the chapel in the midmorning sun looking toward the Flatirons that sit just outside of Boulder in the foothills of the Rockies, the sky piercing blue and cloudless. As other people started to show up to the chapel, I stopped looking and went inside to get ready for the wedding service.

When the time was right, I walked to the front of the sanctuary and stood. I could see everyone in the pews. I could see everyone who was there, and I could see everyone who was not there. I had hoped that my father would be true to his word that he gave me in his letter. The empty spaces where my family and friends should have been felt like physical weight on my chest. This was supposed to be the day when people celebrated the start of my new life, but instead it felt like proof that I was still alone.

Soon, Christina came in, looking ever so much the blushing bride, walked up the aisle, and the ceremony started. When I saw her face, the emptiness in the pews faded. This was what mattered.

Pastor Steve was someone who had helped Christina work through part of her story and had made it so she could become the person I was marrying. When we had planned the wedding, we asked him to announce the marriage to the congregation by using powerful, archaic words that asserted our intention to fight any disruption of our union. The words would emphasize the strength and seriousness of our pledge to each other. With Pastor Steve decreeing, "What God has joined together, let no man put asunder!" Christina and I were married.

+ + +

That summer Christina and I moved into her apartment on Bunting Avenue. We would spend the first year of our marriage finishing our degrees, working part time jobs, and figuring out how to live with each other. My mother started calling me on a regular basis. Our conversations were cold and distant things, and she rarely asked about Christina, and she certainly never tried to start a relationship with my new wife.

I got a letter soon after the wedding, and in it my father wrote, "Sometimes I think I might not make it to my own funeral," as some sort of apology.

He called unexpectedly one day to offer an apology.

"Hey, Bud," he started, "Sorry about not being able to make it."

"Yeah, it's alright," I lied, waiting for what came next.

"I'd like to make it up to you somehow."

"You don't need to."

"No, I want to. What can I get you two as a wedding present? I'll get you anything you want," he said, being his turn to lie.

"Anything? Well, we could use help with tuition, but that's too much. A Mac computer at home would help with homework, or it would be nice to be able to make espresso at home," I offered.

We finished the conversation, and as I hung up the phone, I knew he would send nothing. That was the final time that I heard my father's voice.

I had changed my major the semester before we got married, and I now spent significant parts of my days wondering what I was going to do for a career.

While I was in Germany, I found a copy of Esquire magazine that had an announcement on its cover for a short story writing contest. On a whim, I sent in a story I had written. Months after sending the entry in, I received a fountain pen and a letter stating that I was the runner up in the fiction contest.

At Mesa State, I won the best story prize for a short story published in the college's Literary Journal. With these small successes, and since I didn't really know what I was going to do after graduation, I applied to graduate school thinking I would become a writer.

+ + +

As graduation approached, Christina and I started talking about what came next. The acceptance letter from the University of Alaska had arrived in March, along with the offer of a teaching assistantship that would pay a small stipend.

Neither of us had ever lived anywhere that remote, but the idea of an adventure together felt right. We had each other now, and that seemed like enough to handle whatever Alaska might bring.

The August after we graduated from Mesa State, Christina and I packed everything we owned into a used blue Ford pickup truck with a hard shell covering its bed. With all of our stuff packed in, we still had room for a full-sized futon to be rolled out flat. In preparation for our trip, we spent hours looking at maps of Montana, Alberta, British Columbia, Yukon, and Alaska. We read the Milepost Guidebook to plan our overnight stops, and we put all the emergency gear in the truck that was recommended by the guidebook.

On Monday the 26th, we started out on what would be a five-day trek to Fairbanks, Alaska, where I would start graduate school at the University of Alaska. The drive to Dawson Creek, British Columbia, where the Alaska Highway begins, was across the Great Plains of Alberta, with the Rockies always looming to the west. At Dawson Creek, the Alaska Highway veered into the Rockies and the wilderness. The Milepost Guidebook was a necessity as we headed into the last frontier, because it listed where towns, gas stations, and camping grounds could be found, and there were hundreds and hundreds of miles in between each.

On the fourth day of our trip, we drove along the winding road through the rugged Yukon Plateau north of the Rockies veering west straight toward the Saint Elias Mountains which are on the eastern side of the Coast Mountains. Having lived in the Colorado Rockies, we appreciated the beauty of the mountains, but nothing could have prepared us for the spectacular sight of Kluane National Park, with its massive snowcapped mountain peaks, its glacier filled valleys, and the forests at the foot of it all. We spent little time in the park because we still had over a day to travel to Fairbanks.

After Kluane, our trip was downhill. We had arranged to rent a cabin within walking distance to the university, and it would be Sunday before we could get in. So, as we got to Fairbanks, we had to find a place to stay, because we couldn't camp in the city.

That evening we learned by experience that Fairbanks is truly a frontier city, on the very edge of civilization. Our evening spent in a cheap motel, with walls so thin we could hear the occupant in the room next to us on the phone making drug deals all night gave us our first taste of our new home.

Our cabin in the woods just off the campus was a one-room log cabin with a loft, no running water, a fuel oil burner for heat, and a propane tank for the small cooking stove. Our lavatory was a plywood A-frame outhouse with a curtain made from an old sheet for the door, and it was shared with the neighbors.

I started attending classes, and Christina started looking for work.

I met the other students in my department and found that they all had attended either Ivy League or private schools. I was the only student from a state college and I was the only veteran, but they were friendly to Christina and me, and we tried to fit into the little community. The differences went deeper than just the schools we'd attended. They talked about spring breaks in Europe, summer houses, and parents who were professors or doctors. Their casual mention of things I'd never experienced made me realize how wide the gap was between their world and mine. Still, we found a little Lutheran church, and we started to attend worship regularly.

At that latitude, in autumn, the light bled away at five minutes each day. By the final week of September, the days had shortened by two hours from when we first arrived, and they would grow darker still. Then the snow began to fall, and it would not cease.

Fairbanks is a town that runs on tourism, and as the tourist season ended, so did most jobs. Christina was unable to find work. My GI bill money from the Air Force gave us a little income, and combined with the small stipend I got from teaching composition to first year students, we could survive, but just barely and not without a few trials.

The days got darker, the air got colder, and the snow piled higher with each passing week. In October, the propane tank that we used to cook our food ran out before my payday, and we used an electric wok to cook in.

Around this time, I was working in the tutoring center, which was part of my duties to earn my stipend, when the phone rang.

"Mike, it's for you. It's the Alaska State Troopers," my colleague said.

I was expecting the worst, when I answered, "Hello? This is Mike."

"Mike, this is Trooper Johnson. Your wife has been in an accident," he told me, and my heart dropped, but he added, "She is not hurt, but the truck she was driving is in bad shape."

I got the location of the accident and asked a fellow student to drive me to the scene. When I arrived, the truck was still perched on the guardrail that it had somehow landed on after spinning on the icy road, and Christina was sitting in the front of the trooper's cruiser as the snow drifted down.

Christina was shaken but visibly calm. The truck was fixable, but the repairs took weeks, and during most of that time we were without a vehicle, which meant we had to walk to get food and water, in the bitter Alaska winter.

With no money and no vehicle, things got grim. The only bright spot were the cold, dark evenings with the ground blanketed in the silent snow, glittering in the moonlight, when the Northern Lights would unfurl across the black sky, making ribbons of green, and pink, and violet.

We would put all our layers of winter clothes on and stand in front of the cabin and watch as the colors would twist and swirl and twirl above us. We convinced ourselves that these shimmering veils of light were making music that could just barely be heard over the muffled silence of the snow. Standing there together in that vast wilderness, I began to sense something larger than our immediate struggles, something that had been guiding us even when we couldn't see where we were going.

We at least had the truck back when December came, but financially, we weren't doing any better, and I had become disillusioned with the graduate program at the university. The classes felt disconnected from any kind of writing I wanted to do, and the whole academic world seemed designed for people who had grown up in it.

We made the decision to go back to Colorado when the semester was over. After making arrangements to put the truck in storage, we booked a round-trip airline ticket back to Denver. And since these were the days before you had to show your ID to board a plane, Christina's mother and father would use the return ticket to pick up the truck in the summer.

+ + +

The year that followed our return to Colorado tested everything we thought we knew about building a life together. 1991 was a year of economic recession, and an awful time for a recent college graduate to look for a job.

Christina and I took any work that we could manage to get—she worked in daycare, I worked temp jobs and patched potholes. Some days we had enough money for groceries, other days we lived on whatever we could find in the back of the refrigerator.

I no longer questioned my existence by this point. Church attendance helped with the existential crisis, but I did question what I was supposed to be doing. I felt as directionless as I had before joining the Air Force, but Christina and I had our newly married relationship to work on, and we made enough money to be able to pay rent and go get coffee in downtown Denver if we wanted.

That summer, I applied to a position at Northeastern Junior College in Sterling, Colorado to be a dorm director and a part-time English instructor. The job would give us stability and put me back in a classroom, which felt like progress after the Alaska disappointment.

In the fall, I began teaching and managing the students living in the dorm. Being responsible for the care, safety, and discipline of 70 young men who are away from home for the first time in their lives was a miserable and exhausting experience. But the teaching was exciting, and I began to grow into it.

I applied to speak at regional conferences on composition pedagogy, and I sent in articles and teaching tips to journals. I got to give my first academic talk, and I published my first small article while at Northeastern Junior College.

By the end of the first semester, I knew I would not be renewing my contract for the position of dorm director, and I could not be hired on full-time to teach unless I had at least a master's degree, so Christina and I tried to figure out what was next for us.

One day, as I was walking down a hallway in one of the academic buildings, a building that I was rarely in, I glanced at a bulletin board that had recruitment posters and cards from colleges and universities around the country pinned on it. I noticed a card for the English Graduate School at St. Cloud State University. The idea of trying graduate school again, but somewhere that might be a better fit, started to take shape.

That March, while it was Spring Break at Northeastern, Christina and I drove the twelve hours to St. Cloud to tour the campus and figure out if we could live and thrive in Minnesota.

CHAPTER FIFTEEN

The Interstate heading east out of Denver is flat and easy from the start, the only sign that the road had passed through difficult terrain visible in the rear-view mirror—the rugged Rockies with their 14,000 foot peaks falling away behind us.

It was easy to think, as I drove the small yellow box truck along I-76 heading northeast out of Denver toward Nebraska, that all the roads from this point would be smooth. Behind me, Christina drove the 1976 VW van we had bought for a few hundred dollars in cash, and together we headed north and east toward Saint Cloud, Minnesota.

Driving northeast out of Denver the landscape spread before us like a vast, tawny hide, scattered with sage brush and golden grass that bent in the constant wind. The high plains grass gave way to squares of cornfields and thin lines of trees that traced the small rivers crossing the terrain.

In August the corn was yellowing and dry, dulling what would have been green country. As the sun set, we could see thunderheads rising in the distance, their silent lightning flickering inside the storm clouds. Those storms were moving away from us as we drove toward our future.

Having lived in the dry Front Range, we found the weather grew thick and wet as we neared Minnesota, the humidity sticking to our clothes and skin. But with the moisture came green country.

As we drove up from southwestern Minnesota toward St. Cloud, groves of trees appeared—first scattered, then common. The grass and croplands began to yield to forest. The golden grass and corn became edged with saplings and brush. Soon the fields gave way to the city.

St. Cloud sits, as Garrison Keillor used to say, "out on the edge of the prairie." The first evening we were in St. Cloud, we pitched our tent under the thick oaks and maples at a private campground, and as we sat at the picnic table eating dinner we had cooked on our camp stove, we read the St. Cloud Times classified ads looking for an apartment to rent.

+ + +

Christina and I had found an apartment the next day. It was in a very utilitarian brick building that looked like an unadorned cube, with three stories and two one room apartments on each floor.

I would be earning a stipend for teaching at St. Cloud State University, and I would still be getting what little GI Bill money I had left, but Christina had yet to find work, so the apartment was more than we could afford. The financial pressure sat heavy between us as we signed the lease, another reminder that I was asking her to trust me with a future I wasn't certain I could provide.

Still, the location was good, and since the building sat directly across the road from the right bank of the Upper Mississippi, the view was beautiful, so we signed a lease.

We had planned to spend all day apartment hunting, and this took us less than two hours. Christina had a childhood friend named Ramona who grew up in the same Lutheran church and had attended the same Lutheran school as she had. Ramona had also spent her summers in high school and college working at a Lutheran camp in the mountains above Colorado Springs. When Ramona found out that I would be at St. Cloud State, she told Christina about a chaplain from the camp who had taken on the role of campus pastor at the university, so, since the apartment hunting was done, we decided to see if he was in his office near campus.

As we walked into the stucco former two-story home that had been converted into the Lutheran campus mission, the first person we saw was the pastor's assistant, Barb.

Upon seeing us, Barb greeted us with, "Well, hello. Are you two the couple from Colorado?"

I was taken aback and managed, "Uh, yeah. I'm Mike, this is Chris."

"So you're going to grad school here, right? If you haven't found an apartment yet, there is a free apartment available just a couple of blocks from campus."

"I don't understand."

"Well, there is a Lutheran church just a few blocks away that is looking for someone to be their youth leader part time. They have a house next to the church, and you can live there, if you'll be the youth leader."

We agreed to meet with the pastor of the church, and as Barb made the arrangements over the phone, Christina and I talked to the former chaplain of the summer camp. He explained to us that he had known we were coming because Ramona had told him. When the church looking for the youth leader contacted him to see if he knew someone who would take the role, he told them that we would be in town right before school was to start.

Christina and I agreed to meet with the pastor and Joanne, one of the parents of one of the high schoolers who would be in the youth group, after lunch.

We found a sandwich shop to eat at, and we talked about what had just happened.

I started with, "That was weird. That she knew who we were creeped me out a little."

"Yeah, it was kinda strange." Christina paused before saying, "So who is going to be the youth leader? You or me?"

The question hung between us like a test I hadn't studied for. I knew the answer, but saying it out loud felt like admitting something about myself I wasn't ready to face.

"Well, it can't be me. I am going to be teaching and studying. I won't have the time," I argued, though we both knew time wasn't really the issue. "And I don't know how church works."

What I didn't say was that the idea of being responsible for other people's children, for their spiritual formation, filled me with dread. How could I guide young souls toward God when I was still learning that salvation belonged to Him alone, when I was still discovering that grace was His to give and not mine to dispense?

After lunch, we sat around a round oak, pedestal table with Pastor Dave and Joanne. It seemed that the conversation was mostly about Lutheran church doctrine, and Christina had that covered. We all agreed that I would help Christina, but she would be the leader.

Pastor Dave handed us the key to the house, and we cancelled the lease on the apartment we had just signed. With the help of Pastor Dave and his wife, Karen, we moved into the upstairs apartment in the house at the corner of Fifth Street South and Seventh Avenue South behind Holy Cross Lutheran Church.

Although the past few years had brought change for the better, I had spent my entire existence waiting for the next storm to hit me, and as we walked from what would be our home for the next two years, I could not escape the conviction that I did not merit what had just occurred.

+ + +

As a graduate assistant teaching composition classes, I had to hold office hours so that students could come to me between classes and get help if they needed it, and the university assigned me to a desk in the English graduate student office. The university chose to use the word "office" using an extremely creative interpretation.

All of the desks to be used by the English graduate assistants were shoved into the basement of Shoemaker Hall. The building was an active dormitory, and the basement was a former kitchen for the student dining facility in the hall. Walking into the dark brick basement the first time, I could imagine some sort of Cold War espionage operation taking place in there, with the dark unadorned walls, randomly placed sturdy metal desks, and rows of dim florescent lights dangling from the ceiling.

Far from being a hindrance to the work that I, or the other graduate students, had to do, the environment fostered an earned sense of camaraderie. It was as if we were miners trapped deep beneath the earth in a narrow, shadowy vein of knowledge.

We shared a resolve to persevere graduate school in the cramped quarters and the weight of the earth and building above forged a bond among us. Each week in our graduate program came with multiple, lengthy writings as assignments, and all of us, no matter which class we were currently in, had papers due for our graduate classes constantly.

To relieve the stress of this constant production of writing, someone decided to put a jar on an old grey file cabinet near the entrance to the room. The idea was that we should all write random words on slips of paper. The words on the paper slips ranged from the absurd to the erudite—from sea monkeys, to promulgate. Each week we would all gather together and draw slips out of the jar and read them aloud to each other. Then the task was to incorporate the word from the slips of paper into our written assignments.

The first time I drew "phantasmagorical" from the jar, I stared at the slip of paper while the others laughed. Holly drew "kumquat" and started giggling immediately. Mark got "peripatetic" and shook his head in mock dismay. But as we all sat there in that basement, trying to figure out how to work these random words into serious academic papers, something shifted. The absurdity became a game, and the game became a bond.

It turned out that I found it not as difficult as it would seem to use sea monkeys, even in a graduate level assignment about American literature. The exercise taught us to be creative, to find connections where none seemed obvious, to make the academic personal and the personal academic. When Jeff managed to work "flibbertigibbet" into a paper on Transcendentalism, we cheered like he'd scored a touchdown.

That room fostered a near immediate closeness among us, and I formed fast and lasting friendships. I watched and consoled a fellow grad student Mark as he struggled with his relationship with Kathryn, the single mother of three-year-old Ellen, the result of a failed relationship. Other bonds followed. Holly trusted me with the knowledge that she had become unexpectedly pregnant and was unsure what she was going to do. Jeff and Erica danced the awkward dance of two young adults in love for the first time as I and the other students cheered them on. All the students accepted Christina as well, as if she were one of us.

The campus of the school sat on the bank of the river, and as autumn fell on the Upper Mississippi, Christina and I walked along the bluff above the water in the late afternoons before my classes began in the evening.

We could watch the geese gathering, preparing for their journey south before the hard snows arrived, while the Mississippi rolled toward New Orleans. We watched as autumn claimed the trees, and they began their transformation, casting off the green of summer for bolder colors. The leaves turned to crimson, gold, and burning orange, each one like a small fire against the blue sky.

Walking beside Christina, watching this ancient ritual of death and renewal, I felt something I had rarely known—the possibility that beautiful things might last, that I might be allowed to keep what had been given to me.

The scene spoke of both change and endurance, as if the turning and falling of leaves carried some promise meant specifically for those who had known too much winter. It whispered that after the old is shed, something new begins, and perhaps this time, the new might be worth keeping.

+ + +

Christina's approach to youth work grew from her own struggles with faith as a young person. She had grown up in a church culture where attendance at activities was often seen as the measure of spiritual commitment, but she had experienced firsthand how empty that could feel.

Early in her time trying to get high school aged kids to take their relationship with God seriously, she would plan activities that were meant to draw them in, partly because she was pressured by the church to increase the numbers of kids who came to youth events. She felt it was her duty to help the youth foster their faith, but she was beginning to suspect that duty and relationship might be different things.

The house behind the church that we lived in had two levels. The top level was the two-bedroom apartment that we lived in. The bottom level had two rooms with couches and a ping pong table, as if used furniture and the opportunity to play ping pong would lure kids to youth group meetings.

One Saturday evening, Christina had planned an activity and had gotten the downstairs ready. We sat downstairs, with her sitting in the old burnt orange couch, and me sitting in the avocado green couch. I broke the silence by saying, "It's ten after. Do you think anyone is coming?"

"No," was her terse reply.

Minutes later, as we sat in silence, Tara came in followed by her parents.

"Sorry we're late," Tara's mom said, "Where is everyone?"

Christina burst into tears as she blurted out, "No one's coming!"

I watched my wife's face crumple, saw the weight of expectation and failure crash down on her, and I realized I had no idea how to help. This was her calling, her expertise, and I was just the husband who helped move furniture and provided moral support.

This incident convinced Christina that there was a better way to strengthen young people's faith than simply having activities to do, and she set herself the task of figuring out what that better way was. Over the following weeks, I watched her transform her approach entirely. Instead of planning elaborate activities designed to attract crowds, she began focusing on the kids who did show up. She started having conversations instead of programs, asking questions instead of giving answers.

"What if," she said to me one evening as we cleaned up after a group meeting where only four kids had come, "what if the point isn't to fill the room? What if the point is to know the kids who are here?"

She began meeting individually with teenagers, taking them for coffee, listening to their actual concerns instead of assuming what those concerns should be. When Sarah confided that her parents were getting divorced, Christina didn't offer a Bible verse or a youth group activity about families. She sat with Sarah in that pain and helped her figure out what it meant to trust God when your world was falling apart.

On her own, Christina set about transforming the youth group of Holy Cross from kids showing up to do stuff when it was convenient for them to a group of young people who had relationships with each other and, more importantly, with God. The numbers never grew dramatically, but the connections deepened. I could see it in the way the teenagers started seeking Christina out, the way they began bringing friends not because there was a fun activity planned, but because they wanted to share what they had found.

As a neophyte Christian, I helped where I could, but mostly I observed from the margins, and in watching her, I learned something about faith that no sermon had conveyed. Throughout my broken childhood, I had believed my communion with God was transactional. If I disobeyed my mother, or transgressed in some way, I would earn damnation. If I prayed, and had merited God's favor, my prayers would be answered. I learned during my time with the youth group that this transactional understanding of God was largely my own invention. Gradually, I came to comprehend that God desired communion with me, not commerce.

But more than that, I began to grasp that His love was not something I could earn or lose through my actions. It was not wages for good behavior or punishment for failure, but grace—unmerited, unchanging, bestowed not because of who I was but because of who He was. This was not a God who kept ledgers of my deeds, but one who had chosen me before I knew to choose Him.

+ + +

In the spring of 1994, things were going well for us. Christina's and my relationship was going through the normal rockiness that newlyweds experience, but we were in a good place. We had gotten a free apartment in exchange for part-time work; I had found a group of peers who accepted me; my graduate studies were going exceedingly well; and we had found a church home.

To this point, I had kept my past buried like something that might poison the ground if unearthed. I had not even told Christina the full measure of what I had survived. When pressed, I would say only, "My family is broken," as if that explained the wreckage I had crawled out of. No one knew the distance I had traveled from those early rooms where care and harm had been indistinguishable to this place of unexpected grace.

The blessings that had come to us in Minnesota began to feel like accusations. Each good thing that happened seemed to whisper that I was a fraud, that I had stolen what belonged to someone more deserving. The weight of unearned happiness settled on me like sickness.

The day I first met with Rich, dirty snow lay melting in the streets, revealing the winter's accumulated refuse—cigarette butts and rotted leaves and the black grit of months spent under ice. The sky hung pale and threatening, pregnant with storms that might yet come to reclaim what the brief warmth had taken.

The counseling office was a small cave of lamplight in the institutional fluorescence of the campus. I sat in a chair that had absorbed the sorrows of a thousand students before me. Rich waited with the patience of a confessor while I searched for words to name the poison I carried.

"It's just . . . I don't understand why I feel this way," I began, my voice close to a whisper, laden with the weight of what I thought of as unearned success. "I mean, I'm doing well in graduate school. My wife and I have a great gig that gives us an apartment. I have friendships with some good people. And I have a great wife. But every time I receive a compliment, or something good happens, it feels like I'm wearing a mask. Like I'm fooling everyone. I just can't shake this feeling of guilt about it."

"What you're describing sounds like a profound sense of shame, not guilt. Can you tell me more about that feeling?"

Shame. The word hung in the air, heavy and suffocating but precise. "It's like . . . I don't deserve this. I don't come from a place where people achieve things. My childhood was filled with neglect, abuse—physical and emotional. I was abandoned by the people who were supposed to protect me."

He leaned forward slightly, his interest piqued. "Tell me about your childhood. What was it like?"

For the first time in my life, I told someone some of the stories that made up my childhood.

"That sounds incredibly painful," Rich interjected. "And it's understandable that you would carry feelings of unworthiness into your adult life. But can you differentiate between guilt and shame?"

I frowned, contemplating the question. "Guilt is feeling bad about something you did, right? But shame... shame is feeling bad about who you are."

"Exactly. Guilt can be constructive, leading to change, but shame is corrosive. It tells you that you are not enough, that you don't belong. You've accomplished so much despite your past, yet here you are, feeling like an imposter. Why do you think that is?"

I hesitated, the truth clawing at my throat. "Because I've never had anyone believe in me. I did it all on my own, and it feels wrong to take credit for it. Like I don't deserve to take credit."

Rich continued, "We have to figure out why you feel that way. That's what we'll work on for our next few visits."

Over my next several visits, Rich drew my history from me like poison from a wound and made me speak of the ways my family had operated.

At the end of our third session, Rich's brow creased as he studied me with an intensity that made me shift in my chair.

"Mike, I need you to understand something. What you lived through as a child, statistically speaking, kids don't come out the other side of that and end up here, in graduate school, building a life. They end up dead or in jail. But you're sitting right *here*, aren't you? This isn't luck. This isn't just getting by. You didn't just survive what happened to you—you transformed it.'"

I chuckled in response.

"No. I am serious. You shouldn't be here sitting in front of me, and the fact that you are is remarkable."

His words bewildered me. "I don't get it."

"What happened to you as a kid—and what you did with it—that's not typical. Most kids who go through what you went through, they carry those wounds differently. Some get stuck there. Some never find their way out. But you? You didn't just survive it. You turned it into something else entirely. That fighting spirit you had—it saved you."

I swallowed hard, the enormity of his statement washing over me like a tide. "But I'm just me. I don't feel exceptional. I feel . . . broken."

Rich leaned back, his demeanor softening. "Listen, you're not broken . . . not by a long shot. What I see sitting here is someone who figured out how to survive when the adults around you wouldn't protect you. That takes a special kind of strength. You built your own foundation when no one else would build it for you. Those achievements you keep minimizing? They're not accidents. They're proof of something unbreakable in you."

I sat there not knowing what to say.

He finished with, "I don't think I can help you."

As I left and walked to my office in the basement, I struggled to accept that I had made it to where I was on my own. There had to be more to it.

+ + +

Church membership, officially declaring intent to join a congregation, is an important thing in the doctrines of the Lutheran church, and Christina and I became members of Holy Cross. This joining was not merely a symbolic gesture. For us it was a recognition that we had begun to lay roots down in St. Cloud.

The decision to become members forced me to confront something I had been avoiding. When we set out to move to Minnesota, the plan was for me to get my master's degree, and then I would find a Ph.D. program somewhere else, since St. Cloud State didn't offer a Ph.D. in Rhetoric. That plan had slowly started to dissolve from that first day we moved, but I had been pretending it was still intact, still the goal.

Standing in that sanctuary, making those membership vows, I realized I was committing to more than a church. I was committing to a place, to staying put, to building something instead of always preparing to leave. For someone who had spent his entire life ready to run, this felt like the most radical thing I had ever done.

But membership at Holy Cross completed the dissolution of my academic ambitions in a way that felt like relief rather than failure. It wasn't just that we had finally become comfortable in that place and wanted to stay; I realized that I was not suited for academia.

As part of my plan to make myself more attractive to a Ph.D. program, and later a university offering a professorship, I got involved in the "business" of the department. My professors said, publishing articles and presenting at conferences were part what makes an attractive candidate, but serving on committees would help even more. And so I volunteered to serve, and there were plenty of committees to choose from. There were so many, that St. Cloud State had a committee called the Committee on Committees.

The first committee meeting I attended was for the Graduate Curriculum Committee. Twelve people sat around a conference table discussing whether to change the required number of credits for a particular course from three to four. The discussion lasted two hours. Two hours. About one credit. I watched professors I respected engage in elaborate procedural debates about issues that seemed to have no bearing on actual education or learning.

My experience was that absolutely nothing got done in a committee meeting. This, coupled with the political internecine war in all of academia at the time, convinced me that I needed to stop trying to become a professor. The gap between my idealistic vision of academic life and the bureaucratic reality was too wide to bridge. I felt I needed to count my blessings in St. Cloud and try to make life work there.

The decision to abandon my doctoral plans should have felt like failure, but it didn't. Instead, it felt like coming home to myself, to who I actually was rather than who I thought I should become. Christina and I began talking about buying a house, about building a life that wasn't temporary, about putting down roots in soil that seemed willing to receive them.

+ + +

That May, after my thesis was accepted and I graduated, I took work at a catalog retailer in their training department. My service in the Air Force had been done entirely on computers, which at that time was uncommon. I used this computer experience, combined with my teaching experience at the college and universities, to get a job in their computer-based training division.

The work felt like solid ground after years of navigating the shifting terrain of academic life. I was helping people get the skills they could use, developing programs that bore relevance to their daily labor. There was something deeply satisfying about creating instruction that yielded results you could see and touch.

As spring gave way to summer, Christina and I began searching for a house in St. Cloud. The long Minnesota winter was breaking apart, ice releasing its grip on the rivers, and for the first time in my adult existence, I found myself thinking in terms of decades rather than semesters. The seasons would turn many times before I would think of moving again.

Something was settling in me, like sediment finding its place at the bottom of still water.

CHAPTER SIXTEEN

The Minnesota Department of Natural Resources claimed in 1995 that no cougars roamed the state.

Since people with technical skills did not view St. Cloud as a place to build careers, the catalog retailer I worked for constructed a tech center on the northwestern edge of Minneapolis. The company boasted that the state-of-the-art building ensured every desk possessed an outside view and employed white noise generators to keep the cubicles quiet and free from distraction. It even maintained an advanced security camera system that monitored the parking lots.

One early morning, as frost still clung to the windshields and the sky hung pale as old bone, those cameras captured a cougar walking across the asphalt. Both the security technology and the cougar were without precedent in that place. Had I remained at the company, I would have been assigned an office in the building around which the cougar wandered. But even though I eventually left the job, the catalog company proved an excellent place to begin my career.

The work involved teaching people to navigate complex database systems and solve problems that left them staring at incomprehensible error messages. I could see the logical patterns that led to solutions, break down complicated processes into steps that made sense to those who were not technical.

But while the work proved interesting at first, it soon became tedious and repetitive. Like a storm that builds pressure until it must break, I grew restless and began to create friction among my team. The autumn of that year had been unusually warm, as if the world were holding its breath, waiting for something to shift. I had taken the position as temporary work, and I began searching for something permanent.

The world was changing around us in ways we could not yet see, and perhaps I sensed that larger transformations were gathering like storm clouds on the horizon—not just in technology, but in everything that mattered.

+ + +

During the summer of 1995, I started to feel a pain in the right side of my lower abdomen. I went to a primary care doctor who decided that it was not appendicitis. The pain grew increasingly worse throughout the summer. Christina and I sometimes sat in the balcony of Holy Cross, with its dark stained oak trim and fixtures, and unpadded pews.

The congregation below us looked small from our perch in the balcony, families clustered together in the brown wooden pews that stretched in orderly rows toward the altar. Pastor Dave's voice would echo up to us during the liturgy, and we would follow along in the blue Lutheran Book of Worship, Christina's fingers sometimes finding mine during the prayers.

On a Sunday, as I sat in the pew, the pain went from dull to stabbing, and I folded over feeling like a knife had been driven into me. I arranged to see a surgeon that week, and he scheduled me for a hernia repair.

In the late 1990s, the career experts would tell you that you were not supposed to look to classified advertisements in newspapers if you wanted to find a job, but I read the StarTribune from Minneapolis daily even during this spell of abdominal pain, looking for a job. I found an advertisement for a software trainer position at a company called SQL Systems, and I applied. I had a phone interview, with Grant, the hiring manager, just before my scheduled surgery. I had not told Grant that I was having surgery, so when he called the day after to schedule onsite interviews, he was shocked to hear that I agreed to come down to do the interviews two days after the surgery.

On a cold November day, Christina drove me ninety minutes down to Eden Prairie, southwest of Minneapolis, for my interviews, since I couldn't drive because of the surgery. I talked to three executives in the company, and it felt pro forma to me. No one asked questions that I couldn't answer, and no one pressed me as to why I wanted the job. However, everyone was impressed that I would come interview just days after surgery. All I thought was "Why wouldn't I do that?"

Christina had spent her time waiting for me shopping at a store called Tuesday Morning where she bought a Christmas tree skirt because Christmas was only weeks away. The middle to late 1990s was the burgeoning of the coffee culture in Central Minnesota.

Before this there was no espresso to be found in St. Cloud, but by that time there was a small coffee shop called Barrymore's just off the main street in downtown. The shop was dark, painted a deep, forest green, with black and white photos on the walls. They roasted their own coffee on site, and the smell of fresh roasted coffee would permeate our clothes every time we went there. After the interviews one evening, we sat in Barrymore's talking about what might happen.

"What do you think? If they make me an offer, how much would we agree to?" I asked.

"Well, if you make $25,000, and I find a job that pays that much, that would give us $50,000."

"I know that's how much my place now pays their trainers, and they aren't a software company. Maybe I should hold out for more."

"That feels risky," Christina hesitated, "How much more?"

"I don't know. What about $28,000?"

Christina and I drew a line in the sand regarding any salary that I would accept: nothing less than $28,000.

Those were the days before email, and Grant had called me to say that he was going to fax an offer letter to me. I gave him the phone number to the fax machine at the catalog retailer, and I rushed over to stand guard, so none of my coworkers would see the offer. I watched as the fax came in, and I had to catch my breath as I read the offer of $37,000 per year. I accepted the offer, and we arranged a start date in January of 1996.

On the first day of work, before he took me around to introduce me to my coworkers, I sat in Grant's office talking about the role. He told me, "Everyone thought you were a good candidate, Mike, but I almost didn't offer you the position."

"What? Why?"

"I just didn't feel you were ebullient enough."

"Ebullient?" I chuckled. "Of course I wasn't. I had just had surgery. It still hurts to laugh now."

And with that I became a trainer for a software company, which meant traveling to customer sites most weeks and teaching people how to use database systems that could track everything from manufacturing processes to financial transactions. The work felt substantial in a way the catalog job never had. I was solving actual problems for people, helping factory managers understand their production flows, showing accountants how to generate reports that had taken them days to compile by hand.

I would arrive at these places like weather rolling in from distant territory—carrying knowledge they needed but did not possess. In the fluorescent-lit conference rooms of manufacturing plants and corporate offices, I would watch understanding dawn on faces that had been clouded with confusion. There was something satisfying about bringing order to their chaos, about taking the tangled processes they had inherited and laying them out clean and logical as fresh snow.

The travel kept me moving through the landscape of American industry—from paper mills in Oregon where the air hung thick with steam and pulp, to refineries in Texas where the dry heat pressed against the windows like something alive. Each place taught me something new about how people worked, how they struggled with the tools they had been given.

+ + +

One of the benefits of being a veteran is the VA Home Loan. The Veteran's Administration would back a mortgage that has zero down payment, good interest rates, and no private mortgage insurance for me. Christina and I bought a two-bedroom Cape Cod house on the corner of 6th Avenue North and 13th Street North, directly across from the emergency room at the St. Cloud Hospital.

We made our first attempt at creating a home out of that little grey house, with its undersized kitchen and tiny dining room by ripping out the pet urine-soaked carpeting, under which we found hardwood floors. We splurged and paid someone to refinish them, but other than that, we could move right in.

Our furniture had remained the same since we had gotten married and moved into Christina's apartment in Grand Junction. The beautifully restored red oak table remained our dining room table in our new home where we would sit for our meals.

We had been married for nearly seven years by that point, and yet, we were still talking about dreams and aspirations as we sat at that table. We would talk about what plants Christina wanted to add to the yard and about what car I would get if I got a raise.

And sometimes we would talk about children. Conversations about children weren't uncommon. We had talked about them before. Christina, as usual, started the discussion. "If we had a baby, the second bedroom would be the nursery."

"Yeah, we could paint it if you wanted. Painting's easy, but I don't want kids."

"You always say that. Why?"

"You know why. I don't want to be my father."

"Well," she responded, "don't be your father."

"I know, but I am scared it will happen, and I'll be a lousy dad. I don't want that."

"You'll be a good father."

+ + +

Within a couple of months, I was promoted at work, and I became one of the people delegated the task of demonstrating the software to people considering buying it. The promotion came with a slight increase in salary, but I continued traveling most every week. Most of my trips were to factories, refineries, and paper mills in the industrial parts of the country. In November of 1996, the CEO called me into his office.

"There is a problem with a sale in Columbia," he explained. "Our folks in Latin America won't do a demo there."

"Why not?" I asked.

"I'm not sure, but the deal is near to closing, and we need someone to give them one last demo. You're the only one who has availability. We need you to go to Cali, Columbia."

"Okay, when?"

"Tomorrow, and you'll fly back on Friday."

"Uh, that's short notice," I hesitated and then added, "My wife is not going to be happy."

"What if we flew her down to Miami to meet you on Friday, and you two can stay in Miami for the weekend? And the company pays for everything."

In the late 1990s, Colombia was still writhing in the final convulsions of cartel violence and crime, and Cali remained caught between cartels, guerrilla movements, and paramilitary groups. I flew from Minneapolis to Miami where I would change planes for Cali. My connecting flight would not depart Miami until early evening, and I would not reach Cali until nearly midnight, so I sat in the Miami airport feeding my own fears about what I was getting into.

All year, I had been hearing news reports of US businessmen being taken and held until their companies paid ransom. Never one to assume the best outcome, that day I had convinced myself that my company would not pay if I were seized.

The flight started like any other flight, taking off and reaching cruising altitude, with me reading a book.

Toward the end of the flight, in the distance, I could see almost dead ahead reddish gold lighting as it flashed in the clouds as we headed toward them. As we got near the storms the turbulence started to shake and rattle the plane, and people began screaming and praying out loud.

Soon we started crossing the Western Cordillera mountains toward the valley that Cali sat in. Our plane was tossed about by the remnants of the thunderstorm that had preceded us over the mountains as the air currents danced unpredictably over the craggy landscape of the mountains.

The currents, whipped into frenzy by the uneven terrain and the storm's aftermath, tossed the plane in sporadic jolts and heaves.

The screaming and praying became more insistent, and the sewage in the lavatory was tossed back up from the commode, spilling onto the floor and filling the cabin with the stench of human waste.

My silent prayers joined those of the other passengers, and I was seized with a sudden fierce hunger to live, followed just as quickly by a calm certainty that I would.

We landed at the Cali airport, and the other passengers erupted in applause and shouting. Minutes later, we deplaned and were met by paramilitary soldiers who were serving as guards at the airport. The city itself would be full of armed patrols, as well. I went through immigrations and met the colleagues who would host my visit.

My work in Cali seemed mundane and docile compared the flight. The Colombian engineers were sharp and asked pointed questions about system architecture and database optimization that pushed me to explain concepts I'd only theoretical understanding of before.

They wanted to know how our software would handle their specific manufacturing challenges, how it would integrate with their existing systems, whether it could accommodate the complexity of their supply chain that stretched across multiple countries. The days were filled with technical demonstrations and wonderful coffee at break-time, conversations that revealed how little I understood about business operations outside the United States.

Their questions made me realize that what I'd considered sophisticated database management was actually quite basic compared to the challenges they were trying to solve. The visit was successful and unremarkable, and on that Friday, I was ready to be home.

This time, the flight out of the valley where Cali lay was much less violent, but as I sat with my book open in my hands, I found the words sliding away from me, my attention seized by a growing pressure beneath my eyes and a thickness forming in my throat. I felt something urgent clawing at my gut, a need to see Christina that came from some place deeper than thought. The need was so strong I could taste salt at the corners of my mouth.

After I landed in Miami, I had a couple of hours to wait until Christina's plane from Minneapolis landed. The hug we shared unfolded slowly, as if time had paused. It felt like we were reunited after a long separation, and we wanted to savor the moment, even though it had only been days that we were apart.

"Man, I missed you," I told Christina.

"Yeah, me too."

"How was your flight?" I asked.

"It was fine, but I almost missed it."

"Why? What happened?"

"I overslept. I've been so tired lately, and I have been feeling sick."

"Really? How do you feel now?"

"I'm okay. The sickness comes and goes."

We went to our hotel and spent the next day looking at alligators in the Everglades. On Sunday we flew home with every intention of simply returning to our routine of Christina leading the youth group and me helping people understand how our software worked, but our plans were about to be completely upended. God had his own plans for us.

+ + +

While I traveled at least a few days for work most weeks, Christina built the youth group at Holy Cross, and we attended Sunday worship there every week. The interior of Holy Cross was filled with row after row of dark brown oak pews, I would joke that the divider halfway down a pew showed that it was a Lutheran church, because at a Catholic church they wouldn't split a family up like that.

The chancel, where the altar sat, was bounded by a curved arch. At the back of the chancel, on the curved back wall behind the altar, were the letters "IHS" written in black letter, a throwback to the German heritage of Holy Cross. Behind the alter was an ornately carved reredos with a statue of Jesus, his arms lifted as if offering a blessing. The pulpit was to the right of the chancel with the same deep brown oak paneling its sides and top, and to the left of the chancel was a smaller lectern.

Christina and I usually sat toward the back of the right side of the church, not so far back that we would be in the crowded back, and not so far to the front that we would stand out among the mostly empty rows. There were families we recognized week after week: the Andersons with their three young children who always sat in the third pew, Mrs. Kowalski who came alone and always brought a thermos of coffee, the college students who filled the back rows during the school year and disappeared during summer break. Pastor Dave knew everyone's name, would ask about sick relatives and job searches, and made the large sanctuary feel intimate during the passing of the peace when neighbors would shake hands and share brief conversations before settling back into worship.

One Sunday, as we sat in our usual spot, at some point in the liturgy, Christina leaned over to me and whispered, "I think I'm pregnant."

"What?" I whispered back.

"I'm late."

"Oh," I replied.

Neither of us reacted with joy or exultation at the realization that we were going to be parents, and it wasn't just because the revelation came to her in the middle of church service. Rather it felt like we both were resigning ourselves to this new fact. On my part, I made a conscious effort to hold the miasma of my past at bay—to shove it back into the box where I had put it.

That afternoon, after church, we went to the drugstore and bought a pregnancy test. I stood outside our bathroom door as Christina did the test. The instructions said to wait five minutes before trying to read the results, so Christina came out of the bathroom and leaned into my chest as I wrapped my arms around her.

Eventually, I said, "It's been five minutes. Do you want to check it?"

"No, you do it."

As I stepped into the bathroom, my heart hammered against my ribs. The air grew thick as I crossed the threshold. I moved with deliberate care, as if walking through water. The stark white tiles in that small, confined space seemed to burn with their own light. Our lives hung in the balance of what I would find there. That small piece of plastic with its tiny window held the power to remake everything we had planned, everything we thought we knew about what came next.

When I emerged from the bathroom carrying the test, Christina's face had turned crimson and her hands trembled like leaves before a storm.

"Well, it's positive," I said, "You're going to be a mom, and I guess I'd better get ready to be a dad."

+ + +

I had been calling my mother most months by this time, attempting to weave together a relationship that had never truly existed. Nearly every time we spoke, she would ask when we were going to have children. My answer was always the same: "We are not going to have children, so you might as well stop asking." When others would ask about having a child, my reply never varied: I did not want to be like my father. Even without knowing anything about the man, this brief response was usually sufficient to end the conversation.

For all the times I had given that answer, I had never examined what I meant. I did not want to be like my father, but what I truly feared was for a child to endure what I had endured. If it had been my choice alone, I would not have become a father. But it was not my choice to make. God had his own design.

In that moment when we understood that Christina was carrying our child, something fundamental shifted within me. I chose to no longer allow my past to govern who I would become. I would make myself into something new. I decided that I would be the father this child deserved—not the father I had known, but the father I had needed. I knew I would fail in ways I could not foresee, but I would dedicate my existence to ensuring this child would know safety and joy. I wanted them to think of me as someone who could be trusted with their heart.

More than that, my reckoning with fatherhood became the moment I began to understand what my relationship with God was meant to be. I began to hunger for communion with a Father who would never abandon, never break his promises, never leave his children to face the storms alone.

And I wanted that same certainty for the life growing within Christina—that they would know from their first breath they were chosen, beloved, never forgotten.

The boy who had waited in vain for his father to come to his wedding was gone. In his place stood a man who would spend his life ensuring no child of his would ever wait in vain for anything.

CHAPTER SEVENTEEN

When we first arrived in Minnesota, the license plates bore the words "Land of 1000 Lakes" pressed into the metal. The locals would inform us it was closer to fourteen thousand, and flying above Minnesota on my journeys to customer sites, I could see what they meant. If the plane departed as morning mist still clung to the earth, an expanse of lakes spread across the landscape, each one a golden mirror catching the early light like coins scattered among the trees and fields.

As a gift to myself upon completing graduate school, I purchased an Old Town Camper 16 canoe so we could spend time on the waters. In my mind, the canoe with its deep forest green hull and ash thwarts and seats woven with yellow cane was proof that we had become Minnesotans.

Christina found peace on the water, especially when the air hung still and the surface lay smooth as glass. She would sometimes fish while we drifted in the canoe, but mostly she would sit and gaze at the trees or into the depths, at rest. She needed that stillness because she was working through her own buried history with a therapist while she carried our child. On those calm afternoons when no wind stirred the water, she seemed to breathe deeper, as if the lake's tranquility could enter her lungs and settle the storms within.

A few months before the birth, I was brought into some of the sessions to learn how to support Christina through what might prove difficult for her. One technique the therapist wanted Christina to master was visualization to manage the fear and tension she would face during delivery. The method required Christina to picture something that brought calm and safety. She chose to imagine herself on a lake in the canoe, drifting through still water under clear skies. My role would be to support Christina, and when the labor pains came like sudden squalls, I would remind her to "go to the canoe."

+ + +

We had made the decision to not know if the baby was a boy or a girl until it was born, so we went into the ultrasound appointment with the technician agreeing to not tell us if she saw something.

When the grainy image of the baby first appeared on the screen, it was easy for me to have a detached curiosity. As the technician moved the probe around, so she could measure the baby's leg and head in order to estimate its weight, I looked at the lines she would draw on the screen and the numbers being displayed in the upper right-hand corner of the display, trying to figure out the process of the estimation. It was as if the baby wasn't the point of the visit.

As the estimation concluded, the technician moved the probe around a little and we could see the profile of the baby curled up in Christina's womb. While I was just realizing that this was our baby I was looking at, the baby turned its head right toward the probe. Seeing the image on the screen felt like the baby was looking right at us. It felt like the baby recognized us. If there had been any doubt in my mind that I was really going to be a father, that look from the baby completely erased it.

+ + +

As spring turned into summer and the baby's due date in July approached, I found myself with a burst of energy in the evenings and the weekends, which gave me the drive to ready the house for the baby.

We had no intention of decorating the room where the baby would be sleeping to look like a nursery, but I made the effort to touch up the paint on the walls and the trim. I oiled the hinges to the door, so it wouldn't squeak when it was opened or closed.

Then I tried the crib we had bought in several spots around the room, making sure it would ultimately be in the perfect place. Finally, I converted an old dresser that I had repainted into a changing table.

And when the baby's room was done, I started on other projects, such as painting the exterior trim on the house, because I thought it should be done, and I reasoned that I wouldn't have much time for that sort of work once the baby arrived.

+ + +

During early summer in St. Cloud, the afternoon heat would settle like a heavy quilt across the land. The sun, burning in a nearly empty sky, would bathe the lakes, fields and forests in golden light. The shadows grew sharp and brief as the summer solstice drew near, and the heat became a living presence that seemed to arrest time itself, making the afternoons drowsy and still as the birth approached.

Our small house on the corner had no central air, and Christina would grow tormented by the heat in those late afternoons.

Sometimes we would climb into the car, turn the air conditioning to full, and drive without purpose or destination.

In the late 1990s the grocery stores in St. Cloud still maintained open-top freezers that stood in long rows like deep, lidless coffins. Inside the freezers, goods were stacked with precision or sometimes heaped high, and ice had built up along the upper edges and inner walls like crystalline formations in some cave.

The cold air poured from their mouths and offered Christina relief in her final weeks as we wandered the aisles seeking respite from the heat that pressed against the windows like something hungry.

+ + +

Because of Christina's emotional situation, her therapist had spoken with her doctor, and he became an active participant in trying to reduce the stress of her delivery. They had agreed that if she hadn't delivered the baby by July 3rd, she would be induced on July 4th because the doctor was leaving for vacation, and he wanted to deliver the baby himself.

So, on the morning of July 4th, since our house was just across the street from the hospital, I grabbed a little satchel with some clothes, a children's book for the baby, and some playing cards, and Christina and I walked to the hospital so she could be admitted.

We had gone to birthing classes that were offered by the birthing center, so we knew the stages that happened during delivery. We knew the meanings of words like "contractions," "dilation," "effacement," "crowning," and "episiotomy." We had watched videos of deliveries, and Christina had decided that her delivery would be one like the red-headed mother whose labor was short and not severe, where she hardly even grimaced in pain, and the baby came out healthy and beautiful.

As Christina sat in the bed in the backless hospital gown, with an IV line in the back of her hand, we played cards on the rolling table with the brown fake woodgrain vinyl top that would hold the ice chips and water later.

The doctor wanted to start slowly with the induction, so the first thing they tried was to artificially break Christina's water. The invasiveness made Christina physically and emotionally uncomfortable, but it didn't seem to cause pain. While we waited to see if labor would start, we continued to play cards.

After an hour, labor had not started, so a nurse injected Pitocin, a synthetic hormone that induces labor, into the IV line. Soon, the contractions started, and I put the playing cards away because Christina no longer needed to be distracted from the thought of labor. She was in labor.

As part of the delivery process the nurses had to check on how Christina's body was reacting to the labor, and this meant an uncomfortable examination. It was this type of exam that we had prepared for with the therapist, so I went to the side of the bed, took Christina's hand, and tried to comfort her. When she seemed to be getting distressed, I would lean down and remind her to go to her canoe. As the contractions became closer and more intense, the hope of having the perfect, nearly painless, delivery faded.

In our seven years of marriage, I had heard Christina scream in pain one time, when she unknowingly stepped on an underground wasps' nest and was stung over ten times at once, but as the intensity of the labor wore on she would cry and let out an occasional muffled scream.

About three hours into labor, Christina went through what seemed to be the longest and most intense contraction of the delivery to that point.

Beads of sweat ran down as the color started to return to her face, and in a quiet voice, she said, "I don't think I can do this anymore."

Bending down to her ear, I said, "I don't think you have a choice... and I know you can make it. You're doing fine."

In between contractions, I would try to give Christina ice chips and wipe the sweat from her brow. Two more hours went by, and after more contractions and more exams, the baby's head started to make progress. The nurse coached Christina on when to push and when to relax, when to strain, and when to rest.

As the time went on, the labor nurse started to seem slightly nervous. After a contraction, she said to Christina, "Okay, you can relax." And to me she said, "I'm going to get the doctor. You come down to the foot of the bed, while I'm away." Christina was exhausted, and simply lay back, while I stood at the foot of the bed saying silent prayers.

Christina's doctor came in with a sense of urgency. "You can go to the bedside again, please," he directed me. "The baby has been in the birth canal too long, and we need to get it out as soon as possible," he explained.

"Will you have to do a C-section?" I asked.

As he got into position at the foot of the bed, he responded, "It's too late for that. The baby is too far into the birth canal."

More nurses came into the room, and I was shooed away to the far side of the room. Two nurses were at the head of the bed caring for Christina, and another nurse along with the labor nurse who had been there were at the foot of the bed helping the doctor.

The new nurse at the foot of the bed rolled over a stainless-steel cart with sterilized equipment on it. "Episiotomy scissors," the doctor said. And the nurse handed him a pair of curved, blunted scissors.

I flinched but made no sound as he cut Christina with the scissors. I was afraid of making her more concerned than she already was with the pain. As the next contraction came, Christina was told to push as hard as she could.

"I need you to push even harder next time, Christina," the doctor said with what sounded like a serious tone.

To the nurse at the cart he said, "Get the Mityvac ready." The word sounded incongruously cartoonish to me at such a tense time.

Christina grunted and pushed as hard as she could, and I could see the baby's head move a little more, so that the top of its head was now out.

"That was good Christina. On the next contraction, when you push, I am going to use a vacuum extractor to help pull the baby."

I watched as the doctor put a cup over the top of the baby's skull and started to pump, squeezing his fist open and shut over a handle with a spring-loaded lever. As the next contraction came, Christina tried to push once more, and the doctor pulled. Christina screamed in pain.

As the doctor pulled, I could see a little shoulder start to make its way out. Briefly unaware of the contractions or screaming, I clenched my eyelids, so all that I saw was that little baby.

At that moment my world was that baby. As it slipped all the way out, and started crying, I realized that I had been holding my breath. I breathed again as I slipped past the doctor and up to the right side of the bed. Christina and I stared in awe at the little boy they laid on her chest.

"You can touch him," the doctor said, seeing us frozen.

I thought to myself, "I don't know what I am doing, and I don't want to hurt him. I never want to hurt him."

As I gently put my hand on his back, I leaned down to him and said, "Hi, buddy," a lump in my throat and tears welling up in my eyes.

A nurse gently picked up Ethan from Christina's chest and performed an examination. After she weighed him, she announced, "Eight pounds ten ounces. That's a healthy big boy."

"Eight pounds?," Christina asked. She then cried, "No!" as tears started flowing.

As the nurse wrote down the weight, she said, "The time of birth was five twenty-eight pm."

Knowing that Ethan was doing well, the doctor and two of the nurses turned their attention to Christina. There was much more wrong with her than the normal post-delivery issues mothers face.

The extraction had created a huge tear beyond where the doctor had cut her, and she was losing blood rapidly. The medical team seemed to struggle with the extent of the damage. The doctor and two of the nurses started caring for Christina, and I watched as he began sewing her wounds closed.

A third nurse came up to me, put her hand on my arm and said, "Dad, let's go wash your son." The small cart she had wheeled into the room was topped with a thick, doubled over, white terrycloth towel. To one side there was an orange basin filled with water, and directly next to it was a white washcloth and a small bar of Dial soap still in its wrapper.

"You open the soap and get the washcloth ready," she told me, "I am going to get Baby."

As I took the small bar of Dial soap and lathered a washcloth, the nurse lifted Ethan from the bassinet he had been laid in and gently placed his naked and soiled body on the towel.

I used the washcloth dipped in warm water and lathered with soap to wash the bodily fluids and blood off of my son. When he was clean, the nurse showed me how to swaddle Ethan with a stretchy, soft, pink and blue striped blanket, and then she put a little hat over his full head of red hair.

I stood holding Ethan as I watched the doctor and the nurses speaking to each other in hushed tones as they tried to figure out the extent of Christina's injuries.

"You've lost a lot of blood, and we aren't sure why," he finally said to Christina, "I am going to order tests to see what your hemoglobin levels are."

"What if the levels are low," Christina asked.

"We would talk about a transfusion."

Before the test results came back, the doctor and two nurses left, leaving one nurse to continue to care for Christina. While we waited for the blood test to come back from the lab, there were still post-delivery milestones that Christina had to cross before she would be considered stable. For one, she should have been able to void her bladder within an hour or two, and she couldn't.

The sky over central Minnesota in July holds its light until half past nine, and I could see the twilight bleeding through the trees beyond the hospital window when the nurse entered to speak with Christina.

"Maybe you are just having a hard time using a bedpan. Let's get you up, and I'll walk you over to the bathroom."

"I don't know if I can stand," was Christina's reply.

"I'll be right next to you."

Christina winced and groaned as she sat up in the bed. The nurse helped her swing her legs over the side of the bed, and they paused for Christina to get ready to stand.

"Okay, let's try it," Christina said.

The nurse held Christina closely by her upper arm, leaning into her to give her support. Christina pushed herself up, her hand still touching the bed as she got up on both feet.

As soon as she put her weight on her legs, she collapsed, but the nurse was able to keep her from falling and put her back into the bed. "What happened, Christina?" she calmly asked, seemingly to avoid alarming Christina or me.

"I don't know. As soon as I stood, my hips and legs just gave out."

"Was there any pain? Maybe somewhere other than the stitches?"

"Yeah, sharp pain in my pelvis and back."

"Okay, you just lie back down. We'll get this figured out."

Christina lay back down on the bed just as I heard the Fourth of July fireworks start.

The blood test showing the volume of blood that Christina had lost came back saying it was borderline as to whether a transfusion was necessary. She had lost a significant amount of blood, but not enough to justify risking the slight chance of a complication from a transfusion.

It was nearly midnight by the time the nurse who had volunteered to stay past her shift to make sure Christina was going to be okay left for the day.

"You didn't have to stay," Christina told her as she was leaving.

"Don't worry about me," she smiled. "There was no way I was leaving until I knew you were alright." She turned down the lights, leaving one dim light shining to hold the total darkness back.

Christina still didn't know why she couldn't stand or urinate, but she, in her utter exhaustion, fell asleep, with Ethan in the clear, curved bassinet mounted on top of the stainless-steel cart next to the bed.

I sat on the couch in the room and dozed off, only to be jolted awake by the tiny cry of the little baby boy in the room.

Not knowing what to do, I jumped up, went to him, and picked Ethan up, cradling him in my arms and swaying back and forth, not wanting his cries to wake Christina.

As he settled down, I felt the burden of what this day brought drop onto my shoulders.

I knew that I would have to provide care, comfort, and support not only to my newborn son, but to my wife who would be healing from what her body had endured. While I battled the exhaustion so I could hold Ethan, I said to myself, "I do not know if I can do this." I began pleading with God to carry me through what lay ahead.

+ + +

Over the next several days, a series of tests and imaging revealed that during delivery, Christina had sprained her pubic symphysis and dislocated her sacroiliac joint. Both injuries are extremely rare. The medical team seemed as surprised by the complications as we were, and I began to wonder if this was the kind of care we should have expected or if something had gone wrong that no one wanted to discuss.

The very day Ethan and Christina were discharged, a social worker who was part of the process wanted to check our car to see if we had the car seat installed correctly before we went home. She wasn't going to approve the discharge if we couldn't transport Ethan safely.

"I don't have my car here. We didn't drive over," I tried to explain.

"You didn't walk here, so how are you going to get home?"

"We did walk here. We live right across the street."

"What?"

"We live at the corner of 6th and 13th."

"Oh, the little grey house?" she chuckled. I could see her mental adjustment—young parents who walked to the hospital weren't the usual demographic she encountered.

With me carrying Ethan and the small bag that we had brought with us, and Christina pushing her walker with a catheter strapped to her thigh, we walked across the street to our little home.

+ + +

I knew the moment I touched Ethan's back that everything I had been was gone. The physicality of that contact brought what had been distant promise into flesh and blood reality—this child was mine to protect, mine to love, mine to never abandon.

While Ethan was whole, the vacuum extractor had deformed his skull, and though it would heal within days, the child suffered now. As I held him during those times when Christina was too wounded to do so, I felt the weight of his entire future settling into my hands. Here was a soul that would never wonder if his father would come to his wedding. Here was a child who would never stand alone in a parking lot waiting for a man who had given his word and broken it.

But more than responsibility, I was seized by a love so fierce it felt like being torn open and remade. This small, wounded creature had called forth something from the deepest part of me—something I had thought was dead, killed by years of abandonment and broken promises. Yet here it was, burning in my chest like a fire that would consume everything false I had ever believed about myself.

I was no longer the boy whose father had failed him. I was Ethan's father, and that would mean everything.

CHAPTER EIGHTEEN

In some Augusts in Minnesota, the locusts begin their droning high in the trees, and the old-timers say this signals six more weeks until the first killing frost. Just south of the hospital, two blocks from our home, Hester Park with its ancient oaks and carefully tended grass would become the stage for the first locust calls. That August in 1997, the month Ethan was baptized, Hester Park was transformed into a living tapestry of orange and white as thousands of monarch butterflies descended upon the oaks like some biblical visitation. In the first days of their passage, clusters of hundreds fluttered among the branches, their wings alternating between the pale orange of their undersides and the deep orange, white, and black of their tops. By the weekend of Ethan's baptism, the oaks had disappeared beneath countless thousands of butterflies, the trees themselves seeming to pulse with wings and life.

On that Sunday morning, we stood before the congregation of Holy Cross and vowed that we would raise Ethan within the church community, place a Bible in his hands, teach him the Lord's Prayer, the Creed, and the Ten Commandments. We promised to nurture his faith and prayer life. Ethan was baptized and welcomed into the body of believers. After the ceremony, we gathered at our home in celebration.

Soon after the baptism, the monarchs vanished as suddenly as they had come. Since St. Cloud was not a natural waypoint in their ancient journey, the monarchs never returned to Hester Park. But for those few days, they had borne witness to something sacred—a child claimed by grace, surrounded by the congregation of the faithful and the wings of ten thousand pilgrims passing through.

+ + +

Sometime after the baptism, I called my mother. Soon after answering my call, she asked, "I know you said that you guys needed some time alone with the baby at first, but it's been almost two months. Can I come see him?"

"I'm not sure if that's a good idea."

"I want a relationship with my grandson," she insisted.

I didn't say anything about her relationship with me, but I did reply, "You are not going to have a relationship with my son, unless you have a relationship with his mother."

There was no response, and I continued, "And if we let you come, you have to quit smoking. You cannot even smell like cigarettes around him."

I repeated the two ultimatums, "If you want to see your grandson, you have to commit to starting a relationship with Christina, and you have to stop smoking. Can you do that?"

After a pause, she said, "I can."

"Just to be clear, it's your responsibility to reach out to Christina and start the relationship." After her agreement, I used frequent flyer miles and got her an airline ticket.

When I picked her up from the airport, I pretended that I could not smell the cigarette smoke that she was trying to mask with perfume. I also pretended that she was waiting to see Christina face-to-face before she initiated the relationship.

Right after we got into the house, my mother asked, "Where's the baby? I want to hold him!" She had not even greeted Christina.

When Christina brought Ethan in, I had my mother sit in a chair, because I did not trust her to safely hold my son. I watched my neglectful mother, cloaked in a veneer of concern, tightly clasp Ethan. Her hands were not gentle and caring.

It was as if she was driven by a greedy need to assert control rather than comfort, and she gripped Ethan too firmly. I could see the pressure she was exerting on the swaddling blanket. Ethan was a mellow baby that rarely fussed, and when he did cry it was easy to comfort him. Now it seemed he too felt the discomfort of her rigid embrace, and he began to cry a plaintive wail.

My mother made no effort to comfort Ethan.

I was struck by poignant picture of detachment, where my mother's self-serving intentions overshadowed the genuine needs of Ethan. It could have been a tender interaction, and I had hoped it would have been. "Comfort him," I said.

"I know how to take care of a baby," she said through gritted teeth.

"No, you don't," I replied as I took Ethan from her grasp.

He settled down as soon as I said, "I got you Ethan."

My mother was to stay with us for a week, but since I had taken so much time off to care for Christina and Ethan after the delivery, I had to work. On the first day of work, I left my mother with Christina and Ethan, hoping that maybe on that day she would speak to Christina, and they could work on their relationship. When I walked in the back door, Christina was ironing a tablecloth with Ethan in a basinet next to her.

I whispered, "Where is she?"

"I don't know. I haven't really seen her much."

"You guys didn't talk?"

"Nope." Hearing this, I set my things down and picked up Ethan.

We had invited some friends over, because we knew dinner would be awkward, and having them there would help reduce the awkwardness. Our friends would help keep my mother on her best behavior.

The next day when I drove home, I saw my mother walking along the sidewalk next to our house, smoking as she walked. Any hope of her making an effort to have a relationship with Christina and Ethan was gone. She had chosen cigarettes over her grandson, choosing her addiction over the small effort required to spend time with him safely.

When I took her to the airport, I asked her, "How come you didn't do what I asked you to?" She didn't say anything. "I thought you wanted to know your grandson?"

"I do."

"But you didn't make an effort." She sat in silence.

For a few years after that she would occasionally send Christmas and birthday presents of girls' clothing to Ethan.

Eventually she stopped contacting me.

+ + +

Christina and I had planned that Ethan would be our only child, and we played, and camped, and traveled together quite happily.

The three of us tried to learn how to be a little family. Our first road trip was to Red Lake, Ontario, where the pastor who had performed our wedding ceremony was living. Red Lake is almost due north of St. Cloud, and we decided that we would drive up for Easter to visit Steve, Sarah, his wife, and Katie, their young daughter.

Since we were preparing for our trip to where the highway ends and the wilderness starts, to a less populated, wilder place, Christina said, "We should take some formula with us. I don't know how expensive it will be that far north."

Because Christina was breastfeeding, I was shocked by her saying this. I asked, "What do you need formula for?"

"I'm not producing enough milk anymore."

"When did this start happening?"

"A couple of weeks ago. I noticed I wasn't getting as full," she explained, "And now Ethan is still hungry when I am empty."

Leaving St. Cloud and heading north, the landscape began to shed its domesticated skin, transforming from lakes and cultivated fields to something more ancient and untamed. As we reached the Canadian border, the wilderness opened before us like a vast, unwritten page.

The route carried us through the Canadian Shield, where the earth revealed its bones. The landscape was ruled by sweeping expanses of naked bedrock. The world became a patchwork of granite cliffs and dense boreal forests that had never known the plow. Each turn on that serpentine highway revealed new lakes carved deep into the stone, their waters black as obsidian and reflecting the endless sky.

It was as if we could sense the presence of the glaciers that had shaped these waters—ancient ice that had moved across the land with patient purpose, leaving behind this sculpted and beautiful country. The very air seemed to carry the memory of that slow craftsmanship, that deliberate shaping of the world into new forms.

We drove the nine hours north on Good Friday, celebrated Easter with our friends, and returned home Monday.

Just after Easter, Christina confronted me as I came in the door, Ethan in her arms. "I am pretty sure I am pregnant."

"I thought you produced hormones while you're breastfeeding that keeps you from getting pregnant," I said as I took Ethan from her, giving Christina her first break of the day.

"Well, you were wrong." She said flatly.

"So, I guess you need to go to the doctor, huh."

"I have an appointment next week. I already called."

When she came back from the doctor, I learned that the due date was in November and, based on her age and her first delivery experience, this was going to be treated as a high-risk pregnancy. Again, God had his own plans for us.

+ + +

The front door to our little house opened directly into the living room. There was no grand entry, just a small closet to the left and then the room itself. The walls of the house were painted white, and so was the trim.

Set into the left wall of the living room was a brick fireplace, with its soot-stained firebox covered by a metal screen, and its tools standing on the hearth. The wall directly opposite had chairs against it, with a doorway that led to the two bedrooms and the bathroom. In between the two chairs sat a small set of bookshelves.

When we found out that we were expecting, we began to stockpile children's books, and before long the bookcase was full of books.

As Ethan began to crawl, we encouraged him to go to the bookcase to grab books and look at them. Most afternoons, when I returned from work after my ninety-minute commute, I would find Ethan surrounded by open books on the floor. When he would notice me in the room with him, he would happily grab one of the books shake it at me, and say, "Daddo!"

That was his sign to me that he wanted me to read to him, and it was also my cue that I should take over responsibility for caring for him, so Christina could have a break which was well earned with her mothering a toddler while being pregnant. It didn't matter how tired or stressed I was from work, I was committed to being a dad, and I would happily take him in my lap to read.

At bedtime, after putting his pajamas on and placing him in his crib, I would say the Lord's Prayer out loud standing next to him and slip out of the room, resisting his playful pleas for me to stay and interact. Soon it wouldn't be just Ethan that I was reading to, playing with, and tucking in. I was going to have another child to care for.

+ + +

In the late autumn days of 1998, the air carried the sharp scent of dying leaves. The neighborhood had become a tapestry of crimson, burnt orange, and gold as the trees blazed their final defiance before winter claimed them. The sky stretched clear and blue as deep water, occasionally touched with white clouds that drifted like thoughts across its surface. The sun hung low, casting long shadows that bathed everything in amber light.

In the mornings, cold would settle into the hollows and corners, whispering of the winter that waited beyond the horizon. When we walked in the park above the Mississippi, the dry leaves would stir at our approach and crackle beneath our feet, marking our passage through those quiet afternoons when the world seemed to pause between seasons, waiting for what was to come.

Due to the high-risk pregnancy, Christina had frequent appointments with her doctor, and on those days, I would either come home early or work from home, so I could take care of Ethan. It was on one of those days, in the early afternoon of October 8th, as I was standing at the sink washing dishes, and Ethan was sitting in a pile of books, that Christina called me from the doctor's office.

"Hello," I answered the phone.

"I just had an exam, and I am going into labor."

"Really?" I asked. "It's too early."

"Yeah, I have to go to the hospital right now. I am going to drive to the ER, and you'll have to move the car later."

"Well, I'll bring Ethan over and check on you in a while."

In the late afternoon, I grabbed the backpack we used as a diaper bag, put it on, and hoisted Ethan up, and said, "Let's go see your mom." We walked across the street into the hospital lobby and went up to the information desk.

"We are looking for Ethan's mom, can you tell us her room number?" The woman at the desk looked it up and told us which elevator to use to get to the floor. Ethan and I would become extremely familiar with that elevator.

Christina's room was on the labor and delivery floor, so Ethan and I had to check in at a security desk before the guards would allow us to go onto the floor. They gave us bands that we had to place around our wrists to identify me as Ethan's father and as Christina's husband.

The room had beautifully polished linoleum floors that looked like a well-maintained 1960s artifact. There was a burgundy-colored couch against the far wall right against the window, and a wooden gliding rocker with a burgundy cushion tied to its seat, near the foot of the bed.

Christina lay in the bed with the head of the bed slightly raised. On a pole attached to the bed frame two IV bags hung, their transparent tubes dangling down, with one tube connected to the other a short way from the bags. The hand with the IV inserted into it lay on Christina's lap.

"Mommo!" Ethan exclaimed as he saw her.

"How ya doing?" I asked.

"Fine. I drove here as soon as I hung up the phone, and they rushed me upstairs," Christina explained. "I didn't even have to stop at the ER except to tell them why I was there. They already knew I was coming."

"So you'll just deliver the baby?"

"No. The IV has mag sulfate in it. It stops labor."

"Do you just have to get the dose of mag sulfate in and then you get to home?"

"I don't know, the doctor hasn't been here yet."

When the doctor came in to see her, he explained that Christina would stay in the hospital until they were confident that the baby could breathe on its own after delivery. There could have still been developmental problems involving the baby's eating on its own, but that was not as big of a concern as lung development.

"How long will the lung development take?" Christina asked.

"Based on the due date, it will be at least a week, and then after that we will have to do an amnio to check."

"So she'll be here at least a week, and maybe more," I confirmed.

"That's right," he said to Christina, "and once we discharge, you'll need to be on complete bedrest for the rest of the pregnancy."

Ethan and I went home where I fed him his supper, but since we lived so close, we went back to see Christina before it was Ethan's bedtime. We used that elevator that was shown to us when we first went; in all, we visited Christina four times that first day. Ethan and I would use that elevator nearly one hundred times before Christina would be discharged.

I made arrangements with work to take time off, and work in the evenings after Ethan's seven thirty bedtime, and Ethan and I spent our days together.

At that age Ethan was a good sleeper, and he would be quiet the night through. In the morning, as soon as I heard him babbling to himself in his room, I would go pick him up out of the crib. If he needed it, I'd change his diaper, and then put on the day's outfit. I'd give him his breakfast, and then we would head over to the hospital to see his mom.

We would visit, with Ethan's sometimes getting to watch Teletubbies in that rocker by himself, until lunch time and his nap. When Ethan awoke, we would make the trip back over, and stay until dinner time.

Before his bedtime, we would make one more trip. At bedtime, I'd change Ethan into his pajamas, read him a book, pray with him, and let him get to sleep. This was our father and son pattern for ten days.

On the eleventh day, I asked one of the youths from Christina's group at church to stay with Ethan for an hour, while I went with Christina to the hospital lab as she got the amnio test.

An ultrasound technician scanned Christina's womb, giving the doctor, and us, a clear view of the baby, as the doctor guided the needle into the sack containing the amniotic fluid.

The images showed a healthy baby, and after I had gone home and gotten Ethan to bring him to the hospital, we learned that the baby's lungs were fully developed. Christina was discharged the next day, and for the next few weeks, although she would be confined to our bed, she didn't go into labor again.

+ + +

The air had gone from crisp to chilly and the leaves had all fallen off the trees between the time Christina had gone to the hospital to November 6th, the day her cesarean section was scheduled. The doctor scheduled the C-section for her at thirty-seven weeks of pregnancy to minimize her chance of injury again during childbirth. Because of Christina's history of injuries and damage, a natural labor and delivery posed risks of re-injury and complications. He said thirty-seven weeks was the safest time for delivery.

By this point in the pregnancy, the baby would be mostly fully developed. The baby's overall growth and lungs would be mature enough to help avoid the complications that came with earlier preterm deliveries.

We arranged for the family of one of the girls in the youth group to take Ethan for the few days Christina and the new baby would be in the hospital, and on that cloudy and cold November day, we walked across the street to the hospital, and checked Christina in. It was about eleven in the morning when we got to the hospital room where she would be staying for the next few days.

"Christina, you'll need to get undressed and put on the gown that's on the bed," the nurse who met us said. "You can't have anything on under it, so you'll just be wearing the gown and nothing else."

To me she said, "Dad, you need to put on the scrubs I put on the couch. You can leave your underwear on," she explained. "You'll put your shoes back on and slip those covers over you shoes."

When the nurse stepped out, Christina began to change in the room, and I went into the bathroom to change in case someone on staff came in. We sat on the edge of the bed looking out the window of the room at the leaden grey clouds that seemed to be dropping lower toward the trees. "Are you nervous," I asked Christina.

"A little. Not like last time."

"Yeah, it's not as scary this time, is it?" I offered, "I like being Ethan's dad . . . so another son or daughter will be good."

"I wonder how Ethan's doing," Christina said.

I smiled and said, "Funny it's only been a couple hours and we miss him. I can't wait to meet his brother or sister though."

"Just a couple of hours."

The nurse came back in and explained what was going to happen. She said that the surgery would start at one p.m., and they would take Christina into the operating room at about noon and do some preparation. I would be waiting in the hospital room until twelve forty-five when someone from the surgery team would come get me.

The procedure would only take twenty minutes, and after the birth, we would all be brought back to the room. "We'll be back to get you in a few minutes Christina," she said as she left.

They came in with a gurney and helped Christina on it. I gave her hand a squeeze and said, "See you in few minutes." I was left in the room by myself, and I was just nervous enough that I didn't really know what to do with myself. So, I paced around the room throwing alternating glances out the window on the leafless treetops and the slowly moving clock on the wall.

Rather than reciting memorized words, I asked God to keep Christina and the child safe, and I asked Him to continue giving me strength and to help me be the father this child deserved. My prayers were simple and unpolished. They were awkward, like those of someone who had been taught to pray but never learned to speak to God as if He were listening.

I was watching the minute hand climb from the tick mark below toward the "9" when the nurse entered.

"You ready, Dad?" she asked.

I paused just a moment, "Yep, I'm ready."

As we walked down the hall toward the operating room, this tiny woman said to me, "I'm going to be standing next to you for a few minutes as the surgery starts, to make sure you don't fall toward the operating table if you faint."

I fought the urge to say something clever, but the thought of this tiny person supporting my six-foot two frame amused me. I controlled myself and just said, "Okay."

I felt the cold air from the operating room hit my face and hands as we walked in. Christina was on the operating table in the center of the room, with her arms strapped to braces that stuck out roughly ninety degrees from the table. Draped in blue cloth, she had a curtain just below her chin that blocked her face from the surgical area. By her head there was an array of medical equipment: monitors, IV's, oxygen masks, and tubing.

"Hi. Are you ready?" I asked.

"I guess so."

The anesthesiologist came in and took her place next to me. I thought it strange that she was the last person to come into the room immediately as the surgery was to begin. I was on the left side of Christina's head, a little stool behind me that I was supposed to sit in if I felt faint, and the anesthesiologist directly centered on Christina.

The doctor first told the anesthesiologist to begin to administer the spinal anesthesia to Christina; then he removed the small surgical drape from Christina, which exposed her swollen belly and began swabbing her belly with antiseptic.

"I can feel that," Christina said quietly.

I looked at the anesthesiologist who was not paying attention to Christina, but I didn't say anything because I thought it would take more time for the anesthesia to start working. The nurse who had escorted me in was still standing at my side, positioned to catch me if I fainted. Meanwhile, the doctor took up his scalpel and started the incision on Christina's belly.

"Ouch, ouch! I can feel that," Christina said whimpering.

I said mildly, "She can feel that," looking directly at the anesthesiologist, but she showed no signs of hearing Christina nor me.

As the doctor continued to cut her belly, Christina again, cried out louder, "I can feel that!"

This time I said forcefully, "Dr. Thompson, she can feel you cutting her."

As he finished the initial incision, he paused and told the nurse to unstrap Christina's right arm. "Point to where you feel it." Christina pointed directly at the start of the incision.

In a firm clear voice the doctor said, "She's feeling the incision. Increase the anesthesia!" As if waking up from a trance, the anesthesiologist made some adjustments to equipment that I could not see, and acknowledged that she had done as she was directed. They strapped Christina's arm down again, and the doctor continued his incisions.

The little nurse asked, "How are you doing, Dad?"

"I'm fine," I replied not looking away from the surgery.

She pushed the little stool out of the way and said, "You're feeling alright? I can leave you alone, and you won't get lightheaded?"

"Really, this doesn't bother me."

She stepped away to perform some other task in the operating room, as I watched the doctor continue the cesarean section. To the nurses, the doctor said, "I am through the abdominal wall. I am about to incise the uterine wall."

To Christina he said, "You are going to feel a tugging as I lift the baby out, so be ready for that." To the operating room he said, "Get ready for the delivery."

After his final incision, I saw him reach in to where he had been cutting. From my angle, I couldn't see what his hands were doing, but he must have been positioning them underneath the baby.

The next moment, he lifted our baby's head out, followed by the whole body. There was no sound except the medical equipment near Christina's head, the people, and the baby, were perfectly silent. The doctor handed the baby to a nurse who had a towel over her hands. Then the baby cried, and I let out the breath I had been holding.

The nurse said, "It's a little boy. Time of birth is two oh four pm." She whisked Ezra over to a high table that had a heating element above it set him down in the little tray on the table and performed an examination.

The doctor began stitching Christina up, and as he did so the anesthesiologist was unhooking the equipment from Christina. "Dr. Johnson, I want to see you before you leave," he stated.

As he was finishing with Christina, the nurse said, "Dad, do you want to help wash Baby?"

I made my way to the heated table and placed my hand on Ezra. "Hey, little guy. Good to see you." I worked the soap into the washcloth and cleaned my son.

This time I felt none of the crushing weight of responsibility I had carried with our firstborn, and no dread seized me. I was prepared and joyful to have another son. When she told us that Ezra weighed eight pounds four ounces, I could not help but wonder how large he would have grown if he had remained until full term.

Other than the surgery and the pain from faulty anesthesia, Christina had not endured nearly the trauma of Ethan's delivery. By late afternoon, we called for the family watching Ethan to bring him so he could meet his brother.

Though Ethan was only sixteen months old, he seemed to comprehend that someone new had joined our ranks. As the family took Ethan to their home for the evening, we looked through the window to see snow beginning to fall—not the harsh, driving snow of winter storms, but gentle flakes that settled like blessings on the world below. The snow covered everything in its mantle of unmarked white, transforming the familiar landscape into something new and clean.

Outside, the world was being made fresh. Inside, our family had grown larger, and I felt the quiet satisfaction of a man who had built something that would endure the seasons to come.

CHAPTER NINETEEN

The first few years of Ethan's and Ezra's lives were spent in that small house on the corner across from the hospital. That 900-square-foot Cape Cod was finer than any dwelling I had ever inhabited, but it possessed small flaws that grew large in my mind.

In the brutal winter, cold would seep inside, with icy drafts threading through every gap around the windows and doors. The radiator labored and barely held back the bone-deep cold. We wrapped ourselves in layers while the house groaned and settled and trembled under winter's grip.

In the oppressive summer, heat would transform the interior into a suffocating furnace, especially the upper floor. Being inside felt like being sealed in a hot, humid tomb. The air hung thick and motionless, scarcely stirred by the fans we had positioned throughout the rooms. But even with its failings, it was a pleasant, modest home.

As I advanced in my career, I began to hunger for a finer house in a neighborhood without hospital traffic. And I wanted a house that had central air conditioning.

In 2001, when Ethan was past three and Ezra past two years old, Christina and I purchased a house in a new development in Saint Cloud called Kensington Gardens.

The house at 1123 Somerset Boulevard rose two stories and contained four bedrooms. The exterior resembled an old yellow farmhouse, with a wraparound front porch supported by white balusters and posts. The builder had planted three mature trees in the front yard, giving the house the appearance of having stood there longer than it had.

The first floor contained a living room with pocket French doors, an open design connecting the kitchen, dining room, and family room. The second floor held three large bedrooms, a full bathroom, and a master bedroom with its own bath. The house possessed a full basement and a two-stall garage.

The builder took such pride in his work that he promised if we ever heard the floor or stairs creak, he would repair it without charge.

When the keys were placed in my hand, they struck my palm with weight that seemed disproportionate to their size. I stood at the threshold, each key carrying the burden of unearned good fortune, whispering accusations about the luxury I did not merit.

Here I was, a child who had slept on infested floors and been forsaken by his own blood, holding keys to a four-bedroom house with mature trees and a wraparound porch. The contrast felt like some cosmic jest—as if I were wearing clothes that belonged to another man's life.

The welcoming porch beneath my feet, the solid door before me, and the mature trees at my back stood as silent witnesses, questioning my right to claim such comfort. We settled in with our modest possessions, placing the boys in one bedroom, my office in another, Christina and me in the master bedroom, and leaving one room empty—an extravagance that felt almost sinful. It was more than I had ever dared imagine I deserved.

+ + +

My office was at the left side of the upstairs across the hall from the master bedroom. The spare room and the boys' shared bedroom were at the opposite end of the hall. I had a huge horseshoe of a blonde oak desk that I had inherited from a remote worker at my company who had left.

I would have never chosen the desk, but it was large and functional, and I had to discipline myself to tidy it every day before stopping for the day. I had reduced the amount of travel I did for work, and most days I would sit behind that desk after lunch working on some project or another, as Ezra would be napping in his room, Ethan having given up napping long before.

When I heard Ezra fussing after waking up from his nap, I would climb out from behind the desk, quietly walk down the carpeted hallway, and open the door to the bedroom. Ezra wouldn't be fully awake, so I would gently pick him up, small, heavy-eyed, and drowsy, his arms loosely hanging by his sides. His head would tilt towards me as I lifted him, and I would help him find a soft spot on my shoulder. He would curl up a little, and his tiny hands would sometimes grip my shirt. His soft breaths would become rhythmic against my neck.

This was when I felt most like myself—not the corporate director climbing ladders, not the kid who never had a real home, just a father holding his son.

The weight of him against my shoulder, the trust in his small body as he settled into sleep, was like an anchor to something I had never known I was searching for. In those quiet moments, with his breath warm against my neck, I understood that everything before this had been preparation.

I would carry him back to my office, sit back in my office chair, and steady him with one hand as I typed with the other. Eventually he would wake up fully, and I would take him downstairs so he could do the things toddlers do, while I finished work.

Before Ethan and Ezra came into my life, my plan was to fast burn up the software corporate ladder. I had had a series of rapid promotions, and within three years of taking my first role in a software company I had been promoted to a director level position, and my ambition was to parlay that success to an even more senior level role when the time was right. I had had dreams of catching the dot-com wave, but Ethan and Ezra were more important to me than wild success and money.

+ + +

For Ethan's fourth birthday, I started digging a square hole in the backyard roughly eight inches deep and eight feet on each side. Since the days were as long as they would be in the summer, and the sky would still be light for two hours after the boys went to bed, I worked as they slept.

I built a wooden frame that slipped down into the square hole, and put on a flat, plank border that rested on the ground that served as decking. Ethan knew a hole had appeared in our yard, but I didn't tell him where it came from, and he never saw me digging it.

I had calculated the volume needed to fill the hole back in, and in the course of a few days, I bought bags full of sand from Home Depot.

On July 3rd, after the boys had been put to bed, I moved two tons of sand from in front of our house to the back and filled up that hole.

In the morning, Christina decorated the edge, and when Ethan got up, we gave him his present of a sand box. He was in his pajamas at the time, but he scurried inside to change clothes so he could put some cars and trucks in the sand to play with. In the afternoon, we had friends over to celebrate his birthday.

On the picnic table in the back yard under the trees, as a center piece, we had bought Fourth of July themed helium balloons and some flowers. After a meal and cake and ice cream, the party began winding down, and we cleared the table.

Ethan asked, "Can I have the balloon?" Since it had a weight tied to the bottom of the nylon ribbon that was attached to the red, white, and blue mylar balloon, I consented, thinking it wouldn't fly off.

As I came back out of the house, after making a trip to help clear the table, I saw Ethan raising and lowering his arm to make the balloon bounce. I watched as he lifted his arm and dropped the balloon, the weighted packet bringing the balloon down fast enough that it hit the ground harder than I would have expected.

I saw him pick the balloon up and drop it again. The bag that held the weights broke, and the metal washers that had been used as ballast spilled out.

Predictably, the balloon shot up into the air, and Ethan screamed as he watched it soar up through the break in the trees.

I rushed over to him, saying, "It's okay, Buddy. There'll be other balloons," but he was not so easily consoled.

The next year when we talked about his birthday, Ethan firmly declared, "No balloons!"

+ + +

Christina and I took to calling Ethan and Ezra "The Boys" collectively. Those early years of their childhood felt like something precious I was responsible for protecting—a childhood I wanted to be everything mine wasn't.

It was easy to imagine their first few years of their childhood as a journey through a storybook forest, where wonder was a path to follow, and just around every turn on the path was adventure—and Christina and I were the Boys' guides.

Those years were filled with vignettes, like old photos spread out on a table. The sun setting, spreading its pink and violet streaks across the indigo sky, behind the towering hardwoods in the state park while camping.

The small fire popping and crackling as its orange flames danced above the glowing embers. The sudden explosion of fireflies in the brush that surrounded our campsite.

Catching a firefly in my cupped hands, opening my hands inches in front of Ezra's face, and the firefly lighting up as if on cue, to bathe his face in a green glow, his eyes wide at the sight.

The Boys scrubbed and groomed and dressed in their Sunday best to go to Orchestra Hall in Minneapolis for the Young People's matinee.

The cavernous hall with its misshaped cubes jutting from the ceiling and back walls. The stage full of black clad musicians sitting in the orchestra.

Ethan and Ezra leaning forward, eyes wide, enrapt by the resonance, the drama, the shimmer of the symphony. The Italian meals served family style at the restaurant on the way home in the late afternoon.

The quiet calm of the Montessori classroom. The low shelves of instructional tools. The counting beads. The number rods. The binomial cubes. Sitting with Ethan as he prepared himself a snack, ate it, and washed his dishes, confidently and proudly.

The conferences with their teacher who let us know, that Ethan would need extra attention in the future so he wouldn't get bored in school and Ezra should be evaluated as soon as possible because in her thirty years she had never seen a child like him.

The chatter before their first piano recitals. The Boys the youngest performers on the program. The boost they had to give themselves to get up on to the piano bench. Their legs dangling down and swinging to the rhythm as they played their short pieces.

The grins as they acknowledge the applause and slid down off the piano bench.

The musical note shaped sugar cookies after all the students had performed.

The bedtime routine of changing into pajamas, even if the sun was still up on those long summer days in the North.

The reading from the Little House on the Prairie books while the boys lay in their beds.

The practicing of the Lord's Prayer and praying out loud, grateful for the chance to give them what I had never had—the security of knowing they were loved.

Ethan saying "Tuck me up!" instead of "Tuck me in," still coming to terms with the subtleties of grammar. Kissing their foreheads and gently shutting the door on the way out.

That was a time that Christina and I tried to gently lay the foundation for what we hoped would become their character.

We wanted them to be ready for the adventures that awaited just beyond the storybook forest.

I wanted them to be prepared even for those adventures that in my experience had been cruel and terrifying.

While I did whatever I could as a father to try to protect them, there would come a time when I wasn't around and life would throw a challenge at them, and they needed to be ready for that.

+ + +

The winter of 2002 brought with it upwards of sixty inches of snow to St. Cloud. The year before had brought heavy snow as well, enough that I had bought a snowblower, so that I wouldn't have to spend nearly every other day shoveling out our driveway.

That year, as I ran the snowblower down the sidewalk and over the driveway, I made sure that the snow was thrown into one large pile in the center of the front yard.

Before the sun was up, I would guide the auger along the concrete, gathering up the newly fallen snow, carefully turning the directional crank to point the chute at the pile as the showers of lumps and chunks of snow fountained out and fell in an ever-growing mound.

After each snow blowing session, I took a broad, grain shovel that I used to move large amounts of snow that the blower couldn't reach, and I hammered the pile of snow compacting it and making it firm.

It was just a few weeks into the snow season, and the pile was taller than I was. I used the shovel to carve stairs at the back of the firm pile of snow, and on the opposite side I carefully sloped and smoothed the face of the mound. When I had finished, we had a small sledding hill in our front yard.

On those short, intensely cold Minnesota winter days, Christina and I would help the Boys get their sled to the top of the hill and watch as they slid downhill tumbling to a stop at the bottom of the tiny hill more often than not.

When the boys were too cold to slide and tumble anymore, we would put the sled away in the garage and trundle into the warmth of the house.

The living room had a gas fireplace, and somehow a fire appearing in it without any effort, just the flip of a switch, always felt like cheating. Most of those cold days were followed by one of the boys and their mom standing in front of the fireplace, their backs turned to the flames, their hands behind their bottoms, warming up.

I would often describe Ethan as an "interesting" kid to others, because I didn't have the words to give justice to what type of boy he was.

Christina and I would often say he was an old soul in a little boy's body. He was strikingly different from other kids. He had little time for play, wanting serious, adult work to do.

We started jokingly calling him Earnie because he was so earnest about work. In addition, he had no time for fiction. In his world everything was concrete, so much so that fictional characters suffering or dying caused him grief.

The day I unceremoniously flushed the dead pet fish we had kept in a little fishbowl, Ethan wailed as I pressed the toilet handle, "We should have celebrated the good life he had!" I was astounded to hear this from a four-year-old.

On one of those bitter winter days, after playing outside in the killing cold, I sat in the living room chair while Ezra played elsewhere. Ethan stood beside his mother as they warmed themselves by the heat.

Without warning or preface, Ethan looked up at Christina and announced, "I am going to die young." I could see he was serious—he was always serious about the things that mattered—and I suppressed the urge to laugh, not wanting to wound him with my disbelief.

Christina asked, "Really? About how old?"

"Nineteen," came his certain reply.

The certainty in his voice struck me like a physical blow. Here was this four-year-old child, solemn as a prophet, speaking of death with the same matter-of-fact tone he used for trucks or dinosaurs. But this was different. This carried weight that pressed against my chest until I could barely breathe.

I felt the desperate need to correct him, to flood him with reassurances, to insist that children live long lives filled with graduation days and weddings and children of their own. But something ancient and terrible held my tongue. Perhaps it was the knowledge carved into me by my own childhood—that sometimes the world breaks its promises to the young, that sometimes children are asked to bear what should never be theirs to carry.

The room grew silent except for the furnace's labored breathing. Outside, the wind drove snow against the windows like thrown sand, and I felt winter settle into my bones in a way that had nothing to do with temperature.

Christina and I exchanged no words about his prophecy. I filed his statement away, but not in the same place where I had stored his declaration about becoming a FedEx pilot. This one went somewhere deeper, somewhere dark, where it would wait and grow cold and patient as the winter that surrounded our warm house.

Even then, some part of me knew that this child who spoke so simply of dying had seen something the rest of us had not. And I was powerless to unsee it.

CHAPTER TWENTY

By the fall of 2002, I had begun to feel as though we were inhabiting someone else's existence, and I was desperate to make it ours. In 2003, Christina and I started contemplating a new setting for our family. Though our yellow house on Somerset Boulevard possessed its charm, with its brass fixtures and red oak woodwork, it never felt like home. The country aesthetic, once appealing, had begun to feel like a costume we could not remove.

Beyond that, we began thinking about the boys' future—though we could not know how brief that future would be. We spoke of a large backyard, a yard I had never possessed except in dreams. In my mind, such a place would hold endless possibilities, adventures that would stretch through years of growing up. It would be a sanctuary from the chaos of the world where I had been raised, a place where my sons could build the childhood I had never known.

In time, our conversations became a deliberate search for the proper piece of land. One drive beyond town led us past a billboard advertising Waters Edge, a new development in the small town of Avon. With its eight quiet lakes and a population just over a thousand, Avon offered the promise of community, nature, and the chance to dwell beside water.

We purchased a lot and worked with a builder to design what we believed would be our forever home at 902 Waters Edge Circle. As construction began, so did what we thought was the foundation for our family's future. This house, set on the shore of Lake Ochotto, would become the stage for a brief but luminous chapter—the boys' laughter echoing across water that would remember them long after we were gone.

+ + +

That yard was a half-acre bounded by the lake, holding two distinct worlds within its borders—one wild, one tamed. Closest to the water, the lot had been restored to prairie, with native grasses and wildflowers that bent in the wind, tall goldenrod and purple coneflowers creating a tapestry of color that would outlast whatever human claims we made upon it.

We could look from the house onto the small prairie with its soft whispers and earthy scents, a picture of nature's stubborn beauty blending with the wild shoreline. Closer to the house, the lot spread in an expanse of emerald grass, manicured and thick, offering smooth carpet that invited games and laughter—though we could not know how many seasons that laughter would echo there.

The lake lay down a short bluff below our property, reflecting the changing sky and the sunsets that would continue long after we ceased to witness them.

Our backyard became what we believed was our sanctuary, where grass met prairie and prairie met lake in what seemed a seamless promise of permanence. In that space, we thought the water and the gold and purple of the prairie and the emerald grass had come together to create the perfect place for nurturing our dreams.

We imagined ourselves like that prairie grass, sending down deep roots to anchor firmly and flourish even in harsh conditions. We embedded ourselves in that house and yard, believing we could grow and thrive with resilience and grace. Like the prairie itself, we were determined to weather any storm and bloom where we were planted.

But prairie grass knows something houses do not—that the deepest roots cannot always hold against the storms that matter most.

+ + +

By the time we moved to Avon, I had a list of things in my mind that my sons should know how to do by the time they were adults.

The list was long, and I made sure the boys knew how to sort and wash their clothes, how to iron a shirt, how to tie a tie, how to drive a manual transmission, and on and on.

One of the things on the list that we worked on early was how to catch and throw a baseball. Ezra took to it begrudgingly. He was a good sport about it, but he never really grew to like it.

Ethan, on the other hand, reveled in every catch and throw. He would lose himself in the rhythm of a game of catch. While Ezra was content to participate out of duty, Ethan embraced every opportunity to play catch.

For a summer or two we had the boys try to play little league baseball, but it wasn't a fit for either of them. Not surprisingly, Ezra simply wasn't interested; Ethan lacked the gifts of the athlete. He had suffered static encephalopathy during delivery, and while it wasn't debilitating, it impacted his strength and coordination, but he grew to love baseball.

Even though, as he grew, Ethan still insisted he was going to be a pilot and became obsessed with airplanes and flight, he allowed a passion for baseball to creep into his world.

Starting in February, with the first Spring Training games, Ethan would drag out the portable radio and start listening to every game the Minnesota Twins played. "The Twins are playing the Tigers, Dad," he would say, "Scotty Baker is starting tonight."

He would turn the pregame show on and listen to Cory Provus and Dan Gladden talk about the teams, the players, and the game that was going to be played. He would go over to the cabinet where he would hang his coat in and store his baseball mitt in. As he walked past the cabinet that held my things, he'd grab my mitt.

"Wanna play catch?" he'd ask.

I knew that he would be asking that question, because, as long as it wasn't raining, he asked it every time the Twins played.

"Yeah, sure. Let me finish this real quick, and I'll be right out," was my reply.

In the golden glow of those summer evenings, with the bugs and the birds flitting around, he would go to that big back yard, with the cool, lush, green grass, and toss the ball high into the air underhanded and catch it as it came down.

He usually wouldn't have to wait long before I had my shoes on and headed outside, breathing in the smells of damp, freshly cut grass. When he was younger, the tosses back and forth would be gentle, and there were often dropped catches, but as he matured, he got taller and stronger. With all the practice throwing every summer, listening to the 150 games the Twins played, Ethan's throwing got faster and more accurate.

More importantly, each throw he made to me and each throw I returned to him was a connection between the two of us, and we threw thousands and thousands of times those summers.

+ + +

Ethan took things seriously. Beyond his being earnest about things he set out to do, he had no room for fiction or irony. This inability to separate reality from fiction, played out as the drama in *Monsters, Inc*, spilled into the theater when Ethan screamed, "Noooo!" embarrassingly loud as the characters Mike and Sully, who are in a panic to hide the fact that Boo is with them, flush her toys down the toilet. *The SpongeBob SquarePants Movie* set him to crying as he watched SpongeBob and Patrick drying up out of water; he thought they were dying.

On one of our visits to the library, he picked out a series of books about a fictional scouting organization called Pee Wee Scouts. He became enamored with the idea of the friendships and adventures in the books, and he decided he would join the Avon Cub Scout pack.

He took to it with the zeal of a new convert. When it came time to sell popcorn as a fund raiser, he set his sights on earning a pocketknife. He went door-to-door in our neighborhood, took his sales sheet to church, and contacted everyone we knew in the area. He easily earned the pocketknife.

His experience with the pack was not as positive as the fund raising. St. Cloud State University, where I had gone to graduate school, was hosting an open house at their planetarium, and the pack leader had arranged for the pack to attend.

Since I knew the campus, and none of the other parents did, they asked if I would drive and lead the way. As we met at Avon Elementary School to load up into the cars, the boys whose parents were not driving began to argue about having to ride with Ethan. The cruelty of their words hit me like a physical blow.

"I'm not riding with that freak!" one stated.

"Nah, I don't want to sit near that weirdo!" said another.

I could feel my temples tighten in rage, but I kept myself calm. The pack leader stood nearby, hearing every word, but said nothing. He just looked uncomfortable and started dividing the boys into different cars.

No correction, no teaching moment about kindness, no consequences for the cruelty. Just accommodation of their meanness.

I wondered as Ethan kept wanting to be a part of this group, but I knew why. He wanted to belong somewhere, to be accepted, to have the friendships he read about in those Pee Wee Scout books. Eventually, he did become disillusioned with the Cub Scouts and quit.

The library didn't have all of the Pee Wee Scouts books, so we occasionally bought one for Ethan. One day, he announced, "We can get rid of these books."

"Oh, why is that, Buddy?"

"Because they aren't real."

Not long after that, Ethan found he liked James Heriot's All Creatures Great and Small series of books, because they weren't fiction.

He lived in a very real, concrete world.

+ + +

We knew Ezra was a smart kid with a voracious appetite for learning. I should have realized, based on my own experience, how miserable at school he would be.

By the time he was five years old, he could read and write at a second-grade level, so having worked with the staff, we enrolled him in second grade, skipping first.

There was no gifted program at the school, so I volunteered twice a week to help the students who were ahead in their reading. I would meet with Ezra and three other students from his class in the hallway where we would read poems by Emily Dickinson, Robert Frost, and William Carlos Williams and fiction by Roald Dahl, Madeleine L'Engle, and J.R.R. Tolkien.

And I would walk them through structure, metaphor and simile, alliteration, symbolism. I would do the same for Ethan's class, and the school appreciated that someone with a master's degree would spend time with the students.

One day having finished working with Ethan's class, I walked past Ezra's classroom. Peering in, I saw Ezra sitting at his desk staring at the wall with a sad look on his face as the rest of the students diligently worked on an assignment.

Pictured in his look was the feeling I had had when I was his age. Soon after this, Christina and I had a meeting with his teacher, a woman who supported the idea of gifted education but whose hands were tied.

"Ezra is upset with school," she began.

Having seen him at his desk, I had expected that she would say something. "What makes you say that?" I responded.

"Well, the other day, I saw him hanging around his locker when the other kids had already shut theirs," she explained, "I walked over to him, and I noticed his locker was messy and had some old lunch bags in it. I said to him, 'If you don't keep your locker clean, it'll attract mice.' And he said, 'I don't care if mice infest this place, and they have to burn it down.'"

"Oh, no," Christina said.

I had thought he was unhappy in school, but I had no idea how miserable he was.

At this time, Christina and I started having conversations about the boys' education. The bullying of Ethan had not stopped, even with repeated conversations with the bullies' parents, and an unchallenged Ezra was now so miserable he wanted the school to burn down. We pulled the boys out of Avon Elementary School and enrolled them in an online public school.

Now, Ezra could set his own pace in his coursework, and Ethan found a safe place, free from bullying. The living room with the wood burning stove set in to the stone fireplace became their classroom, and they thrived.

Ethan excelled at math and flew through the assignments. He quickly outpaced my math knowledge, and while he enjoyed baseball, his true love remained airplanes. He saw every school research project as an opportunity to explore his passion.

Whenever he received a new assignment, his eyes would light up, and he'd immediately begin transforming it into an aeronautical adventure. History projects morphed into detailed accounts of the Wright brothers' first flight; science reports delved into the mechanics of jet engines; geography assignments mapped out famous flight routes across the globe.

Ezra's interests were capricious. Subjects would catch his fancy, and he would dive in until he mastered them.

He was like an explorer charting unknown territories. Each subject he encountered became his world, capturing his undivided attention. He would immerse himself completely, mastering every detail with relentless focus.

Once he had conquered a topic, he would leave it behind like a well-worn map, ready to embark on his next intellectual adventure.

Two subjects he stuck with however, Latin and music. By the time he was twelve, he had finished high school Latin, and the school arranged for advanced coursework, and in the same time period he had published his first CD of music.

+ + +

In those years the Minnesota Twins were not a great team. They had winning seasons, but if they made it into the playoffs, they would usually be eliminated quickly. By late September, the days would get shorter, leaving little time to play catch in the backyard after school as the sky transformed into hues of deep purples and soft pinks, fading into dusky blues as the night approached.

The crisp air would start to carry the scent of fallen leaves and wood smoke, hinting at the colder days ahead. The trees, dressed in bright reds, oranges, and yellows, would rustle softly in the breeze. Lake Ochotto beyond our backyard would reflect the twilight hues, its surface rippling gently. As darkness fell, the stars would begin to twinkle brightly in the clear, cool sky.

As the season of the year changed, so did our backyard activity. We would go from Ethan and I playing catch, while Ezra read and Christina cared for her garden, to the four of us huddled around the flames and warmth from our fire pit.

Our Friday routine became one of finishing supper, clearing the dishes, and rushing the patio of the back yard to build the bonfire, so we could watch the logs pop and crackle releasing their sparks while we listen to the Albany Huskies high school football team play their games.

As the boys grew up and could take some of the household workload off their mom, I started to travel more for work. I would plan most of my meetings, so I would be home by Friday because I didn't want to interrupt our routine.

At that time, I was flying to New York City mostly, and air travel in and out of the city could be unpredictable. One week, I was notified on a Thursday that my flight that day was canceled. The airline informed me that they had rebooked my flight, but I wouldn't be able to leave until Sunday.

When Ethan found out, he started doing research on airports around New York, looking for a way for me to get home.

"Dad, I think you can get out from White Plains. It's not that far from the city."

"I tried that, but Northwest says the flights are all sold out."

"How about ISP out on Long Island? You could fly Southwest."

"Southwest doesn't fly to Minneapolis, Buddy."

"Could you get to Boston and fly from there?"

"I don't think so, Ethan. I'd have to buy a new ticket, and the company won't do that. It's cheaper for me to stay at a hotel for a couple days."

I could hear the disappointment in his voice when he replied, "Oh, so you aren't going be able to get back, huh?"

"Not until Sunday."

It crushed me having to disappoint him.

+ + +

Although we were a close family in that vast backyard, my past clung to me like smoke. There was a voice in my head that would not be silenced, whispering that I was not good enough, had never been good enough, would never be good enough. When I read about leaders in the software industry, that voice would hiss in my ear, "You could have been so much more. If only . . ."

When we met with the counselor who advised us on Ezra's developmental needs, the words tore themselves from my throat: "I don't want Ezra to end up like me."

She paused, looked directly into my eyes and said, "Mike, you are not a failure."

I had never spoken those words to her, but somehow she had seen into the darkness I carried. Beyond the certainty of my failure, I wrestled with the crushing guilt of providing Ethan and Ezra with the life I had never known—the life I was certain I had stolen from someone more deserving.

The voice would come in quiet moments: "Who do you think you are? You don't deserve this happiness. You don't deserve these children. You are still that boy sleeping on dirty floors, and no amount of success can wash that stain away."

Often when I sat in the church pew on Sunday, I would pray desperately, "How did I get here? How did someone like me become father to these perfect boys?" The questions felt like accusations I leveled at myself, at God, at the unfairness of a world where the abandoned could somehow end up blessed.

The bitter irony consumed me—I would sit there listening to sermons about God's unmerited love and grace while simultaneously rejecting the very possibility that such grace could extend to someone like me. I could believe it for everyone else, but not for the boy who had never been wanted, never been chosen, never been enough.

CHAPTER TWENTY-ONE

In 2008, on a cold January day, while we were sitting by the wood burning stove in the living room, the wind blew the newly fallen snow across the backyard, dropping in drifts against the landscaping. While looking out at the grey, leaden sky, I told the boys, "Some night, when it's twenty below, we're going to sleep out in the tent."

Ezra didn't lift his head from his book and didn't respond.

Ethan said, "When are we going to do it?"

"I don't think we're ready this year," I said, "but next January if there is enough snow, we'll do it."

The announcement hung in the winter air like a challenge. We'd been camping together since the boys were toddlers, like the trip to the Boundary Waters where we'd paddled through Minnesota's Arrowhead region, that rugged wilderness of pristine lakes connected by meandering rivers and narrow portage trails.

In the Boundary Waters, no motors, no radios, no lights intruded. The deeper we went, the further we were from the world that provided so many safety nets. As we glided silently through waters that mirrored the deep blue sky, the only sounds were wind, the splash of fish breaking the surface, and the dipping of paddles.

When dusk came in the wilderness, we'd climb into the tent early to escape the mosquitos, listening to the gentle rustle of leaves and the distant hoot of an owl—and on one magical night, the howling of timber wolves. The boys had been camping since they were small, but the isolation and self-reliance still challenged them. We went to the wilderness not only for beauty and serenity, but to push Ethan and Ezra out of their comfort zone, to help build their resilience.

But winter camping would be different. Dangerous in ways that summer never was.

While it was intentional to give Ethan and Ezra opportunities I never had growing up, I knew that a life without challenges would be detrimental to their development. Both boys found academics almost too easy, got good grades without much effort. Ezra could pick up any instrument and play it well. Compared to many families in Avon, we were well off—they never had to worry about a roof over their heads or where their next meal would come from.

I worried that without obstacles, they'd find themselves unprepared when they faced their first real adversities as adults. Growing up under constant stress and difficulty, I'd watched the kids who had the life I dreamed of having—the rich kids, I used to call them—and they seemed to have the least empathy for others. I wanted Ethan and Ezra to care about others while developing strength, confidence, and compassion. Challenges would coax out these qualities. Each small victory would boost their confidence and develop belief in their abilities.

Sometimes I decided we would jointly do something physically difficult with a sense of danger to it, without ever putting them in real danger. When they questioned me, I would say, "Life is dangerous. Get used to it." Tent camping in twenty degrees below zero Fahrenheit presented dangers, but we would prepare for and face them together.

+ + +

As December 2008 unfolded, the days grew shorter with the inevitability of winter's advance. The sun would rise reluctantly, washing the sky with pale colors before climbing into a dome that never escaped its gray shroud. By mid-afternoon, the light would begin its retreat, casting long shadows across the snow-covered earth. Streetlights would come alive at the front of our home, their warm glow caught in the ice, and houses would bloom with Christmas decorations, their colored lights defiant against the encroaching darkness.

Our church tradition included Wednesday evening Advent worship services, and we'd light our own wreath at home every evening during our daily devotions. While we prepared for Christmas, the snow piled up in our backyard. December 2008 was one of the snowiest on record in Avon, with over twenty inches measured.

After Christmas, we started paying attention to the snow that had drifted into the middle of the open space where we spent summer hours playing catch.

"Boys, I think this is it. This January is when we are going to do it," I announced one morning as we sat at the kitchen counter that served as a breakfast bar.

Ezra asked, "Are we really going to do it?"

"Are you going to just pitch the tent on the top of the snow?" Ethan asked.

"Yes, Ezra, we're doing it," I replied, "And we're gonna use the snow for insulation . . . like an igloo."

January rolled in with bitter cold. On days when snow wasn't falling, the backyard became stark and crystalline. The sun would rise on cloudless days but offered little warmth. Cold bit at exposed skin and turned breath into visible clouds that lingered in the frigid air. Snow squeaked underfoot as I walked the backyard, planning.

One day during lunch break, I started layering on protective clothing: insulated underwear, cotton t-shirt, flannel shirt, wool jacket, windproof parka. After slipping into insulated boots and layered mittens, I headed to the garage for the silver grain shovel with the white hardwood shaft that I'd used to build sledding hills when the boys were toddlers.

In the backyard, I stepped out a circle larger than our tent and marked the area I would dig. As I built those snow walls, I thought about all the times I'd faced cold and danger as a child with no one protecting me, no one preparing me. Now I was creating danger, but with protection. Creating challenge, but with love. Shovel full after shovel full, I carefully dug snow out of that circle, putting it in a circular mound along my marking. When I reached the dormant grass, I stepped up and started piling snow on the mounds I'd created.

Our tent was nearly tall enough for me to stand in, so to protect it from wind, I needed walls at least six feet high and thick enough that they wouldn't collapse. Over the following days, working during lunch breaks with Ethan and Ezra helping after school, we created a six-foot high circular shelter with an overlapping opening designed to keep wind from buffeting the tent.

The week temperatures dropped into the low twenties below zero, Friday night came. While it was still daylight, I pitched the tent inside those snow walls, and the boys filled the floor with insulating camping pads and spare blankets. Ground cold would be worse than air cold—sleeping bag insulation on top would protect from air, but lying on ground insulation flattens it, making it less effective.

With everything prepared, we remained inside as darkness claimed the land. I found myself offering a silent prayer about leading them into the killing cold—asking for wisdom, for the proper balance between challenge and safety, for the knowledge to bring them back whole.

"You guys ready?" I asked.

"I think so," Ethan said.

"I have a book and a flashlight," Ezra chimed in.

"I'd go to the bathroom one more time, because you won't want to climb out into the cold," I cautioned.

The cold stung my face as I stepped outside, and I heard the boys scurrying beside me as we walked through snow toward the wall I'd built. Inside the shelter, wind couldn't reach us. We unzipped the tent flap and stepped in. The air was bitter as we stripped off the heaviest outer layers and jumped into our sleeping bags. After some shivering, my sleeping bag started to warm up.

"You guys getting warm, yet?"

"Yeah," said Ethan his teeth chattering.

Ezra replied, "Yeah, but my face is still cold."

"Yeah, you can put your head under the blanket, but it's hard to breathe like that," I offered.

We chatted for a while, then settled into reading our books. Soon Ethan snapped off his flashlight. "Good night."

"Good night, Buddy."

To Ezra I said, "Good night, Ezra. I am going to sleep."

"Yeah, I'm going to finish this chapter."

I woke several times during the night to check on them, finding them snuggled under blankets and in sleeping bags, sometimes with faces visible, sometimes only noses and mouths exposed. When dawn broke, the tent roof—the only part exposed to sky—started to grow light. I heard the boys begin to rustle.

They had made it through the bitter winter night. Not once had either complained.

When I was sure they were awake, I suggested, "Let's go inside and get breakfast."

Without responding, they slipped into boots, grabbed coats and outer layers, and rushed to the house without putting them on.

+ + +

On an October Friday, the Albany Huskies football team was scheduled to play at home, which meant Ethan would want to sit in the stands and cheer. Most home games were simple—autumn air sharp with the scent of dying leaves and cut grass, a light jacket sufficient to ward off the chill as darkness came.

That Friday, we woke to thick gray clouds smothering the sky, casting dead light over the backyard. Rain began to fall, drumming against windows and striking the roof with increasing force. Water gathered on the patio, and the temperature started its descent. I found myself thinking of Minnesota's legendary Armistice Day Blizzard of 1940, when mild morning weather had transformed into a killing storm with 80-mile-per-hour winds and drifts that buried men whole.

"Dad, can we still go to the game even if it's raining?" Ethan asked.

"Well, it depends on how bad it is I suppose."

"How bad is bad?"

"I don't know. Let's decide closer to game time."

As the day progressed, wind picked up, violently shaking trees down by the lake. During a work break, I asked Ethan, "Have you looked at the weather? Do we know what this storm is doing?"

"I haven't looked yet, but I will."

He switched from schoolwork to a web browser. "It doesn't look too bad. It just says, 'Heavy rain with rapidly increasing wind speeds.'"

"I don't know, Ethan," was my noncommittal response.

I took my coffee back upstairs and looked at the forecast myself. "Gusts over 75 mile per hour. Accumulation of 1 to 2 inches. Temperatures dropping rapidly to the low 40s." Seventy-five mile per hour winds—hurricane strength. I said a prayer asking for protection if we did go. Midafternoon I went back downstairs.

"What do you think, Dad?" Ethan asked.

"Sounds uncomfortable and a bit dangerous, to me."

"Life is dangerous, Dad."

"Okay, if they don't cancel the game, we'll go."

Christina and Ezra's response to joining us was a simple "No." Ethan checked the school's and local news websites repeatedly, and at dinner time announced, "They aren't canceling it."

After dinner, we gathered wet weather gear: rain pants, rain jackets, ponchos. Ethan had taken to calling rain boots "wellies" as a nod to *All Creatures Great and Small*, so we collected our wellies for good measure. With the winds, I thought it would be wise to have a poncho over our rain suits, plus a small blue tarp to sit on and wrap ourselves in.

As the sky darkened, gusts shook the house.

"You sure you want to do this?" I asked as we put on rain gear.

"Yep," was all he said.

Kickoff was at seven, and we left with just enough time to get to the school and walk to the stadium. The drive was difficult with winds buffeting the car, but the windshield wipers kept up with the rain. The stands were mostly empty when we arrived—maybe fifteen or twenty people, mostly parents of players, I imagined. Rain was falling sideways as we struggled in strong wind to set the tarp on the bleachers. With rain suits, ponchos, and tarp wrapped around us, we sat down to watch.

When the ball was kicked off to start the game, wind was behind it and blew it far out of the end zone. For the Huskies, the game became a grueling battle against elements as much as the opposing team. The field quickly turned to thick mud, making every play a challenge.

Players struggled to maintain footing, with slippery conditions causing frequent falls and fumbles. I thought the stadium lights were flickering, but it was wind blowing the towers, making them bend and sway. Passes wavered unpredictably in gusts, often falling short or veering off course, forcing teams to rely heavily on running.

The high school band that usually played at every game wasn't there that night. Even if they had been playing, it would have been impossible to hear them over the wind. Ethan and I clapped and cheered, but I don't know if anyone else did—no one was seated near us, and I couldn't hear anything except Ethan and occasional words from the public address system.

Albany was one of the best teams in the state those years, winning all their regular season games, and that night was no different. After two and a half hours of being pelted with rain and rocked by gusts, Ethan and I folded up the tarp and trudged back to the car, wind at our backs. We put the tarp in the trunk, stripped off ponchos and tossed them in too. After climbing into the car and shutting the doors, I started the engine and turned on lights and windshield wipers.

As the wipers slapped back and forth, Ethan said, "Thanks, Dad. That was fun."

CHAPTER TWENTY-TWO

Christina and I learned about "shoulder time" at a marriage seminar when our boys were small. Shoulder time was a way of communicating where couples engaged in side-by-side activities—walking, driving, working on projects together. This approach allowed people to share thoughts and feelings without the weight of direct eye contact, easing tensions and building intimacy. When the instructor explained it, he gave examples of how young men often had their deepest conversations when sitting side by side, their words flowing easier when they did not have to face each other directly.

The concept struck me immediately, and Christina and I began creating moments for shoulder time with each other and with our boys—though we could not know how precious and few those moments would prove to be. Some of our friends called baseball too slow to watch, but Christina and I understood that a baseball game offered perfect shoulder time with the boys.

On warm summer evenings, Joe Faber Field would hum with quiet anticipation before the games began. The sun would hang low in the sky, casting golden light over the grass as players warmed up. We would arrive early to watch each team take the field for practice. The four of us would settle in, relaxed and content, with nothing to do but sit and watch the slow unfolding of the game. Ezra would bring a book to read, and Ethan would carry a pen to keep score in the program we bought at the gate.

The games moved at a gentle pace, offering what seemed like endless moments for conversation. We thought we had all the time in the world for such talk, for such sitting together in the fading light. We believed the seasons would stretch on forever, bringing us back to those same seats, those same conversations, that same quiet contentment year after year.

But time, we would learn, keeps no promises about tomorrow.

In 2011, just before leaving for one such game, I had gotten a phone call from my sister, with whom I had only a couple of years earlier started communicating with again.

The call had been weighing on me since I had gotten it, but I didn't let it interfere with our dinner before going to the baseball game. Along the sidewalk to the main gate to the stadium, towering oaks and maples dappled us with shade as we stood in line waiting for the stands to open. I started to speak a couple of times, but I couldn't find the words.

Finally, as we stood in the shade, I said, "Hey, boys. Your Aunt Bonnie called me right before dinner." I paused as they looked over to me. "She told me my mother has cancer."

There was silence as the boys processed what I had said. Ethan was 14 and Ezra was 13 at the time, and they were certainly old enough to know that my mother would be their grandmother, but they had never met her.

The only time we spoke about her was when the boys had brought home an assignment from school that required them to describe their family, and the sheet had boxes for the names of grandparents. I had to explain that my mother struggled with mental illness, and I told them that my father suffered from PTSD from Vietnam.

Ezra watched as Ethan asked, "How sick is she?"

"We don't know. They did a biopsy and found cancer, but the doctors don't know how bad it is. They don't know how far it has spread."

"Is she gonna die?" Ezra asked.

"She's not young, that's for sure. And she's been smoking since she was your age. I can't imagine she can live too much longer."

The gate to the stadium opened, and the line started to move forward. As we walked, I told them that the doctors were going to stage the cancer to figure out how far it had spread, and after that we would know how bad it was.

I let them know that I would likely have to take off to Colorado before long. We slowly walked in the sluggish line toward the gate, the news I had just delivered hanging awkwardly in the air. I listened to the sounds of shuffling feet and the hum of other people going to the game.

The shadows seemed to stretch longer, matching the weight of the silence that had settled between us. It was clear the boys did not know how they were supposed to respond to news of a grandmother they had never known, and I found myself relieved by their uncertainty. I did not know how I was supposed to feel either about the dying of a woman who had never been a mother to me.

After we reached the gate, surrendered our tickets, and entered the stadium, I broke the silence with, "Ethan, you want to get a program?"

+ + +

A couple of weeks later, I got a call from my sister.

"Hey, Bonnie. What's the news?" I asked.

Bonnie, who had made her way through the education system on her own and earned a Ph.D. in biostatistics, had a career of working in cancer research. She knew exactly what was happening with our mother.

"Well, they did a bunch of imagery. PET scans. MRIs. They didn't do any more biopsies because of where the tumor is," she paused and then started back up. "They decided that it's stage IV."

"Oh," I muttered. "Were they able to give a prognosis?"

"Not really. The major tumor is huge though, and it is wrapped around her aorta. They won't be able to do surgery on that," again, she paused to collect her thoughts. "The cancer spread to her lungs also."

"That doesn't sound good," I offered.

"No, it's really not."

"Did they give her a plan, yet?"

"She's going to try radiation first to see if they can shrink the tumor around the aorta."

"And if that doesn't work, she'll be on palliative care, right?" I asked Bonnie to keep me posted.

Before we hung up, Bonnie asked, "You're going to go see her, right?"

"I don't know what I am going to do" was my honest reply.

+ + +

I let my boss know that my mother was really sick and that I might need time off at short notice, but I tried not to let the news interfere with work. At that time, I had a standing desk in my office, the huge blond oak desk having long ago been cut up and burned in our backyard fire pit. I somehow managed, even standing, to hunch over my desk, in front of the keyboard, motionless. Time would slip by while I stared at my office wall.

In the afternoons, as the sun crossed over the roof of the house, light would fall through the window behind my left shoulder and cast long shadows across the floor—shadows that seemed to carry the weight of questions I could not answer.

On those days when I found myself wrestling with the tangle of anger and sorrow and longing, the weather would conspire to mirror what churned within me.

Some days, darkness would begin to mass on the horizon, the first hint of storm appearing as a distant, threatening cloud with edges torn and restless. Gradually, the cloud would swell, growing blacker and more ominous, like charcoal smeared across the sky. The wind would shift, leaves rustling with urgent whispers of what approached. The towering clouds would become a wall of gray and black, lit sporadically by veins of lightning that split the darkness. Thunder would roll across the distance. The sky would darken as if night had chosen to fall before its time.

In those storms I would wrestle with the confusion that had no name—anger at what she had been, sorrow for what she had never become, longing for the mother who had existed only in my imagination. I struggled to understand which version of her I longed to grieve: the mother I had needed, or the woman who had raised me with her fists and her abandonment.

Even beneath the hurt, there remained a small ember of something I could only call mercy—a flicker that had somehow survived all the years of her coldness. I prayed that God would show me what justice looked like for parents who never learned how to love.

On a weekday, while I was at work, Bonnie called me.

"Hey, how's it going?" I asked.

"I'm okay . . . The radiation didn't really work," she said flatly. "The tumor didn't shrink."

"That's bad."

"Yeah, they tried to talk her into doing chemo, but she refused."

"So, I guess that's it then, right?"

"That's right. She has requested to be put on hospice," Bonnie continued. "I think you should go see her. I already asked if she wanted to see you."

"Can you give me her phone number?" I promised to let Bonnie know when I would be going to Colorado, so we could coordinate our flights to be there at the same time.

I went downstairs where Christina was working in the kitchen, and the boys were avoiding the heat of the summer day, and said, "My mother is in hospice. I should go see her."

+ + +

Bonnie had gotten to Fort Collins a day before I had, and she stayed in our mother's rented two-story condo. We agreed to have the reunion between my mother and me take place at a Panera not far from my mother's. It was less likely she would overreact in a public space.

I drove to the restaurant right from the airport after letting Bonnie know when I would get there. I had just walked in and sat at a table to wait for them when they walked in through the door.

My mother was painfully thin from the cancer. She was almost skeletal. The woman I had last seen fifteen years ago had been reduced to fragile bones draped in loose, sagging skin.

I let her hug me and said, "Hey. I'm sorry to hear what you are going through."

"Oh, Michael. It's so good to see you," she gently cried.

After we ordered our food and sat down to eat, I learned that, hidden in her rib cage, the tumor was so large that it prevented her from swallowing easily. She was no longer eating regularly and was living on Ensure.

As Bonnie and I ate, and our mother took tentative spoonfuls of soup, we talked about a plan for the visit. This wasn't to be just a social call. There were necessary decisions to be made and a move to a care facility to be arranged.

Bonnie spread out on the table some of the resources the hospice team had given my mother, one of which was a list of assisted living facilities, and their approximate monthly costs.

"How much money do you have saved?" I asked.

"Oh, I don't know for sure," my mother hesitated.

"We need to know, so we can help you," Bonnie insisted.

"About twenty thousand in savings, but I don't want to spend it."

"If you are saving for a rainy day, guess what, it's raining right now," I told her.

Bonnie had let me know that the prognosis was a maximum of six months if my mother was perfectly and lucky. "We'll make sure your rent won't be more than you can afford," she added.

By the end of the meal, my mother was exhausted, and Bonnie took her back to her condo, and I went to check in to my hotel. We agreed to meet for coffee in the morning and start visiting apartments. Bonnie and I also arranged to meet with the hospice staff for lunch, while my mother would be at home resting.

+ + +

The first facility we toured that next morning was a stucco clad building that must have been built out of cinder blocks. It looked more like a prison than a care facility, with its steel doors on the apartments and lack of decoration. We spent little time there, and simply thanked the person who showed us around and left.

The second facility was nicer than the first. It had a country motif, with red oak crown molding and flowered curtains, but it also had linoleum floors that were polished to a mirror finish. It looked as if it were designed to be a hospital with the clinical feel papered over with some nice trim and fixtures. The dining room looked like a middle school cafeteria, and although it might have been my imagination, it smelled like stale milk. The people were nice, and if we found nothing better, it would do.

Pulling up to the entrance of the final facility we would look at, I said, "This looks like a resort."

Bonnie agreed, "This is nice."

I dropped Bonnie and our mother off and parked the car. When I walked in, I felt like I had stepped into a full-service hotel and began to get that familiar but uncomfortable feeling that I was somewhere so nice that I didn't belong.

The salesman ushered my mother around showing her the full-service dining room where she would eat all her meals, the exercise facilities, the pools, the movie theatre, the bar. He mentioned that Mackenzie Place was all inclusive, meaning there would be no additional costs for any of what he showed her.

When he asked what size apartment she was interested in, my mother told him that she wanted to see a studio. He gently nodded and took us to the second floor via the elevator and opened the door to a beautifully maintained one bedroom apartment painted in subtle neutral colors with tan walls, beige carpets, and blond wooden kitchen cabinets. He showed us the button my mother would need to press every morning when she woke, so that the staff would know that she was up. If the button wasn't pressed, they would come see if she needed help.

As we stood in the room, I had decided, without talking to Bonnie or my mother, that this was the right place. "How much does it cost?" I asked.

He started to describe the value of the services and how they were included in the price. Then he went on to tell us how they calculate the rates.

"I'm going to ask again. How much is a one-bedroom apartment?"

"A unit like this is two thousand one hundred a month."

"Inclusive?"

"Yes. There are some services that your mother can request, that would be extra, like the hair salon, for example. But that includes everything."

"Can you give us some time to talk, please?" I asked.

He left us in the apartment.

"What do you think?" I asked.

"You were rude," my sister said.

"I was just conducting business. It's nothing personal. He was wasting our time. I was already sold on the facility."

To my mother I said, "Do you think you could live here?"

"It's too expensive."

"Really? Were you going to buy something else with your savings?"

"No."

"Then you can afford it. But can you live here?"

"It's so nice. Yes."

We took the paperwork from the salesman and took my mother to her condo so she could rest. Then Bonnie and I went to meet the hospice chaplain and nurse for lunch.

+ + +

When Bonnie and I got to the restaurant, the chaplain and nurse were already seated, and we joined them at their table. The chaplain stood to shake my hand when we arrived at the table.

"You must be Mary's Lutheran son," he smiled.

"Yeah, I'm Mike," I responded as I shook his hand.

After we sat down, I asked, "How did you know I was Lutheran?"

"Mary mentioned it when I first talked to her."

Even though Christina, the boys, and I were active members of a church, and a Lutheran one at that, this was the first time my identity was defined by how I worshipped.

If someone had asked me who I was I wouldn't have said, "I am a Christian," much less, "I am a Lutheran." Not wanting to dwell on his definition of who I was, I quickly changed the conversation to questions about the chaplain. "So, how long have you worked in hospice?" I asked.

Soon we ordered our food, and we started to talk about what we could expect the team from hospice to do for my mother. With the chaplain at the table, the nurse began by mentioning that they would provide emotional and spiritual support as needed. I found this to be ironic in the context of my mother.

I thought, "Funny since she didn't provide that to us. Does she deserve that?" I quickly pushed that aside and agreed that it was important for her.

The nurse spoke about coordination of my mother's health care, which wasn't much really, since she had decided to not have treatment. She told us that as her health declined, they would provide personal care, such as bathing, dressing, grooming, to help her have dignity and comfort.

"We'll also give her a comfort kit," the nurse explained. "The kit has medication and supplies that will help your mother manage symptoms if any come up suddenly."

"What sort of supplies?" I asked.

"There are some first aid supplies in there, but it also has medications like Ativan for anxiety and morphine for pain." She paused briefly, then added, "The kit will be in her refrigerator, and she'll be able to administer the medication herself if she needs to."

+ + +

The foothills just west of Fort Collins were punctuated by clusters of ponderosa pines and junipers. They dotted the sides of the hills with deep green making a striking contrast to the earthy tones of the terrain. Even from the town I could see the rocky outcrops set against the sky that shifted from bright blue to deep blue as I looked straight above.

Bonnie was a long-distance runner at the time, and she would often run for hours at a time. That next morning, she went to the foothills toward Horsetooth Reservoir to run, which left me alone with my mother. She had stopped smoking in her condo, but she still smoked outside.

My visceral reaction verged toward incredulous anger, thinking "What is wrong with you? You have lung cancer!" But I realized that she had so little time left that being angry would accomplish nothing. She asked me if I would walk with her while she smoked.

As we walked, I didn't tell her how hurt I was that she had chosen to live her own life rather than care for me or how alone and scared I felt as a little boy.

I didn't tell her about the existential crises I went through doubting that there was a loving God and being convinced that my life was not worthy of living.

I didn't complain about how hard being a little boy having to forge my way alone was.

I didn't tell her because I wasn't thinking of myself during that walk. Like a smoldering ember in my gut, I had one thing on my mind.

From the time I had learned of her cancer, I was haunted by the question of whether I would see my mother in heaven. In heaven she would be the person she was meant to be before this world had twisted her into what she became. Whatever transpires in that place, the sins and stains of this existence would be washed away, the cruelty and abandonment burned clean.

Now, though I had never spoken anything overtly Christian to anyone beyond Christina and the boys, I felt a weight pressing down on me to say something to my mother that morning—words that might bridge the chasm between the woman who had failed to raised me and the soul that might yet be saved.

Taking a deep breath, I began, "I have a question for you, and if it makes you uncomfortable, you don't have to answer."

She inhaled from her cigarette and said, "What is it?"

"Do you believe that Christ died for you?" She stopped walking and looked at me. "Yes."

"Good. You don't have to be afraid of what is going to happen to you then." That was all I needed to hear.

+ + +

I had to return to work, but Bonnie stayed in Fort Collins for a day or two longer and arranged for our mother to be moved into the beautiful apartment at Mackenzie Place.

I had steeled myself for what I thought would be the inevitable slow decline of my mother's health; nevertheless, I found myself struggling to focus on my work that first week I returned to Minnesota. In the afternoons, as the sun shone through my office window, I would again be staring at the wall.

On a Friday, August 26th, 2011, late in the day, I got a call from my mother.

"Hey, how are you? Everything okay?" I asked.

"Yeah, I am fine," she said, her voice cheerful. "I just wanted to make sure you got home safely."

"I'm good. The trip was fine."

"How's Christina? How are Ethan and Ezra?"

We chatted for a few minutes, and she said, "I love you."

I told her, "I love you, too."

Four days later, on Tuesday, Bonnie called me and told me that our mother had died. I went downstairs and cried as I told Christina.

A day later, when Bonnie and I got to our mother's apartment, we found that the seven-day supply of morphine was gone.

+ + +

After I returned from Fort Collins following her memorial service, I held the letter from my mother to the judge again. I sat in my office holding that paper, reading her words again. The familiar anger started to rise—all the years of wondering why, all the nights as a boy when I had needed her and she wasn't there.

But as I sat there, something shifted. The anger felt pointless now. She was gone. No amount of rage would change what had happened or give me the childhood I had been denied. I folded the letter and put it away.

When I had asked my mother if she believed that Christ died for her, it wasn't because I thought she deserved forgiveness. It was because I understood, finally, that none of us do. That's what makes it grace.

CHAPTER TWENTY-THREE

Late summer and early fall on the edge of prairie was a time of deceptive beauty. The hills that surrendered to the flat fields would be bathed in golden light that seemed to promise peace. The corn would turn from green to pale yellow and bend in the wind like something already mourning what was to come. Along the roadsides, the last wildflowers—mostly goldenrod by then—would bleed their yellow into a scene that felt like the world's final blessing. The sky, usually a brilliant blue stretched tight to the horizon, would hold its breath above this false tranquility.

But this calm was always temporary, always fragile. On warm, heavy days when the air itself felt like a burden, dark clouds would mass on the horizon, their edges tinged green as old bruises. The sky above Avon would darken, and dread would settle over the land like something alive and hunting. Wind would rise, lifting dust and bending trees, making the earth itself seem restless.

Then would come the stillness—that terrible calm before nature reveals what it is truly capable of.

From the heart of the storm, a column of air would descend, twisting and tightening with ancient fury. The tornado would touch earth, connecting sky to ground in a slender, deadly dance. Though small, it would be merciless—a coil of wind and debris that carved its hunger through the landscape. As it moved, it would seem to choose its victims, touching down with devastating force, then lifting, then descending again like some capricious god deciding who would be spared and who would be consumed.

The path it left behind was a wound upon the earth—a scar that spoke of how quickly beauty could be torn apart, of how little control any of us truly possessed over the forces that could destroy everything we had built.

+ + +

When I returned from Fort Collins after finding the lawyer's letter to the judge, I drove the silver Oldsmobile Aurora that someone in my mother's family had given to her.

In the center console, precariously balanced, I found a coffee can filled with cigarette butts with some sort of liquid at the bottom. The odor from the toxic stew in the can permeated the car. I could feel the retching crawling up from my stomach, and I fought to hold it down, as I grabbed the can to throw it out of the car. Eventually, I paid a car detailer to try to remove the stench of cigarette smoke from the interior of the car, but despite his best efforts, the odor lingered.

A trip that should have taken two full days of driving took closer to three because I was forced to stop to have the car repaired twice on the way.

Those three days were spent with the windows rolled down trying to remove the smell and with me constantly seeing, as if projected on the windshield, the words of the letter that I had found. On that third day, I approached Avon from the southeast, much as a late summer tornado would have approached.

When I got home, I couldn't bring myself to tell Christina what was happening inside me. She'd ask questions with concern in her voice.

"Mike, it has to be hard. How are you doing?"

"Yeah, it sucks, but it's not that big of a deal."

The words came out automatic, like I was reading from a script. But inside, something was building. Dark clouds gathering on the horizon of my mind, and I was choosing to face whatever was coming alone.

+ + +

My personal tornado hit without warning. I started drinking heavily. Not because I thought it would help—I just did it. The alcohol opened doors I'd kept locked for years, and I went stumbling through them, tearing apart everything I'd carefully stored away.

I started seeing a counselor, a kind, gentle woman who described herself as a Christian. She had soft eyes and spoke in measured tones.

"I'd like you to try journaling what you're going through," she said during our second session.

"No."

"It might help you process—"

"I'm not writing any of this down. Having it on paper would make it worse."

She nodded, making a note. I wasn't a good patient from the start.

At night, I'd lie next to Christina, trying to be as still as possible so I wouldn't wake her. I was hiding both my pain and how much I was drinking. I thought I was being clever, but I was only fooling myself.

One morning, after another sleepless night, I walked over to the couch where she was sitting in the dark.

"I have a problem."

She looked up at me, her face calm in the dim light. "I know."

+ + +

We made a plan to help me stop drinking. The first thing I had to do was apologize to Ethan and Ezra. I sat them down in the living room, their faces serious and attentive.

"I haven't been the dad you deserve lately," I said. "I've been drinking too much, and I'm sorry."

Ethan nodded. Ezra looked down at his hands.

"Are you going to be okay, Dad?" Ezra asked.

"Yeah, I am."

I forgot to apologize to God.

+ + +

On a Friday evening, when Christina, the boys, and I were getting ready to go out on the lake fishing, something snapped. We couldn't find the key to the chest where we kept our life jackets down at the lake, and instead of looking for it, I went to find something to cut the lock.

All I could find was a hack saw.

Christina watched me attacking the hasp with the useless blade. "Mike, that's not going to work."

"Shut up. I know what I'm doing."

The saw wasn't even scratching the metal. Ethan came over.

"Dad, it's not even making a mark."

"Fine! We won't go out then!"

Christina stepped closer, her voice quiet. "Mike, you're scaring me."

The words hit me like cold water. I looked at the hacksaw in my hands, at my family watching me with worried faces.

"You probably should take me to the hospital," I said. "I don't know what's going on."

+ + +

At the emergency room, I walked up to the admitting desk and said, "I have an incredible headache, and my wife says I've been acting irrationally."

They took me back immediately. Hours of tests followed—blood work, urine samples, a spinal tap. The doctor kept disappearing and returning with more questions.

Finally, he came back with results. "After all those tests, we can't find anything that could be causing your symptoms."

"What happens now?"

"We'll get ready to discharge you."

A new nurse came in for the shift change. She took my vitals and clipped the little sensor on my finger.

"Eighty-five percent?" She looked at the readout, then at me. "Has your oxygen saturation been this low the entire time you've been here?"

"Maybe a little higher, but it's been in the eighties."

The doctor returned. "Before we can discharge you, we need to see why your oxygen level is so low."

After the CT scan, a different doctor appeared.

"You have a blood clot in your left lung. We're admitting you."

By then it was three-thirty in the morning. Christina and the boys had been with me the entire time.

"I guess we'll go home," Christina said, gathering her purse.

"I love you guys," I said as they prepared to leave.

Three days in the hospital on blood thinners. Over the next several months, I'd be back three more times—twice for bleeding in my stomach, once for headaches that wouldn't stop. My body was keeping score of what my mind had put it through.

+ + +

One Sunday in 2012, while I was putting my health and sobriety back together, a woman named Maggie stood up in church.

"I'm forming a team to go to Uganda to work at an orphanage," she announced. "It's a construction project in Gulu, in northern Uganda. The area is recovering from war."

I sat up straighter, leaning forward.

She talked about the devastation, how the median age in Gulu was fifteen compared to thirty-nine in the United States. More children than adults, mostly homeless. Watoto Childcare Ministries was trying to help the widows and orphans, and we'd be helping Watoto.

I thought about Christina's and my goal of teaching the boys compassion and grit. Pushing them out of their comfort zones was part of our plan. Going to a war-torn area to do hard labor for widows and orphans—that was exactly what we needed to do.

Later, when Christina and I were alone, I said, "I think we should go to Uganda. It'd be good for the boys."

Christina looked surprised. Usually she was the one suggesting ministries to support.

"Oh, really? Why do you think that?"

"Widows. Orphans. Construction. It'll be a great experience."

As I said it, I realized I needed the experience as much as Ethan and Ezra did. I'd been feeling sorry for myself for months, and I needed to be pushed out of my own comfort zone.

When we told the boys, Christina said, "We'll have to work with the team to raise money for building supplies. If we don't raise the money, we can't go."

"So we'll do fundraising, right?" Ethan asked.

"Yep, but we're going to have to make a sacrifice too. If you want to do this, you each need to put in a hundred dollars from your savings."

+ + +

Monday, August 5th, 2013, a meeting invitation from my boss appeared on my work calendar. Subject line: "Catch Up." Scheduled for Tuesday morning at nine, the start of the workday. We were leaving for Uganda the day after the call.

I assumed Chuck just wanted to make sure my work was covered while I was away.

Tuesday morning, I grabbed my coffee and went upstairs to call him. Before I could dial, my phone rang.

"Hello?"

"Mike, this is Chuck. I have you on speaker phone, and Mark from HR is with me on the call."

"Hi, Mike," Mark said.

My stomach dropped. "Hey."

"Mike, we've decided that it's just not working out anymore, and we're going to sever our relationship with you."

"Not working out? Can you give me more information?"

"Texas is an at-will employment state, and we don't have to provide cause for termination."

"So that's it. I'm fired, and you won't tell me why?"

"That's right. I'll let Mark take over from here."

Mark explained about returning my laptop, about unemployment eligibility, about how he'd tell the state the termination was without cause if they called. He wished me luck. They hung up.

I knocked over my coffee cup and watched it spread across my desk.

"Of course this would happen," I said to the empty room. "Especially today."

While we finished packing for our seventeen-day trip to Africa, I told the boys I'd lost my job.

"Don't tell anyone else on the trip what happened," I said. "I don't want sympathy or concern for us to overshadow what we're doing in Uganda."

+ + +

By the time we landed at Entebbe Airport, we'd been traveling for over thirty hours. Christina, Ethan, and Ezra looked rested. I felt like I'd been dragged behind the plane.

Boniface—Boni for short—met us in the arrivals hall. He'd be our host from Watoto for the next fourteen days.

Boni and our driver Steven loaded us onto a bus for the drive to Kampala. The road wound along the northern shores of Lake Victoria, shimmering water visible through lush, green vegetation. Roadside markets lined the route with names like "One True God Meats." The smell of burning charcoal from cooking fires filled the air.

Saturday, we went to the main Watoto facility for orientation. By evening, we were all jet-lagged and exhausted.

Sunday morning, we prepared for worship at a local church before departing for our build site in Gulu.

The church exterior bloomed with people dressed in soft pinks, greens, yellows, and blues. The muted pink stucco building was sheltered by towering trees, the dusty rose walls gentle against the emerald foliage under the brilliant sky. Our group was led into the worship hall and seated in the front two rows.

The worship we knew from home was Lutheran liturgy—ordered ritual, ancient hymns, organ music, a pastor in vestments leading prayers and readings by candlelight. Here at Watoto, worship burst alive with energy. The band ignited the space with contemporary songs, guitars and drums creating celebration that seemed to lift the very roof. Through most of the songs, the congregation raised their hands in spontaneous prayer and praise, each worshiper seeming to possess an intimate communion with God.

I knew these songs from the radio. As I sang along, I felt uncertain and out of place, but I sensed with growing clarity that everything would be well. I was not thinking about the jobless future that awaited me. I was not dwelling on the recent past of wrestling with the darkness that had nearly destroyed my health. I was not remembering the abandonment and isolation of my childhood. I felt peace in that exact moment, complete and unearned.

During one of the songs, I glanced left. Ethan stood there with both arms raised, joy transforming his normally serious face, as if he had been born to this kind of worship.

A realization struck me with the force of revelation. In that instant, the confusion that had clouded my vision for months scattered like smoke before wind. The boys were going to be well. They would become confident, compassionate, resilient men. And Ethan's faith—it was different from mine, stronger perhaps, more certain, untainted by the doubts that had marked my own journey toward God.

As the moment passed, I felt something too quiet to hear but strong enough to sense settle in my chest. Peace in my life was not just possible—it was promised.

+ + +

The days in Gulu, we worked with local tradesmen to construct a room at a high school. The process took on an almost primal, rhythmic cadence. The rough-hewn blocks, made on site with cement and local red dirt, were each a testament to solid earth and the men from Gulu who formed them.

Two young men mixed mortar in a pile, and I spent most of my days shuttling it by wheelbarrow to the walls being built. Ethan and Ezra worked on scaffolding, lifting bricks with gloved hands, hats shading them from the equatorial sun. With methodical effort, they laid blocks one upon another, sticky mortar slathered between them like ancient binding paste.

As the sun climbed over the rising walls and sweat began to flow down our faces, we labored to the rhythm of trowel scraping against block, the harsh grinding of sand and cement binding together, the occasional grunt of effort woven through steady conversation between our team and the local workers. Slowly, deliberately, the structure took shape.

+ + +

Boni had been a gracious host, guiding us through the country with quiet dignity and assurance. I learned of his wife and young son, how he sought to be a faithful Christian husband and father. We learned of the loss of his brother to AIDS, of his homelessness after his brother's death. Through his actions, we witnessed his compassion toward every soul he met.

Before entering Murchison Falls National Park, we stopped at the overlook above the falls. We watched the water hurl itself over the cliff and thunder down, creating a churning cauldron of white fury at the bottom.

As we prepared to load back onto the bus, Boni called to me.

"Mike, can I have a word with you, please?"

"Sure."

"Let's walk over here, away from the others."

We walked beneath some trees beside a bus that was not ours, apart from our group.

"Ethan told me that you lost your job just before coming here," Boni began with gentle care.

I dropped the hat I had been holding. As I bent to retrieve it, I said, "Yeah. On the Tuesday before we departed the States."

"I want you to understand that you will survive this. This is temporary." His voice carried certainty I had not heard directed toward me in years. "I have watched you with Ethan and Ezra. You are a good father. You will not allow this to defeat you."

After convincing myself that our journey to Africa was to serve the people of Watoto, I was struck to realize that I had traveled to Uganda to receive what I most needed to hear.

"Can I pray for you, Mike?"

He prayed for peace regarding my employment, asking blessings upon me and Christina, Ezra, and Ethan—speaking our names as if they mattered to God, as if we were worth divine attention.

"Ethan and Ezra are fine boys," he said after the prayer. "They will become good men."

This conversation with Boni, and the prayer he offered, settled something in me that had been restless for years. I had not failed as my father had failed. Whatever else might be uncertain, I had managed to raise sons who spoke of their father with respect to strangers. I had given them what I had never received.

+ + +

When we visited the Watoto orphanage in Kampala that cared for the smallest children, I saw words painted on the wall in bright blue letters: "I know the plans I have for you," declares the Lord, "plans to prosper and not to harm you, plans to give you hope and a future."

I stood before those words while infants cried in the rooms behind me and Ugandan women moved between the cribs with tender care. The verse seemed written for this moment, in this place, for a man who had once been abandoned but had learned not to abandon others. I did not understand why I needed to see these words here, among children who had been left behind as I had been left behind, but I knew with certainty they were true.

What I could not know then was how desperately I would need to remember this promise. How these words painted on an orphanage wall would become the anchor I would cling to when everything I thought I understood about God's plans would be tested beyond measure.

The neglected boy who had slept on dirty floors was gone. In his place stood a father who believed he had learned all the hardest lessons life could teach. But some lessons, I would discover, come not in the learning but in the letting go.

CHAPTER TWENTY-FOUR

The Minnesota we returned to from Uganda was one of mellowing heat and cooling evenings. It was the end of summer's intensity, the beginning of brilliant blue skies unmarred by haze or storms. If I looked closely, I could see the first few leaves beginning their transformation, touches of yellow and red emerging in the dense green foliage—nature's earliest warnings of what was to come. The air carried a hint of freshness, a whisper of crispness, the promise that change was approaching whether we were ready or not.

We arrived home on the Friday before Ethan, still technically a junior in high school, was to begin classes at St. Cloud State University on Monday. Minnesota offered a program where Ethan could enroll in college full-time and earn both high school and college credit simultaneously, and the state would cover his books and tuition.

Ezra would start his sophomore year of high school online a few days later, eager to finish that year so he, too, could enter university.

For me, seeking employment felt like returning to basic training—as if I had to shoulder my fifty-pound pack once more to begin the road march that would be my search. After polishing my resume, I began the long campaign of job hunting.

The journey to Watoto had transformed us all in those brief weeks, and I could see no signs of trouble gathering on the horizon. The sky stretched clear and blue above us, deceptively peaceful, holding its secrets close. We had no way of knowing that the clearest skies often precede the most devastating storms, or that sometimes the greatest tempests rise not from the weather, but from the very ground beneath our feet.

+ + +

In late September, Christina found out about a one-night-only screening of a Christian documentary that would be showing at the large movie theater in St. Cloud.

"I think we should go to *Unstoppable* at Crossroads," she told me.

"We don't really have the money to go to a movie, do we?"

"I know . . . I just feel like we are supposed to go."

The way she spoke made me go still. Christina had cultivated an instinct for such moments over the years, a sense that God was drawing us toward something we could not yet perceive.

"How much is it?"

"Thirty dollars for each of us."

"Ouch!" I blurted out.

But something in her certainty made the decision for us. We had learned to trust these promptings, even when they stretched our budget.

On that Tuesday evening, we walked up to the ticket desk at the theater, and I scratched a mosquito bite on my thigh, as the attendant swiped my credit card to pay for our tickets.

Inside, I was so distracted by my job search that I only remembered fragments of the show: a live gathering of university students in a huge arena; black and white, beautifully filmed cinematographic imagery; perfectly framed vignettes of the host sitting on a porch drinking coffee.

During the event, the advertisement for Liberty University felt intrusive and disruptive, but of the entire two hours we sat there, I recalled one moment in the ad most vividly. The words "School of Aeronautics" superimposed in the upper left of the screen, with a panning shot of a young woman and young man in polo shirts standing in front of a perfectly clean Cessna airplane, with a deep blue sky as the backdrop.

Ethan had made it to his junior year of high school, and his ambition of becoming a pilot had not faltered. Now instead of "I want to be a FedEx pilot," his answer if you asked him what his plans were would be "I want to fly the heavies overseas," meaning he wanted to fly wide-body, long haul jets.

When we got home that night, I told him about the advertisement we saw for Liberty's flight program, and in typical Ethan fashion, he decided that was where he would go to school. I tried to convince him to look at three schools and make a decision after that, but he could be a stubborn boy, and in this he dug his heels in.

"Dad, I know what you saw," he said. "That's where I'm supposed to be."

+ + +

By late November of 2013, I had found a new job, and we had repaired the damage my firing had caused. Ethan had been asking to visit the Liberty University campus from the moment he found out I was working again. In January, I decided we could pull off a trip to Virginia.

"Buddy, can you check your class schedule to see if you have President's Day off from class?" I asked.

"Yeah, I can do that. Why?"

"I have it off, and I think we should go visit Liberty to see if it is a good fit." Even though his face looked serious, I could tell he was ecstatic.

On that Friday in February, we landed at the airport in Lynchburg and checked into our hotel. Ethan had arranged to tour the campus on Saturday.

We were supposed to spend Sunday getting to know the area, and on Monday we would tour the aviation school at the airport. I called Christina from the hotel room. While looking out the window, I told her, "I don't know about this place."

"What do you mean? What's wrong with it?"

"I don't know. It just seems a little rough."

However, my concerns about the area were immediately erased when Ethan and I toured the campus. My experience my first year at university had been one of loneliness and isolation, and it was clear that Ethan would not be alone.

The people from residential life promised they prayed for each student by name every day. Walking across that campus, I could sense something I had never encountered in any educational institution—a genuine conviction that these people cared for more than enrollment numbers or graduation statistics. They cared for souls.

On Monday, when Ethan woke up he was vomiting and said he had a pain in his lower abdomen, but he convinced me that he just needed breakfast.

He seemed better after eating, and our appointment wasn't until one p.m., so we went to a museum that was open on President's Day. While I was looking at an exhibit, Ethan quickly left to find a bathroom.

When he came back he said he had vomited again, and he said he didn't feel good. I felt his head, and he had a fever, which had come on so quickly, I decided to find an urgent care to take him to.

We ended up in the emergency room at Lynchburg General Hospital, and after nearly eight hours of waiting, Ethan was admitted. The system moved slowly, with forms and procedures that seemed designed more for the hospital's protection than patient care, but the nurses who actually worked with Ethan were genuinely kind.

On Tuesday a call came to Ethan's room. I answered, "Hello?"

"Is this Ethan LaFleur's father?"

"Yes."

"This is Larry with Liberty University. I understand that Ethan was touring the school this weekend and ended up in the hospital. Is that right?"

"Yeah, they don't know for sure what happened, but he seems to be doing better."

"Is there anything we can do for either of you?"

"I don't think so. They are letting me stay in the room with him, and they are bringing me meals, too, so I think we are as good as we can be."

"Let me give you my number in case you need anything." He gave me his contact details, and I hung up the phone.

The fact that someone from the university had called, without being asked, told me everything I needed to know about the kind of community Ethan would be joining.

Ethan's mind had been settled long before we toured the campus, but the visit had changed my perspective completely, and the concern I had shared with Christina was gone. We never learned what had made Ethan so ill so suddenly, and I returned home with a clear sense that God had plans for our son that were bigger than anything we could imagine.

+ + +

Ethan thrived at St. Cloud State, even finding enough time with his schoolwork to start working at a pizza restaurant. Ezra made it through his sophomore year, and he, too, started taking classes at St. Cloud State.

In December of 2014, I started talking to someone I knew at a software company that was headquartered in New York City. Paul had an opening on his team, and we started talking about what it would look like if I took the job.

The opportunity felt different from anything I had experienced before—not just another job, but a chance to provide opportunities for my family that I had never imagined possible.

When I came back from the trip to New York to meet the rest of the people I would be working with, I sat down at the table with Christina and the boys.

"I might get a new job in New York," I told them.

"Oh, that's cool," said Ezra.

"No, I won't be working from home," I said, sensing he didn't understand completely, "We'll have to move to New York." I was expecting some sort of disappointment or some sort of push back.

"That's awesome! When do we leave?" he asked.

Ethan was a little more taciturn, and said, "Well, I'll be going to Liberty soon anyway."

Christina looked at me with that same expression she'd had about the documentary. "I think this is what we're supposed to do," she said.

We all decided it was the right thing to do, and I took the job. Ethan was already graduating high school in June, and Ezra adjusted his course work and applied for an early graduation. He finished high school at sixteen, graduating in June, also.

The company gave me six months to make the transition, and we sold our house and moved to Cold Spring, New York, an hour's commute by train north of the city.

+ + +

Cold Spring was a village with tree-lined streets and 19th-century buildings filled with shops and cafes. From nearly any point on Main Street you could see Storm King Mountain and Breakneck Ridge reflected in the river below. After we had lived there for a while, I said to Christina, "What are they thinking? This isn't Disneyland," as I watched a tourist wander into the middle of Main Street in wonder.

The day I had been searching for houses, I turned left onto Main Street from Route 9D at the only stop light in town. I felt the weight of uncertainty lift as I saw the heart of the village—five young boys walking up Main Street alone, carrying candy, safe and unafraid. In that moment I understood I had found something that looked like what I had been seeking my entire life: a place where children could walk without fear, where neighbors knew each other's names. This could feel like home for a while.

In the spring of 2015, we bought a house on Constitution Drive.

+ + +

Before we found out we were leaving Minnesota, Ethan and Ezra had been working on a return trip to Uganda. Just weeks after we moved into the house in Cold Spring, Christina and I took the train with our sixteen-year-old and eighteen-year-old boys to LaGuardia Airport and watched them go through security to get a plane to Washington, D.C. They would meet the rest of the group at Dulles Airport and make the trip to Uganda.

When they found out that Christina and I would not be going, they did not hesitate or question. They were determined to go back to Africa, even if it was on their own.

Watching them walk through that security checkpoint, I felt the same pride I had felt years earlier when they had first insisted on going to Uganda. These weren't boys who needed their parents to validate their choices anymore. They had become young men with their own sense of calling.

When they returned and we sat on the train from Grand Central heading to Cold Spring, even though they were exhausted from jet lag and the more than twenty-hour journey they had just endured, they chattered on about their adventure.

It was just weeks later that we loaded up Ethan's stuff in the car and we all drove down to Virginia to drop Ethan off at school.

On August 18th, we drove eight hours down to Lynchburg. We stayed in a hotel that night.

The next morning, we awoke to see the foothills of the Blue Ridge Mountains bathed in the soft, golden light of the early morning sun. The air was warm and heavy with humidity, carrying the sweet, thick scent of vegetation that seemed to press against our skin. The sun touched the tops of the trees, highlighting the early signs of autumn—leaves that looked weary from their summer labor, some already beginning to curl at the edges as if preparing to surrender.

To the west of the university campus, the Blue Ridge Mountains stood like ancient sentinels, their silhouettes sharpening as the sun climbed higher. The sky stretched cloudless and blue above us, deceptively serene. The air hung still—too still—with the peculiar heaviness that often precedes a change in weather. There were no visible signs of storms, yet something in the atmosphere felt charged, as if the very molecules were holding their breath, waiting for some signal to unleash what they contained.

The morning felt suspended between peace and whatever was gathering just beyond the horizon, beyond sight, but not beyond sensing.

We waited in line in our car to reach Ethan's dormitory. When we got to the entrance, a crew of students emptied Ethan's stuff into a cart, and ushered him, along with Christina and Ezra to Ethan's room while I found a place to park and walked back up to the dorm.

The rest of the day was filled with wandering around the campus, not wanting to say goodbye. Christina and I lingered at Liberty but finally said our farewells and drove back to New York.

+ + +

The next months were filled with phone calls with Ethan about his classes and friends, and Ezra exploring New York City on his own since he had taken a gap year.

Ezra filled his days with reading, exploring, and performing music with local artists. Ezra made enough money from playing music for Broadway artists and other professionals that our neighbor across the street one day asked me, "Why doesn't Ezra get a job while he's waiting for school to start?"

"Elliot," I told him, "you would be shocked if I told you how much money he makes at a gig. He doesn't need to find work."

That first Thanksgiving, Ethan took the train from Lynchburg to New York, and we met him at Penn Station in the late evening, shoving past panhandlers and crowds trying to get to Madison Square Garden.

When Christmas came, we bundled up against the cold and made the same trip to Penn Station again.

When the boys were young, Friday was pizza night, with Christina making the dough from scratch, and one of the boys grating the mozzarella cheese, and Christina and I had kept the tradition of pizza night when we moved to Cold Spring. We didn't make our own pizza though.

We started going to Angelina's Pizzeria a couple of blocks from our house. Ethan had five weeks off from school that Christmas break, and that Friday, as we sat in Angelina's talking to Mary Ellen, who was our server, Ethan piped up, "Uh, excuse me, Mary Ellen. Do you guys need help? I used to work at a pizza restaurant."

Smiling, Mary Ellen said, "I know we need help, but let me go ask the manager." She walked to the back of the restaurant, came back, and told Ethan, "You need to come back and talk to Robby, the manager."

Ethan came back from talking to Robby, and calmly said, "I start as a bus boy tomorrow." He spent every break from school for the next year and a half working at Angelina's, bringing the leftover pizza home with him after his shifts.

+ + +

The spring of 2016 in Lynchburg was windy and stormy. Ethan told us how the calm skies of the previous fall were filled with threatening clouds and torrential rains, storms that would howl through the foothills, bending trees and rustling the fresh green leaves.

He told us of thunderstorms that came up sudden and fierce. Too many times, the storms forced his flight instructor to cancel his flying lessons, and each cancellation meant more money we would have to spend to keep him on track for graduation.

He reluctantly came back to Cold Spring, and I promised him I would pay for local lessons, so he could get his private pilot's license that summer and stay on track to graduate.

The summer was filled with visits to Manhattan, the Catskill Mountains, and pizza Ethan would bring home after work.

Ethan flew all summer, and his final check ride—the one that would grant him his license—was scheduled on the day we were to leave to take him and Ezra to Liberty for the school year.

Liberty University had offered Ezra a full-ride scholarship—tuition, fees, books, room and board—something that still amazed me, considering how different his path to higher education had been from anything I had imagined possible.

On August 17th, we packed the rented SUV with the boys' stuff, and drove over to the airport where Ethan was flying out of to take his test. Ezra, Christina, and I went to a coffee shop to wait while Ethan flew with the examiner. I was so anxious for Ethan that the coffee seemed cold and bland.

We went back to the airport and watched as the little Cessna airplanes took off and landed, each of us guessing which one was Ethan's. Finally, one of the planes taxied to a spot near the hangers, and as the doors opened, we saw Ethan and the examiner climb out.

As the examiner walked away from the airplane, Ethan hung back a little, his head hanging down after he looked over at us.

"Oh, no!" Christina exclaimed.

"Crap. He didn't pass did he?" I said.

Ezra offered, "It doesn't look like it."

As the walk started to look like a funeral dirge, Ethan suddenly stopped, put his two thumbs up and smiled.

+ + +

That school year, Christina and I traveled often to Lynchburg to witness what our sons had become. We would attend performances where Ezra's fingers moved across piano keys with the grace of someone born to create beauty, and Ethan would take us to the airport to show us the planes he was learning to command, his face bright with the joy of flight.

Ezra was the kind of person others were drawn to like moths to light. When he was young, we walked into a Starbucks we rarely visited, and the woman behind the counter said, "You're Ezra's parents, aren't you?" We heard that often. Seeing him among his friends at Liberty, surrounded by laughter and easy conversation, we were happy but not surprised.

Ethan had struggled more with connection as he was growing up, so watching people smile and call his name as we walked across campus filled something in my chest I had not known was empty. Students would rush up to embrace him, their faces genuine with affection. These were my sons—no longer the boys I had worried about, but young men who had found their place in the world, who were loved not because they had to be, but because they deserved to be.

As their father, watching Ethan and Ezra flourish at Liberty, I felt the quiet satisfaction of a man who had built something that would last. The abandoned child had raised sons who would never be abandoned. The cycle was broken. The work was done.

CHAPTER TWENTY-FIVE

Looking back, I can see how the seeds of Ethan's passion were planted years before he drew breath. I do not know where our set came from, but World Book Encyclopedias in the 1960s were sold by door-to-door salesmen who worked the daylight hours, using charm and persistence to convince housewives that their children needed these books to succeed in life. How or why my mother bought that set remains a mystery. The books were an extravagance kept on a shelf in the living room, each volume representing a letter of the alphabet, spanning the entire width of the bookshelf like a promise of knowledge.

Before I could read, I would pull one of the books from the shelf and turn through the pages. My favorite was "A"—for airplane, for airline. I would spend hours studying the logos of airlines, gazing at photographs of aircraft as if they held secrets I needed to learn. When I was ten, I found a postcard meant to be filled out and mailed for information about joining the Air

Force. I completed it, including my birthdate, and sent it away. The Air Force replied: "Thanks for your interest. Please contact us when you are old enough to enlist."

An airplane changed the course of my existence—that image of an F-16 soaring during the national anthem as I watched the television station sign off the night I had failed out of college. In the Air Force, I would spend idle hours studying Jane's All The World's Aircraft, memorizing what I could not touch.

Even after all that, I never considered myself obsessed with aviation, but I flew for work, and flight was often the subject when I spoke with anyone, even when Ethan was small. It was no surprise to hear him announce at age three, "I want to be a FedEx pilot."

What I could not know then was that he would get closer to the sky than any of us ever imagined.

+ + +

These childhood fascinations carry deeper weight when you understand that Ethan was not like other children. His declaration at age four that he would die young had been our first glimpse of this, but there was more.

Over the years, I had come to believe that Ethan could perceive what remained hidden from the rest of us—something we all sense lurking at the edges of consciousness but cannot name or grasp.

Sometimes he would speak words that made me go still and wonder how he possessed such knowledge.

Like the afternoon I came home for lunch and mentioned I needed to leave early to stop at the drugstore. Looking up from his plate, Ethan said, "You are going to buy a new toothbrush." I had told no one—not his mother, not him, not anyone. I had not even spoken of going to the drugstore until that moment.

But Ethan knew. He dwelt in a country the rest of us could only visit in dreams.

+ + +

On June 6th, 2017, I was on a business trip that took me from Cold Spring to South Bend, Indiana. Christina was in Newburgh, New York at her job at the WIC office. Ezra was at home in Cold Spring, during his summer break following his first year at Liberty University.

My Tuesday had not started out all that great. It's not an easy thing to fly from New York to central Indiana, so I had made the decision to fly to Chicago, and spend the night near the airport, since my meeting in South Bend was first thing in the morning.

When I had landed at O'Hare and got to the rental car facility, they were all out of cars, so they gave me a minivan as a rental. I grumbled about that minivan when I got into it that morning after staying at the hotel.

Knowing it was going to take me two hours to drive to where my meeting was in South Bend, I left three hours before I was supposed to arrive, thinking I would have plenty of time to find parking and get to the meeting.

I was wrong about the time. South Bend is in the Eastern time zone, while Chicago is in Central. This meant I had exactly two hours to get to my meeting, and I didn't know this until nearly an hour into my trip.

During the drive, I stopped by a coffee shop to get a cup of coffee and a breakfast sandwich. I should have checked the lid of the cup, because the server had not put it on tightly, and I ended up spilling coffee down the front of my dress shirt and suit.

By the time I was on the road to South Bend, I was running late, driving a minivan, with spilled coffee on my clothes.

I figured, "Well, my day can't get much worse."

I ended up arriving at my meeting only 15 minutes late, but the meeting went well, followed by a pleasant lunch with my colleagues and business partners. After saying our goodbyes, I got back in the minivan and started toward Chicago.

My flight out of Chicago was early evening, so after a two-hour drive back to the airport, I thought I would have a couple hours to drop off the car, go through security, and catch up on email. Around 1:30 pm or so, getting into the rental car, I thought to myself, it's not so bad after a rough start.

+ + +

State Route 2 from South Bend toward Chicago unfolded like a testament to the Midwest's dying grace. Farmhouses and red barns stood sentinel among the geometric rows of crops, remnants of a world that still believed in permanence. I drove the divided highway through country that had been carved into squares by men who thought they could make the earth obey their lines.

Occasional woodlands and gentle swells interrupted the flat expanse, and I would cross low bridges where small creeks wound through the land with the patience of water that knows all roads lead to the sea. The farmsteads sat like islands in an ocean of corn and soybeans, each one a small fortress against the vastness that stretched beyond sight.

The sky that afternoon hung vast and open above this ordered world, but to the west I could see thunderheads beginning to tower on the horizon—great pillars of white and gray that climbed toward heaven like the dreams of fallen angels. The air had grown still in that particular way that precedes violence, and the light had taken on the strange, yellow cast that warns of storms.

I drove through this false peace, not knowing that the tempest gathering on the horizon was nothing compared to the one that waited in my phone, that the real storm would come not from the sky but from words that would tear apart everything I believed about the natural order of fathers and sons.

1:56 pm: my phone rang, and the caller ID showed that it was Ethan. As school was winding down, Ethan had taken a job at the library on campus, and the job would allow him to work all summer.

Normally, I don't pick up the phone while I am driving, but since it was Ethan, who was spending his first summer alone in Virginia, and who never called me during the day, I picked up, thinking something might be wrong.

The voice on the other end of the line identified himself as a Liberty University police officer. He sounded very young and very nervous. His speech was rapid but halting, and I was having difficulty understanding him.

"Mr. LaFleur, does Ethan have any conditions that we should know about?" he asked.

"Conditions? I don't understand," I told him.

He tried the question again, and I eventually understood that he was asking if Ethan had any medical conditions. While I was attempting to answer, an older, firmer voice took over the phone asking the same question.

"Mr. LaFleur, this is Mark Johnson, I am an EMT and we need to know if Ethan has any medical conditions that you know of," he explained.

"No, not that I know of. He just passed his aviation physical," I replied.

As he tried to hang up, I asked for some sort of context.

"Can you give me some context here?"

He said that they were helping Ethan with an issue he was having and that he had to go.

As I drove along that flat stretch of highway toward the thunderheads massing in the distance, I began to conjure possibilities about what sort of trouble could have befallen Ethan. Had he been assaulted? Struck by a vehicle? Suffered some break with reality? Taken to drinking in the daylight hours like his father once had?

Each scenario I constructed felt more plausible than the last, yet none of them approached the unthinkable truth that waited ahead. I was a man trying to solve a puzzle with pieces that did not exist, mapping territories of worry that would prove to be the wrong continent entirely. The mind, faced with the incomprehensible, will fashion explanations from familiar fears rather than venture into the country where sons die before fathers, where the natural order breaks down like a machine whose gears have seized.

2:12 pm brought a call from a different number. The caller ID on this one showed it was from Lynchburg, Virginia. It was the same young police officer that had initially called me.

"Mr. LaFleur, this is Officer Kimball. I wanted to let you know that Ethan went into cardiac arrest at the library. After working on him for nearly 45 minutes, EMS was able to get a pulse. They are taking him to the ER right now."

"Okay, thank you." was all I said.

As soon as I hung up the phone, I called Ezra. Christina was not allowed to have her personal phone on her while she worked, and since I was driving, I didn't have a way to find her work number.

"Hey, Buddy. I just got a call that Ethan is on his way to the emergency room."

"Oh, no. What happened?"

"They aren't really sure, and they didn't really tell me anything. I just need you to answer your phone if I call again. You're going to have to call your mother if something happens."

"Okay. Just let me know."

"Thanks, Buddy. I love you."

"Love you, too."

In my mind, Ethan was going to be fine, and Ezra wouldn't need to call Christina. I thought that since they had gotten a pulse, we might have to deal with some brain issues from temporary lack of oxygen, but it wouldn't be too bad. He was going to be okay. I told myself, I would just need to get to Lynchburg to help Ethan recover.

While still driving through that deceptive calm, I called the airline and changed my flight. God's comfort in our tribulation began at that moment, though I could not yet name what tribulation meant. After ending the call with the airline, my phone rang again. A chaplain from Liberty University spoke from the other end of the line.

"Mr. LaFleur, my name is Pastor Doug D____. I am part of a team called the LU Shepherds, and I am the chaplain on duty at Liberty. I'm calling to let you know your son is on the way to the emergency room."

"Yeah, someone from the PD let me know that."

"Okay, good. Are you able to get to Lynchburg?"

"Yeah, I am on a business trip, and I am heading back to the airport right now. I changed my flight, so I will be flying into Roanoke. I couldn't get to Lynchburg."

"Roanoke, good. That's only about an hour from Lynchburg. I'll come pick you up. Will your wife be able to make it?"

"For right now it's just me. We'll see how Ethan is doing and then decide."

"I want y'all to know that when you get here, we'll be taking care of you. Don't worry about anything except Ethan. We'll handle everything else."

In my mind, Ethan was simply going to be going through recovery, so I thanked him and asked that if he heard anything that he let me know. I didn't think we would be needing help from the chaplains.

+ + +

2:39 pm brought a call from a different Lynchburg number.

"Hello?"

"Mr. LaFleur, this is Doctor D_____. I'm an emergency medicine physician at Lynchburg General. Your son, Ethan, came in a bit ago and I attended to him."

As he paused, I still held on to the thought that Ethan had just been through some trauma, and Dr. D_____ was just going to tell me Ethan was stable and that he was going to recover.

"Ethan experienced cardiac arrest due to tachycardia while he was at the library. First responders and EMS worked on him at the site for a good deal of time. They then sent him here to the ER."

Dr. D_____ then went through a litany of procedures they performed on Ethan and medications that they delivered to Ethan while he was in the ER. I tried to keep track, but I soon gave up and started thinking only of Ethan. Even at this point, I still thought, "Well, cool. They did all of that, and they resuscitated him. We'll just be getting ready for a long recovery."

Dr. D_____ paused. I could hear his breath trembling across the distance between us. His voice broke as he began to weep. "Ethan did not make it."

The bright, sunny day on the plains of Indiana went black, as if some great mouth had devoured the sun itself. I was cast into darkness so complete it seemed to have weight. The warmth and light died in an instant, leaving only the cold void where my son had been.

"I want to let you know that I have children Ethan's age, and I can't imagine hearing the news I am giving you," he trailed off.

My reply was likely the typical stoic response I would have given, "Thank you."

2:48 pm: I called Ezra. The burden I was about to place upon his shoulders was not what any seventeen-year-old should bear, but he accepted the weight with a strength that belonged to men twice his age. I gave him the task of calling his mother's workplace and delivering the news that his brother was dead. I carry the shame of that decision still.

"Ezra, I just got a call from the ER," I explained, "Ethan died."

"No."

"Yeah, can you call your mom? I don't have her number."

"Sure, I can do that."

"Thanks, Buddy."

I felt trapped in the minivan, stuck heading toward Chicago, unable to deviate from that path. In my state, it never occurred to me that I could pull over and call Christina myself. Right after I had hung up the phone with Ezra, I got a call from Pastor Doug.

"Mike, this is Pastor Doug. It's about Ethan."

"I already know. A doctor from the ER called me."

"Oh. I can't believe they called. I wouldn't think they would deliver that news."

He told me again that he, Pastor Tim, and other staff would be taking care of us, and he made sure that I would get back to him with my flight schedule and that I would let him know when Christina would be arriving. This is when it hit me that when he said he was going to take care of us, not only did he mean it, but we were also going to need it. We had just found ourselves in the middle of the worst storm a parent or a brother can imagine.

+ + +

I finished my drive to O'Hare, turned in the minivan, and got on the airplane. I had to change planes in Charlotte, and as I waited, I sat in one of the white rocking chairs that dot the airport there.

Ezra and Christina were driving through Pennsylvania at the time, and as I texted Ezra, since Christina was driving, I was finally able to let them know what had happened. I got on my flight to Roanoke and arrived around 11:00 pm. As I landed, Pastor Doug texted me that he was there to pick me up.

When I walked out of the airport terminal, it felt like I was walking on the deck of a storm-tossed ship. As I got to the curb and to the white SUV that Pastor Doug had let me know he would be driving, I saw another man was with him. Paster Doug had brought Jim M_____, who at that time was the dean of the School of Aeronautics, with him.

Initially, I said, "Nice to meet you," and then something dawned on me. "Dean M_____? Ethan's talked a lot about you . . ." I realized that I had said Ethan's name, and I started to cry. I was exhausted and I wanted to collapse both physically and emotionally.

In the darkness of the Virginia night, we drove to the hospital, and I got to see Ethan.

Meanwhile, Christina and Ezra were driving through the tip of West Virginia, across a narrow band of Maryland, and down into Virginia. They journeyed eight hours through a landscape that no longer held any meaning, carrying the knowledge that her son and his brother was gone from the earth. While they traveled this changed country, staff from the university maintained contact to ensure they remained safe on the road and to confirm that someone would meet them at the hospital.

Around 12:30 am, Christina and Ezra showed up. I rushed to hug them as I saw them. I took them to the room Ethan was in. The three of us all had a good cry with Ethan, and then we headed to the hotel that Pastor Doug had arranged for us to stay in; they had made it clear that the university was going to pay for everything associated with our stay.

They weren't going to merely take care of our emotional and spiritual comfort. They made it clear that they were going to take care of our physical comfort as well. I could feel some of the burden lifting off my shoulders as we stepped into the beautiful suite they had provided for us.

+ + +

We arranged to meet the chaplains in the morning at their offices on campus to start the process of taking care of Ethan's burial arrangements. After talking a little bit about what needed to happen, the pastors started talking about eating. Pastor Doug told us, "Just so you know. We are going to go into parent mode. We are going to make sure you take care of yourselves. Don't think we're being bossy. We just want you to be okay."

The chaplains walked beside us through every hour of the aftermath that followed Ethan's death. I came to understand this as God's comfort made flesh—His mercy given hands and feet and voices that could speak into the silence where our words had failed.

Others in Lynchburg started caring for us, too. Especially the School of Aeronautics where Ethan studied. They went out of their way to shower us with God's comfort as well. Leann, an administrator at the school, arranged for us to spend most of a day in the school at the airport. As we walked around the buildings, we were introduced to staff that had worked with Ethan and instructed him.

They showed us the equipment Ethan used and the desks where he planned his flights. They introduced Ethan's friends who shared their favorite memories of Ethan. Some of the professors showed us some of the coursework he had turned in, explaining what a fine young man he was, also telling us about how happy Ethan was at the airport, in the classroom, on the flight simulator, how he always had a smile on his face when he was in the hallways.

Ethan had become a pilot and earned his instrument rating before death claimed him. The child who had been captivated by aircraft had achieved his dream of flight. It was grace itself to spend time among the people who had helped guide Ethan toward the sky and to be in the presence of his friends.

People from around the country started to arrive after that. My sister from Tucson, Christina's childhood friend, Ramona, from Colorado Springs, our family friend and her son from St. Cloud, Ethan's godparent from Minneapolis, and even the pastor from our little church in Cold Spring all came to pay their respects.

In the evenings before the funeral, we would gather on the hill behind the School of Medicine overlooking the valley and watch the orange sun die behind the Blue Ridge Mountains.

+ + +

There was a small white chapel on campus that stood like a beacon among the red brick buildings that hemmed it in. We arranged to hold Ethan's funeral there. When we entered to ensure it would serve our needs, I found myself drawn along the walls, studying the stained-glass windows where scripture verses had been painted in careful script.

At the back, to the left as I faced the altar, I stopped before words that brought sudden comfort to my chest: Jeremiah 29:11, "I know the plans I have for you," declares the Lord, "plans to prosper and not to harm you, plans to give you hope and a future."

The same words that had been painted on the orphanage wall in Uganda. The same promise I had read while surrounded by abandoned children, not knowing then how desperately I would need to cling to them in this chapel where we would lay my son to rest. Those words became my anchor in the storm—the assurance that Ethan's death was not random, not meaningless, but part of some greater design I could not yet comprehend.

God's plans, I began to understand, encompassed territories beyond earthly prosperity, hopes that reached past this world's boundaries. Perhaps Ethan's nineteen years had been complete in ways I was only beginning to grasp, his journey from earth to sky exactly as long as it was meant to be.

I spent a day writing something to read to the people who would be attending Ethan's funeral. I had no expectation that there would be many people, but I wanted those that were there to hear about Ethan.

When Saturday came, Christina, Ezra, and I went to the chapel surrounded by those who came to support us. We greeted some people as they filed in, and said their farewells to Ethan, dressed in his blue dress shirt a Rubik's Cube resting on his hands.

We sat down in the front row, before the service began. As I stood and walked up to speak and turned around to look at the congregation, I was shocked at the number of people that came. The room was packed with people standing around the full pews, and the back doors were open, and people were standing in the sun trying to come inside.

That chapel, far from where Ethan was born and raised, far from where his home address was, was filled to overflowing with people whose lives he had touched.

After the burial service at a cemetery in the countryside, with the Blue Ridge Mountains standing witness in the distance, the School of Aeronautics transformed their annual summer gathering into a celebration of Ethan's life. We spent the afternoon among his friends and those who had known him at the school, sharing stories and laughter that seemed impossible yet necessary.

While we sat at the picnic tables beneath the open sky, Pastor Jonathan from a local church approached and offered his condolences. His presence felt like another manifestation of grace—that strangers would seek us out in our grief, that a community we barely knew would fold us into their care.

"I'm sorry to hear about Ethan. I can only imagine how hard this is." After we thanked him, he said, "We will be taking up an offering after our service tomorrow, and we'll put that toward Ethan's funeral." What a comfort and blessing it was when we found out that the church paid the entire bill.

When we got back to Cold Spring, our little church took care of us the best they could. For weeks we had no worries about where our next meal would come from as they brought food to us every day.

Over the following few weeks, Christina and I slowly slipped back into trying to live our lives.

In the evenings, after dinner, we would walk through the neighborhood down the hill toward the Hudson River.

As we stood on the dock that reached into the water, looking west toward Storm King and Sugarloaf Mountains, I would search the sky for signs of storms, perhaps expecting another tornado to tear through what remained of my life. No tornado came.

The storms I had feared—the ones that destroy from without—had already done their work. What remained was the deeper transformation that comes not from wind and debris, but from the hand of God remaking a man according to His purposes. The boy who had once cowered from his mother's rage, the man who had drunk himself toward oblivion after his mother's death, was gone. In his place stood someone God had carried through the valley of ultimate loss and shown that His grace was sufficient even for what I had thought would destroy me utterly.

I had learned that God's plans truly do prosper us, though not in ways we expect. That His comfort comes not in preventing the storm, but in walking with us through it. That even in the depths of grief, even when sorrow threatened to silence every note of praise, the song continued. The cloud that had once seemed so thick and impenetrable—the cloud of abandonment, of pain, of loss—had grown thin enough to let heaven's light break through.

I no longer needed to fear the storms. God had taught me that His music plays even in the darkest valley, that no earthly trouble can stop the song He places in the hearts of those He loves. The cloud grows thin, and in that thinning, we see not the end of sorrow, but the eternal melody that carries us through it.

CHAPTER TWENTY-SIX

In July, the early morning train from Cold Spring wound down the bank of the Hudson River, moving through daylight that seemed somehow altered. Through the windows on the right, the river caught the light with occasional whitecaps stirred by wind, the Hudson Highlands rising from the far bank like ancient guardians. Before Ethan's death, the rhythmic clatter of wheels on track had pounded a rhythm that built anticipation as I approached the heart of New York City. I would watch for Bear Mountain Bridge spanning the Hudson with its steel arches connecting the forested hills, a sight that had once seemed like a promise.

But the summer after we buried our son, the scenery had lost its clarity. The views through the window were no longer sharp and vivid but appeared as if seen through gauze, the colors muted, the edges soft. When the train entered the tunnel beneath Manhattan, it would leave the daylight behind and descend into shadow more quickly than I remembered, as if darkness were more eager now to claim what light remained.

Pastor Tim, from our little church in Cold Spring, had counseled us soon after Ethan's death, that it would be easy to make life decisions in the year after his death that we would regret in the long run. As the grief clouded my view of the world, his words rang true. Heeding Pastor Tim's advice, Christina and I agreed to make no major life decisions for two years.

On the day of the anniversary of Ethan's death, we got the sample image of what would be engraved on his granite memorial. The front side had his full name, Ethan Oak La Fleur, with the date of his birth—July 4, 1997—and the date of his death—June 6, 2017—with a Cessna 172, the plane he became a pilot in, above. The back had the Bible verse he had chosen to be his personal verse when he was confirmed in the Lutheran church: Colossians 2:6-7 that speaks of stability, growth, and gratitude.

The fall after losing his brother, Ezra had returned to Liberty University, and Christina and I seized every opportunity to make the journey to see him: Parent's Weekend, three-day holidays, his piano performances, plays where he would sit in the orchestra pit. In our grief, we sought to surround Ezra with the presence we had learned was precious—trying to fill the space that absence had carved in all our lives.

On one of our journeys from Cold Spring to Lynchburg, we went to Ethan's gravesite to see the memorial for the first time. As we pulled into the cemetery and approached his burial place, I noticed the half-wilted flowers scattered across other graves—small offerings left by the living for those who could no longer receive them.

I stopped the car beside the new headstone that marked where Ethan lay. Seeing the airplane etched above his name brought both pain and comfort in equal measure. I studied his name and those dates that marked his nineteen years, then moved to read the inscription on the back. As I read the Bible verse Ethan had chosen with such care, I came to the sixth line and saw "TRENGTHENED" where the word should have been "STRENGTHENED." There was an error carved in granite.

I stared at the misspelled word, feeling something unexpected settle in my chest. After everything we had endured here was this flaw etched in stone. The irony was not lost on me: a verse about being strengthened, with "strengthened" broken.

I traced the malformed letters with my finger, this permanent imperfection on something meant to honor my son and God. But instead of the rage I might once have felt, instead of the despair that had marked so many months, I felt something like recognition. This was the nature of things, wasn't it? Our most careful plans marked by human frailty. Even our most sacred gestures, even when we attempt to do everything right, carry the flaws of mortal hands.

And maybe that was as it meant to be. Maybe perfection had never been the point. Maybe the love behind the gesture mattered more than its flawless execution.

"Of course there is a typo," I said to the granite and the sky and the memory of my son. And for the first time in months, something in my chest loosened enough to allow a smile on my face.

+ + +

The realization that we needed to be closer to both Ezra and Ethan's resting place had been growing for months. In April of 2019, nearly two years after Ethan's death, someone contacted us seeing if we were willing to sell our home in Cold Spring.

I decided that if we were going to sell, it had to be on our terms, which meant no realtor commissions would be paid, the house would be sold as is with no repairs done by us.

Finally, I asked for more than we owed on it. By June we had left Cold Spring and moved to Lynchburg, to be with Ezra for his final year at Liberty and to be closer to where Ethan was buried.

+ + +

Years had passed since I'd had any meaningful contact with my father, and I'd made peace with that distance. Then, in the summer of 2020, in the heart of the Covid-19 pandemic, my phone rang, and the number showed it was Bonnie.

I picked up my phone from next to the notebook that I keep on my desk. "Hey, Bonnie. What's up?"

"It's about Dad," she said, "I don't think he's doing well."

"What's going on with him?" I wondered out loud.

Some years prior, Bonnie had taken a professional position at the University of Arizona, in their biostatistics department.

She was living in Tucson, and my father was living in a town called Cottonwood, having moved there sometime after retiring.

"Well, according to him, he was at a doctor's appointment and got angry at the doctor during one of the tests." She paused, then continued, "The doctor scheduled him for a cognitive exam because of it."

"So, they suspect some sort of decline?"

"It looks that way," she said, "You might want to think about coming and seeing him . . . I know you felt better seeing Mom."

"I don't know." I flipped the notebook to a blank page and looked at it while I waited for Bonnie to continue the conversation.

"He also told me that he was working with some sort of living trust company. He is going to put this guy John in charge of the trust."

"Who's John?"

"Some guy Dad says he adopted."

Before we hung up the phone, I didn't commit to seeing my father. I just asked her to let me know if something changed. I had no clear idea of how much money or property or assets my father had, but I did know that he had started to create a small empire of rental houses in Lander, where Jean, the woman he took to Wyoming, lived.

At one point, Bonnie had told me that my father groused about having to give Jean money after they had broken up. He told Bonnie that he had given her at least a million dollars.

After the call, I couldn't concentrate on work, so I paced in the air-conditioned room that faced our backyard. The summer breeze caressed the trees, gently rustling their leaves in soft, flowing movements. The midday sun dappled the ground as the branches swayed, casting shadows that danced across the shrubs and grass below.

My first instinct was to get on an airplane and get to Arizona as quickly as possible to stop this stranger from taking advantage of my father. Then I began to think about the possibility of my father slipping into dementia. I wondered who was going to care for him.

When Christina came home from work that evening, I told her that Bonnie had said my father was likely going into cognitive decline.

"What do you think you'll do?" she asked.

"Nothing," I said.

As evening began to claim our backyard, I looked toward the Blue Ridge Mountains to the west, searching for signs of weather that might approach. The horizon stretched clear and untroubled. There were no storms gathering.

* * *

A couple of months after Ethan's funeral, I was on a business trip to Singapore. At a business lunch, an executive from Southeast Asia's largest bank, an ethnic Chinese man, asked how many children I had. I hesitated for a moment, and then told him that I had one son alive, and one son who had just died.

He paused, put his utensils down, looked at me and asked, "Are you a believer?"

I said, "Yes."

He picked up his utensils, relaxed, and said, "Then you know you will be reunited with him in eternity." That thought carried me through those first years after his death.

+ + +

On that first trip to see my mother when I found out she was dying, I went into her condominium one evening after eating dinner on my own.

I took out that round lacquer box that my father had brought from Japan, and I started going through the old photos from the sixties and seventies.

My mother was sitting at the table watching me pull out pictures and study them briefly before placing them on the table.

I came across a set of pictures that were all taken in what seemed to be a small apartment.

The photos were filled with American sailors, some in uniform and some not. Among them was my father in uniform next to a young Japanese woman. They were seated together in several of the pictures.

"I think your dad had an affair," my mother commented.

"With her?"

"Yeah, and with other women."

"Why do you say that?"

"Because he could."

"What does that mean?"

"He got a vasectomy, so there couldn't be any consequences."

"He had a vasectomy, huh?"

"Yeah, he got it when he was in Vietnam . . . right after I wrote him and told him that I was expecting you."

I looked in the lacquer box and saw that little metal picture frame I used to swap out the photos of my father in. The glass had broken, and the frame was bent.

My mother continued, "Your dad never wanted kids, and he made sure he would never have another one."

It wasn't until I heard that my father was planning on leaving his legacy to a stranger that I began to understand the true weight of the vasectomy I had learned about years before.

The memories came not as a flood but as an avalanche, each one striking with the force of stone falling from impossible heights. Snow driving into my face like punishment. Sitting in the emergency waiting room alone. Facing my mother's madness alone as a child. Being abandoned in Lander like cargo no one wanted to claim. Standing alone during every milestone of my youth—graduation, wedding, the birth of my sons—waiting for a man who had made certain he would never have to care about another child.

The revelation struck with the violence of lightning splitting the night sky, illuminating every dark corner of a lifetime. Every excuse I had carefully constructed, every rationalization I had built to shield myself from what I had always known, crumbled to ash in an instant. The truth stood naked and merciless before me: my father had not simply failed to want me. He had taken medical steps to ensure I would be his only mistake.

I was not just unwanted. I was the accident that had taught him to be more careful.

+ + +

By the time spring of 2021 came, I had been praying and thinking about what I should do about my father, the man that had made it so clear that he wanted no part in my life. In the spring, Bonnie called me.

"He's getting worse," she said.

"Oh, what's going on now?"

"His COPD is really bad, and he can hardly talk," she explained. "And the last time I went to see him, I could really tell the dementia is getting worse."

"That doesn't sound good," I hesitated before finishing. "I think I'll go see him. Can you check and see if he's okay with that?"

"Yeah, I'll ask the next time I see him. He can't really talk on the phone."

+ + +

The message appeared on LinkedIn like a ghost from my past, something I never expected to see.

On June 2nd, 2021, I got a message from a Bill Lafleur. The message said:

> "Hi Mike . . . I am William (Bill)) LaFleur as more info I am retired Navy I was raised in upstate New York and am presently 81 year old My bad news is that my voice is about gone and the only way to communicate is Email kokbill@gmail.com. If you want to answer i would enjoy it Thanks Me."

My father was adamant about spelling our name with a capital "F," so I was suspicious about the source of the message, and when I read the barely literate rambling without punctuation, I was even more suspicious. My father could write.

I texted Bonnie to see if she had my father's email address. I didn't tell her the one in the message, but she responded with kokbill@gmail.com. Knowing that it was my father's email address left two explanations. The first was it was actually my 81-year-old father writing that message, and the grammar and punctuation was due to his dementia. The second was that John, the person my dad was leaving everything to, had access to my father's LinkedIn account and was baiting me for some reason.

I sat at my dimly lit desk, looking at the glow of my laptop. I would start to type a reply, but then I would erase all the words and start over.

The message from my father's account felt like an apparition, haunting and alluring at the same time. It didn't seem real. I wrestled with the decision on how best to respond.

My gut was a battlefield of resentment, longing, and a flicker of hope. Each passing second felt like an hour as I mulled over whether I should cross the chasm of thirty years with a few keystrokes, or I could wait until he responded to my request to see him.

Or I could let the silence stretch on forever. I told Christina about the message, and she encouraged me to write to him. I found a soft cloth and dusted the keyboard of my laptop, and I sprayed glass cleaner on the display and gently wiped it clean.

Finally, I sat down and began to write, beginning with a salutation that hinted at the impending end of his life and compared it to being in the Navy and getting to leave the ship for the last time.

I told him I would offer him two pieces of encouragement before I wrote a long letter. "If you read nothing more of this missive than the next four or so paragraphs, at least two things you will know: 1) You are bound for heaven if you choose, and 2) I have forgiven you."

After I explained that he could make it to heaven because God's grace is given to those who believe in His Son, I wrote: "And I am done with that topic. Somewhere along the way since the last time we communicated nearly 30 years ago, my faith began to get stronger and stronger, and it has sustained me in the hard times and has shaped into who I am right now—but I am not going to proselytize to you. My peace comes from knowing that I offered the key to heaven to you, and your peace will come if you choose to acknowledge the truth of what I offered. The next thing I have to do is tell you that I have forgiven you. Now, you may not feel that you need to be forgiven for anything, but, in order for me to have as few regrets in my life as possible, I know that I need to forgive people who have wronged me. If you choose, you can stop reading now, and you can consider yourself ready for Liberty Call."

The rest of the letter became a chronicle of the previous thirty years: my education, our marriage, our sons, my transformation from the boy he had abandoned, our journeys, our tribulation in losing Ethan. I told him of the boys growing into men he would never know and of Ethan's life being severed before its time. I closed with telling him, "I hope you choose to go see your grandson. As I said, the price of your admission to the place he is has already been paid."

+ + +

Only occasional clouds drifted across the blue sky above our backyard as I took my break for lunch a few weeks after speaking with Bonnie and sending that letter to my father. As I walked through the yard, I stopped before a Gerbera daisy in a large ornamental pot. The season's final flower clung to its stem, wilted and bent, reaching for renewal that would not come.

Bonnie's text arrived like a judgment: "He doesn't want to see you." I had been holding onto some hope for reconciliation between us, nursing some faint dream of the assurance of my father's redemption as well. "Oh," I replied.

In the soil beneath the flower, I could see the petals that had already fallen, and I understood the flower was finished. As was I with waiting for a father who had spent a lifetime choosing absence over presence, rejection over acceptance. The boy who had once stood in parking lots and sat in waiting rooms hoping his father might show up was finally, completely gone.

+ + +

In the early morning of November 10th, 2021, I was glancing at the latest cheap fitness band that had broken—I had started unintentionally collecting them, mostly because when one would quit working, I would get another and try again. I kept the bands in a little organizer shoved to the side of my desk. Bonnie called so early in the morning for her, three hours behind me, that I knew it was something definitive and final.

"Dad died sometime last night. John just called me."

The words hung in the air between us. After thirty years of estrangement, after learning of the vasectomy, after his final refusal to meet, after decades of wondering what reconciliation might have looked like, it came down to this: a phone call from a stranger to report to my sister that the man who had never wanted to be my father was dead.

I sat in silence, processing not merely his death but the absolute finality of it—all the conversations that would never be spoken, all the explanations that would never come, all the understanding that would remain forever out of reach. The questions I had carried since childhood would die with me, unanswered. The apologies I had sometimes imagined would never be offered. The reconciliation I had once hoped for had been buried before he was.

Yet in that silence, I found something unexpected: not the devastation I had feared, but a strange, quiet peace. The boy who had waited in parking lots was finally free to stop waiting. The son who had sought his father's approval could finally stop seeking. The man I had become—husband, father, follower of Christ—had been forged not because of this man's presence, but in spite of his absence.

"I guess that is it then," I said, but even as the words left my mouth, I knew they were not quite true. It was not "it"—it was the end of one story and perhaps the beginning of understanding another. A story where a son does not require his father's approval to know his own worth. A story where forgiveness can exist without reconciliation, where grace can be extended without being received. A story where some questions remain forever unanswered, and that must be sufficient.

The boy who had once believed his father's love was necessary for his survival was gone. In his place stood a man who had learned that the most important approval comes not from those who gave us life, but from the God who redeems it. I had become the father I needed, raised sons who would never doubt their worth, and found peace that did not depend upon the blessing of a man who had chosen to withhold it.

This was not the end I had once hoped for, but it was, perhaps, the end that was meant to be.

There would be no funeral. My father's soul would not be commended to the mercy of God by a Catholic priest. No memorial service to celebrate the life my father had led. No gathering of friends, or family, or loved ones, because he had labored so hard to make sure he had none of those. There would be no offer of comfort to the bereaved because he made certain there would be no bereaved to comfort.

Even though no funeral was planned and his estate had been secured in a living trust that required no arrangements from me, I knew I needed to go to Arizona. Christina and I flew there the following day.

+ + +

On the evening we arrived, we met Bonnie at a resort on the outskirts of Tucson. We sat outside on wicker furniture with soft cushions as the sun began its descent, transforming the desert and the distant mountains into something almost sacred. The sky blazed with streaks of orange, deep rose, and soft purple, bleeding seamlessly into the azure that stretched directly above us. The final light bathed the stark, treeless mountains, casting them in fire that made them glow like ancient altars against the darkening sky.

As the conversation danced around trying to find the right groove to settle into, Bonnie said, "You know he built the lighthouse, don't you?"

I was incredulous. "What!"

"Yeah, in Queen Creek when he was with Barb."

Christina asked, "What lighthouse?"

I told her about the blueprints that were to have been drawn and the lighthouse that was to have been built. I spoke of the coins I had scavenged and sacrificed at thirteen years old, how he had promised me I would finally have my own bedroom when we built the lighthouse, how he had sworn everything would be different. As these words left my mouth, my chest constricted with sharp pain radiating outward from my heart. I felt as though the earth had shifted beneath me and I was no longer on that couch but standing at the edge of some great precipice.

The brilliant colors of the desert evening drained away, replaced by gray uniformity. I began to feel the familiar dread of approaching storms, but as I looked toward the horizon, I saw the golden light still bathing the mountains beneath a crystalline sky. In that moment, I felt something I had not expected—peace settling over me like a weight being lifted from my shoulders.

"It's in Queen Creek?"

"Yeah, I'll give you the address, if you want to go see it."

Christina and I spent time with Bonnie letting her process her emotions about my father's life and death—and her own life—by talking it through to us. On Saturday, Christina and I started out on the two-hundred-mile drive to Cottonwood where my father had died, but along the way, I would look for that lighthouse.

+ + +

The drive to Queen Creek was bright, flat, and hot. We followed the GPS directions to a roughshod development of mismatched, poorly maintained houses with wire fences or stucco walls. The dirt road we drove on toward 35434 Sierra Vista Drive was bordered by a weed filled ditch and scrubby mesquite.

As we got closer to where the GPS showed the address should be, I had expected to see a lighthouse rising up out of the desert, but all that was there was a low-slung, awkwardly proportioned house behind a cinderblock and pipe fence.

I gave up searching and went to a coffee shop where I took out my laptop and looked at satellite images of the address. I looked at the top of the building we had just seen, and I could make out a octagon shaped framework on the roof that must have been where a lighthouse had sat at one time. Sometime after he left that house, the new owners had torn down that lighthouse as if it were meant only for my father just like everything else in his life was.

But as I sat there studying the satellite image, I understood that something profound was taking place within me. Here was evidence that my father had built the lighthouse he had promised me forty-one years before. Not for me, not with me, not when he had sworn he would—but he had built it. The childhood dream that had carried me through those crushing months in Lander, the promise that had kept alive my belief in the possibility of home, had taken form in the world. He had the knowledge and ability to make it real; he simply had not wanted to make it real with me.

The pain I felt was not the sharp sting of fresh betrayal, but something deeper and more intricate. It was mourning for the child who had gathered those coins, who had believed in blueprints and promises that were never meant for him. But it was also a strange form of liberation. The lighthouse had not been mere fantasy designed to quiet a desperate boy—my father had held the vision and possessed the skill to build it. He had simply chosen to share that vision with someone else.

I closed the laptop and settled back in the coffee shop chair, watching ordinary people order their ordinary drinks, living their ordinary lives that did not involve fathers who build lighthouses for strangers while abandoning their sons. But I felt something I had not anticipated: a kind of completion. The lighthouse had been real. My dream had been founded on something solid. And now I understood that the true lighthouse—the beacon that guides you home—is not something another builds for you. It is something you construct yourself, with the people who choose to remain.

I had spent decades wondering what was wrong with me that made my father unable to love me. Now I saw the question had been backwards. There had been nothing wrong with me. The boy who collected coins and believed in promises had been chosen and beloved long before he knew to seek such love. The man I had become had built something better than any earthly lighthouse: a home where children know they are wanted not because they earned it, but because grace itself had claimed them. Where promises are kept not out of duty, but out of the overflow of unmerited love. Where sons never have to wonder if their father will show up because they belong to a Father who never abandons His own.

The lighthouse my father built would stand on some distant shore, marking supposed safe harbor for someone else. But the home I had built was founded on the rock of divine election—that God had chosen me before the foundation of the world, not because I was worthy, but because He is faithful. This was the inheritance I would pass to generations yet to come.

Even though I was not swept away by emotional tempest when Ethan died, my world did not become sunshine and ease. For years, I would lose hours staring into the distance. During those times I was not necessarily dwelling on anything particular, not necessarily thinking of Ethan, simply existing in a place where he was not. Normal activities had lost their vibrancy, their color drained away as if I were seeing the world through gray glass, a muted reproduction of what life had been.

I look back at the time we first visited his grave with the new memorial installed. The moment I saw the error carved into the stone, I said aloud, "Of course there is a typo." I thought to myself, "Why should I have expected anything different?" And why should I have expected that the man who had never wanted me would have wanted to see me before death claimed him? I had wanted to preserve that small flame of hope that perhaps I was wrong about him. Perhaps it had been merely a series of misunderstood events that led to our estrangement.

I do not regret sending the letter to my father, even though he refused our meeting. Perhaps, like the Catholic Saint Dismas, the penitent thief who found grace in his final moments, my father discovered his redemption just before death. The God who had pursued me through every abandonment, who had transformed the unwanted boy into a beloved son, was surely capable of extending mercy even to fathers who had never learned to love their children.

www.ingramcontent.com/pod-product-compliance
Lightning Source LLC
Chambersburg PA
CBHW031325230426
43670CB00006B/244